P9-DUE-777

The Completest Mode

I.A.RICHARDS AND THE CONTINUITY OF ENGLISH LITERARY CRITICISM

'It is the privilege of poetry to preserve us from mistaking our notions either for things or for ourselves. Poetry is the completest mode of discourse'

I. A. Richards

JOHN NEEDHAM

for the University Press
Edinburgh

© John Needham 1982
Edinburgh University Press
22 George Square, Edinburgh

Typeset in Monotype Plantin
by Speedspools, Edinburgh
and printed in Great Britain by
Redwood Burn Limited
Trowbridge

British Library Cataloguing in Publication Data

Needham, John
  The completest mode: I. A. Richards
  and the continuity of English literary criticism.
  1. English poetry — History and criticism
  I. Title
  821'.009   PR504.5

ISBN 0-85224-387-1

TABLE OF CONTENTS

PREFACE

This book is about a variety of critics but its general emphasis is on continuity and change in English literary criticism. Since the continuity is in elementary critical principles, to dwell upon it is to risk labouring the obvious; but the risk is worth taking because 'elementary' means 'important' and because the general conclusions reached, particularly about Dr Johnson and I. A. Richards, are less obvious.

Changes in literary criticism can only be properly estimated if continuity is clearly understood. Changes of the kind one sees when considering together such critics as Johnson, Coleridge and Richards are neither radical nor merely a matter of the same things being said in different words; they are real changes but within a common tradition. What follows is an attempt to see in detail how this is so within one central area.

I have tended to quote other commentators on the critics with whom I deal, chiefly when I wish to disagree with them. I am acutely conscious that any changes of emphasis I wish to suggest are within a tradition that I inherit from them.

JOHN NEEDHAM
December 1981

ACKNOWLEDGEMENTS

I should like to thank Professors R. G. Frean, W. W. Robson and D. W. Harding for help and encouragement at various stages in the preparation of this book. I am particularly grateful to Mr A. R. Turnbull, of the Edinburgh University Press, for editorial assistance of the most thorough and valuable kind. And I owe a great debt of thanks to May Needham, without whom the work could not have gone on.

ABBREVIATIONS OF BOOK TITLES

Richards

CI	*Coleridge on Imagination*
MM	*The Meaning of Meaning*
PC	*Practical Criticism*
PLC	*Principles of Literary Criticism*
PR	*The Philosophy of Rhetoric*
SI	*Speculative Instruments*

Johnson

Yale	*The Yale Edition of the Works of Samuel Johnson*

Leavis

ELT	*English Literature in our Time and the University*

INTRODUCTION

1. Aims

In this book I argue that the central continuities of English literary criticism are currently much neglected, with damaging consequences. The book is a series of studies of particular critics, and does not attempt to chart the continuities exhaustively or chronologically. Since it deals at length with I.A. Richards and Dr Johnson, and considers, by way of Richards' interest, the significance of Coleridge, it can however be said to touch on the chief sensitive points of English criticism. I seek to enforce and enlarge the conclusions by looking at two other influential modern critics: Eliot and Leavis.

Richards is considered first, because his work, being theoretical and methodical, most readily permits a discussion of basic principles. To establish a continuity between him and Coleridge is not in itself difficult, since he himself points in that direction. Richards' view, however, was obscured by his special philosophical interests; and later commentators have obscured it even more, so that some detail is necessary in order to describe the real nature of the continuity. The continuity between Johnson and Richards is more difficult to define and this difficulty determined, to a large extent, the structure of the book.

The first section is devoted to Richards. It argues that the idea of 'interinanimation', developed chiefly in *Coleridge on Imagination*, is his most useful contribution to thinking about the analysis of poetic language, and that both his earlier and later work is less satisfactory. To enforce this point of view an account is given of his overall development, beginning with the early work on language and on the theory of 'complexity' and ending with a critique of Jerome Schiller's study, which sees Richards' later work as his most valuable. To trace Richards' story in this way gives a necessary sense of a persistent and acute intellect struggling, without being precisely aware of it, to restore a broken tradition, in such a way as to make it valuable to the modern critic.

The second section discusses the basic identity of the idea of 'interinanimation' and the eighteenth-century concept of 'propriety of diction'. These central concepts are similarly related to other key principles common to both neo-classical and modern criticism. Johnson's Shakespeare criticism was chosen as the chief source of evidence in this section, for several reasons: it is an ideal point at which to see eighteenth-century criticism in practice, it is of intrinsic interest, and, since it is usually seen as a *locus classicus* of disabling neo-classical prejudices about poetic language, peculiarly apt for our purpose.

It is argued that Johnson and Richards possess a common core of principles and that they each have their particular biases within it. This approach is then applied to Eliot and Leavis; the common core is outlined and the biases, or, to put it more neutrally, the distinctive features, discussed. The critical line traced is a long one; it is easy to look back from Johnson to Renaissance and classical criticism, and forward from Richards to current criticism, and though these longer views are not taken in detail, they are suggested at various points.

2. 'Interconnection' and 'propriety'

Since the first section, on Richards, is lengthy, the tenor of the book may not immediately become apparent. Thus a brief account of the central material may be useful; and, in this, Empson, a third important modern critic, is used as an introductory model of the book's approach.

The eighteenth-century doctrine of *propriety* of diction and Richards' concept of *interinanimation* both refer to the ideal of interconnectedness in poetic language; all the aspects of a given word should interconnect to a high degree with all the aspects of the other words in the context. 'Aspects' here means the senses, the implications and the physical qualities of the words. In the language of modern criticism this is a 'complex' use of words, constituting a 'realisation' of whatever experience the poem is presenting. In this usage 'realisation' is something of a pun, meaning both vivid presentation and conscious awareness of the experience. Further, that element of conscious awareness is intimately related to the idea of 'impersonality'; in detaching himself from his experience the poet identifies it as a common human property. In the language of eighteenth-century criticism, propriety of diction creates images of such clarity that the reader feels himself to be in the presence of things and experiences rather than of words, and he is enabled to do so because the images are general as well as particular. 'Generality', for (say) Johnson, has the same import as does 'impersonality' for Leavis, and both terms refer in their moral aspect, which is never far away, to the idea that poetry is a means of 'self-realisation': the reader's becoming aware in himself of the human fact. These familiar ideas, simple to outline, though they present problems when pursued theoretically, constitute what has been referred to above as the common core of principles.

Two points should be made immediately. First, though Richards' thinking is Coleridgean, it translates the idea of imaginative fusion or unity into one of multiple interconnection. Richards notes that such a step is necessary if analysis is to go on at all, but adds the equally necessary warning that the translation is merely a device and that multiple interconnection is not to be simply equated with imaginative power: no matter how dense the demonstrable system of verbal relations, there is always a leap from the demonstration to the claim that the work in question is imaginatively realised. Secondly, to establish the presence of the common core outlined above is an urgent need, because current studies of English criticism tend to exaggerate to an absurd degree the distinctive features of a given critic or critical school. Professor Wellek's account of Johnson, for example, in *A History of Modern Criticism*, isolates and elaborates the neo-classical elements, neglecting the common features, with the result that Johnson, who after all lived in England not very long ago, begins to resemble a critic from Mars. This tendency is accentuated by suggesting that criticism is closely linked with philosophy, so that, for instance, a critic in the age of Locke is seen as a radically different creature from one in the period of Kant or Wittgenstein. And that procedure, in turn, is furthered by an emphasis on critical theory with a corresponding neglect of critical practice, for it is from the latter that philosophical questions are most remote. The following chapters try to consider in detail what critics say about particular lines and poems, in the belief that such a procedure is necessary if the historian is to keep in touch with critical realities.

To return, the distinctive features of modern criticism largely revolve around the notion of fruitful conflict in poetic language, whereas the eighteenth-century bias reveals itself in an emphasis upon consonance. One can readily pinpoint this by thinking of Shakespeare criticism. The modern critic admires Shakespeare's free use of language, in which words are connected in such a way that their normal senses are slightly modified. The old sense and the new one imposed by the context react upon each other in a way which resembles the process of metaphor but without its formal features. This verbal complexity is seen as an index of the realising power of Shakespeare's poetry. Eliot, for example, in a well-known passage, finds in poetry of the Shakespearean kind,

> that perpetual slight alteration of language, words perpetually juxtaposed in new and sudden combinations, meanings perpetually *eingeschachtelt* into meanings, which evidences a very high development of the senses, a development of the English language which we have perhaps never equalled.

The phrase 'development of the senses' refers to the power of creating images. The eighteenth-century critic, on the other hand, is more anxious to detect the point at which the new meaning so dislocates the old that the word disintegrates, producing 'harshness' or 'obscurity', and his anxiety, being notorious, requires no immediate illustration. Yet he too (as we shall see when we look at Empson's critical method) rests finally on an appeal to the criterion of dense interconnection which is implicit in Eliot's remarks.

3. A critique of Empson

To apply the ideas outlined above to *Seven Types of Ambiguity*, is revealing. The chief points to seize are as follows: the first type of ambiguity resembles the doctrine of propriety, is the most important type,

and is different in kind from the later types; and the later types are
symptomatic of a continuing modern bias that entails a neglect of the
essential nature of poetry.

The first of these points can be illustrated from the opening pages or
Seven Types. Empson defines 'ambiguity' as what occurs when 'a word of
a grammatical structure is effective in several ways at once', and goes on
to give his well-known (notorious, one might say) commentary on the
line from Shakespeare's seventy-third sonnet, 'Bare ruined choirs, where
late the sweet birds sang':

> the comparison holds for many reasons; because ruined monastery
> choirs are places in which to sing, because they involve sitting in a
> row, because they are made of wood, are carved into knots and so
> forth, because they used to be surrounded by a sheltering building
> crystallised out of the likeness of a forest, and coloured with stained
> glass and painting like flowers and leaves . . .; these reasons, and
> many more relating the simile to its place in the sonnet, must all
> combine to give the line its beauty, and there is a sort of ambiguity
> in not knowing which of them to hold most clearly in mind. Clearly
> this is involved in all such richness and heightening of effect, and the
> machinations of ambiguity are among the very roots of poetry.
> (2–3)

The phrases 'holds for many reasons' and 'relating the simile to its place'
are sufficient to relate Empson's approach to those generated by the ideas
of propriety and interinanimation. Johnson, of course, pursues his points
less exhaustively, but a brief comparative sample of his analytic manner
will serve to indicate the community of spirit.

In the second part of *Henry VI*, Captain Whitmore, about to commit
murder as darkness falls, says:

> The gaudy, blabbing, and remorseful day
> Is crept into the bosom of the sea.

Johnson comments:

> The epithet 'blabbing' applied to the day by a man about to commit
> murder, is exquisitely beautiful. Guilt is afraid of light, considers
> darkness as a natural shelter, and makes night the confidante of those
> actions which cannot be trusted to the 'tell-tale day'.

Johnson is here sketching in the network of implications through which
the metaphor of day as informer is realised. It is worth adding, here,
Richards' remark (following Coleridge) that the reader, confronted with
a Shakespearean metaphor, 'finds cross-connexion after cross-connexion'
between the tenor and the vehicle (*Coleridge on Imagination*, 83).
Empson's own interest in eighteenth-century analytic criticism, which
clearly emerges in his later work on Milton, in *Some Versions of Pastoral*
and *Milton's God*, is already discernible in *Seven Types*.

The second and third points (that the first type of ambiguity is both
different from and more important than the remaining types) have both

been recognised by Empson himself, though the import of the recognition has gone unnoticed.

Empson notes the difference in a discussion with F. W. Bateson, in *Essays in Criticism*. Pressed by Bateson about some of the details of his commentary on 'bare ruined choirs', Empson remarks, 'my first type is meant to be different from the other ones' (*Essays in Criticism*, iii, 362). The difference is that in the later types there are conflicts between the various implicit meanings, whereas in the first type there are only different emphases, all of which are, so to speak, unidirectional (*Seven Types*, 48).

That the first type is by far the most important is recognised by Empson from the beginning. After the basic definition of ambiguity quoted above, he says 'such a definition of the first type of ambiguity covers almost everything of literary importance'. He adds that his chapter on the first type ought, therefore, to be his 'longest and most illuminating', but goes on to give reasons why this is not the case (3). The most important is the difficulty of proving the remoter meanings which Empson claims enrich 'bare ruined choirs'. This is true of analysis as subtle and fertile as Empson's, and most of the adverse criticism levelled against him has tended chiefly to accuse him of, to use his own phrase, 'spinning fancies out of his own mind' (49). He seems to have invited that sort of criticism, remarking, in a rather casual way, near the end of the book:

> I have, in fact, been as complete as I could in cases that seemed to deserve it, and considered whether each of the details was reasonable, not whether the result was reasonable as a whole. (244)

This is an important reservation, and it is typical of Empson not to have helped the reader by giving it more prominence. Had Elder Olsen, for instance, noticed it, his critique would have had to be abandoned since his intention is precisely to charge Empson with piling up meanings in that way.

Even allowing for Empson's reservation, detailed analysis of that kind runs the risk of squandering itself in fancifulness. This is true even of the rigorous-looking style of grammatical analysis practised by Jakobson. Empson's error, indicated by the word 'complete', was to attempt exhaustiveness. In his own case this is not important, since he is making the attempt only out of curiosity, and is well aware of the limitations of analysis. But his manner fell into the hands of practitioners who had not the restraining experience of being poets as well as critics, and were thus prone to feel that a complete account is possible, with the result that they tend to confuse their analyses with the poems themselves. They forgot that analysis can only, to recall Leavis' formulation, 'point to' or 'draw a line around' (discussed in *Scrutiny*, xi, 267). Exhaustive analysis, having confused the signpost with the place to which it is pointing, tries to put too much information on it; with the result that the reader who wants to get to the place – the poem – becomes impatient, while the one who is afflicted with the same belief as the critic is further confirmed in his feeling that, by looking at the signpost, he is actually travelling somewhere.

To turn to Empson's positive side, consider one of those analyses that command assent, leaving the reader with an increased sensitivity to and understanding of the poem in question. In a curious way he seems to anticipate a point that Richards, to the annoyance of his philosophical readers, occasionally develops in his later critical work: that imaginative language can be analysed only by imaginative language. Empson at his best not only points but moves the reader in the right direction. His comments on Nashe's famous lines are characteristic.

> Beauty is but a flower
> Which wrinkles will devour.
> Brightness falls from the air.
> Queens have died young and fair.
> Dust hath closed Helen's eye.
> I am sick, I must die.
>   Lord have mercy on us,

On 'dust hath closed Helen's eye', he comments:

> one must think of Helen in part as an undecaying corpse or a statue; it is *dust* from outside which settles on her eyelids, and shows that it is long since they have been opened; only in the background, as a truth which could not otherwise be faced, is it suggested that the *dust* is generated from her own corruption. As a result of this ambiguity, the line imposes on *brightness* a further and more terrible comparison; on the one hand, it is the *bright* notes dancing in sunbeams, which *fall* and become dust which is dirty and infectious; on the other, the lightness, gaiety, and activity of humanity, which shall come to dust in the grave.

This is primary criticism; it concerns itself with that without which other kinds of criticism can have no useful existence. It helps to put the reader in full possession of the statements and feelings about decay and death of which the poem consists, and in doing so it concentrates attention on what Johnson called 'the force of poetry': 'that force which calls new powers into being, which embodies sentiment, and animates matter' (*The Rambler*, 168). Even though Empson is speaking in terms of multiple interconnection, he contrives to keep the reader vividly in touch with the unitary imaginative effect.

It is necessary therefore to disagree, as Empson himself does, with James Smith's limiting criticism. Smith complains that Empson uses the word 'ambiguity' ambiguously, and continues:

> Is the ambiguity referred to that of life – is it a bundle of diverse forces, bound together only by their co-existence? Or is it that of a literary device – of the allusion, conceit, or pun, in one of their more or less conscious forms? If the first, Mr Empson's thesis is wholly mistaken; for a poem is not a mere fragment of life; it is a fragment

that has been detached, considered, and judged by a mind. A poem is a noumenon rather than a phenomenon. If the second, then at least we can say that Mr Empson's thesis is exaggerated. (*The Criterion*, x, 741)

Ambiguity of the *first* type does not involve a 'bundle of diverse forces'. It does not involve, either at a conscious or unconscious level, 'irony', 'tension', 'paradox', or whatever word of that kind one chooses to employ. It is much more than 'allusion, conceit, or pun'. Miss Tuve, wanting to take the wind out of Empson's sails, once remarked that his analytical method is an old one that has been 'resuscitated after some four or five hundred years and given a new slant' (Tuve, 'On Herbert's "Sacrifice"', 74). The essential idea is, indeed, old; Quintilian, speaking of 'proprietas', singles out that form of it 'which deserves the highest praise: the employment of words with the maximum of significance' (*Institutio Oratoria*, Act VIII, Scene ii, Line 1), and that is what Empson means by the first type of ambiguity. That it is centrally, not marginally, traditional should be seen, of course, not as a disadvantage, but as confirmation; and that Empson should have revived it seen not, as Miss Tuve implies, as a suspect critical dodge but as one of the remarkable features of his achievement. That Empson, though he never spells it out in detail, knew what he was doing is indicated by his comment on Johnson and on the state of criticism in the 1920s. There is now, he says, no 'positive machinery' of analysis such as Dr Johnson thought he had, 'to a great extent rightly', and the

> result is a certain lack of positive satisfaction in the reading of any poetry; doubt becomes a permanent background of the mind, both as to whether the thing is being interpreted rightly, and as to whether, if it is, one ought to allow oneself to feel pleased. (*Seven Types*, 255–6)

He then adds:

> It is not that such machinery is unknown so much that it is unpopular; people feel that, because it must always be inadequate, it must always be unfair. (*Ibid.*)

The contribution of Empson, and Richards, was a recall to what seems elementary – a reminder rather than a discovery – but people are still, as in Johnson's day, more frequently in need of being reminded than of being told; and to re-state in modern terms a 'machinery of analysis' of that kind, and to give good grounds for it, required a great and sustained effort of enquiry.

The fourth point (that the types, apart from Type I and its extension into Type II, represent a characteristic modern bias) requires discussion at slightly greater length, because, although the point is obvious enough in itself, it raises an interesting problem.

The later types owe much to Richards' concept of 'irony', though they tend to give it more psychoanalytical weighting than is present in Richards. The debt can be seen, for instance, in Empson's comment on

Herbert's poem 'The Sacrifice': 'the contradictory impulses that are held
in equilibrium by the doctrine of atonement may be seen in a luminous
juxtaposition' (*Seven Types*, 224). The phrasing here echoes that of the
definition of irony in *Principles of Literary Criticism* (see, for example,
242). And that sort of contradiction is central to the later types, as is made
clear by Empson's definition of the fourth type:

> An ambiguity of the fourth type occurs when two or more meanings
> of a statement do not agree among themselves, but combine to make
> clear a more complicated state of mind in the author. Evidently this
> is a vague enough definition which would cover much of the third
> type, and almost everything in the types which follow. (*Seven Types*,
> 133)

Empson, pressed by his own theory, tends to find conflict where none
exists and, also, more important, the nearer a poem approaches to his
seventh type (the purest in the series) the less value it has as a poem. The
argument needs discussion only of a key poem from the seventh type,
since this can be related to a general principle, which can be conveniently
outlined by referring again to James Smith's adverse comment on
Empson's approach. The point on which to agree with Smith is that a
poem is a 'noumenon' rather than a 'phenomenon'; that it has been
'detached, considered, and judged by a mind'. Empson assumes, in
crucial instances, an intolerable degree of unawareness on the part of the
poet.

The problem of the poet's awareness and of the success of the poem is
best handled by using our original cluster of ideas, where the term 'realisation' refers both to vividness of presentation (which can be analysed
as complexity of language) and to awareness of what the experience presented *is*. The process is different from any mere immersion in experience,
no matter how vivid it might be. Further, verbal complexity, in this connection, shows itself as a system of interrelated meanings. If we apply
this to Empson's approach we find that, when he is pursuing meanings of
which he claims the poet is unaware, he unbalances the total system
which *is* the poem. The usual cautionary note has, of course, to be
sounded; it is not a question of demonstrating that a high degree of coherence is equivalent to realisation, but of making analytic suggestions
that the reader can pursue and test for himself against a reading of the
poem. However, apart from one's ultimate views on that question, it is
easy enough to show that the poems considered by Empson have more
coherence than he allows.

His analysis of Hopkins' 'The Windhover', a key poem of the seventh
type, is characteristic. Empson puts the poem in this category by claiming
that Hopkins, without knowing it, is juxtaposing two contradictory impulses, one towards spiritual, the other towards physical, fulfilment. In
Empson's view the crucial word in the poem is 'buckle', which he says has
two meanings:

Brute beauty and valour and act, oh, air, pride, plume, here
Buckle! AND the fire that breaks from thee then, a billion
Times told lovelier, more dangerous, O my chevalier!

Empson defines the two meanings as follows:
> *buckle* like a military belt, for the discipline of heroic action, and
> *buckle* like a bicycle wheel, 'make useless, distorted, and incapable of
> its natural motion'.

This double meaning reflects, for Empson, the conflict to be found in the
poem as a whole:
> Confronted suddenly with the active physical beauty of the bird, he
> [Hopkins] conceives it as the opposite of his patient spiritual re-
> nunciation; the statements of the poem appear to insist that his own
> life is superior, but he cannot decisively judge between them, and
> holds both with agony in his mind. (225)

'Conceives', 'judge' and 'in his mind' are rather questionable, because
Empson wants also to insist that Hopkins is *unaware* of the second
meaning of 'buckle': 'he would have denied with anger that he had meant
"like a bicycle wheel", and then after much conscientious self-torture
would have suppressed the whole poem' (226, footnote). It is more
profitable to examine the point in terms of realisation and interconnection
or unity, rather than to tackle directly the question of awareness. What
Empson calls the second meaning of 'buckle' is the primary and obvious
meaning, because it is insisted on by the surrounding context. This is
most obvious in 'fire that breaks', where the vehicle of the metaphor refers
to something bending under pressure and sending out sparks – a metaphor, probably, from the forge. 'Buckle' is immediately connected with
that, and more widely with the two final metaphors of the poem; the
bright, bending movement is repeated when the downward pressure on
the ploughshare makes it shine and when the falling of the embers makes
them break and glow.

This repeated metaphoric effect grows from the central statement of
the poem, which says that submission is both more exciting and beautiful
than self-assertion; and the interconnected meanings just outlined are the
realisation of that statement.

To return to 'buckle', the sense 'collapse' is also accentuated by the
sound and movement of the lines, which closely connect 'buckle' with
'breaks'. Further, it is not difficult to find a place for the other sense (as in
buckling a belt); the poet's feeling for the 'brute beauty' of the bird has
to be *gathered* and *concentrated* before it can be collapsed. The two
meanings taken together thus describe that readily recognisable action of
the mind by which an impulse is gathered to clear definition and then
dealt with.

Empson's interpretation destroys not only this system of meanings but
almost everything else in the poem. It cannot recognise, for instance, the
clear and consistent *tone* in which the poem speaks about the bird. The

tone is one in which delighted admiration is tempered by a critical note, a
note particularly clear in such phrases as 'brute beauty' and 'air, pride,
plume', and which has been introduced in the first line of the poem with
the arresting word 'minion'. 'Air', for instance, has a double range of
meaning; as well as referring to the free element in which the bird dis-
plays its power and thus continuing the sense of delight, it also carries the
meaning which appears in such stock phrases as 'he gives himself airs'.
This latter sense is brought out by contact with 'plume', which has a hint
of the phrase 'to plume oneself', as well as a reference to beautiful plum-
age. Further, the tone generated by these meanings is transmitted, by way
of 'minion', to 'dauphin'; the air, pride and plume are those of a courtly
hanger-on; and, finally, that atmosphere surrounding the bird is contrasted with the images in which the bird is rejected: the forge, the
ploughshare and the hearth all implying the reverse of courtly display.

Empson is, of course, himself aware of the problem raised by his
method. To speak of a poem as a system of interconnected meanings is,
evidently, to speak of its unity, and Empson tackles that issue as follows:

> all the subsidiary meanings must be relevant, because anything
> (phrase, sentence, or poem) meant to be considered as a unit must
> be unitary, must stand for a single order of the mind. In complicated
> situations this unity is threatened; you are thinking of several
> things, or one thing as it is shown by several things, or one thing in
> several ways. A sort of unity may be given by the knowledge of a
> scheme on which all the things occur; so that the scheme itself
> becomes the one thing which is being considered. (234)

It follows that Empson's view, that 'The Windhover' embodies un-
resolved conflict in the poet, itself becomes the 'scheme' which incorpor-
ates all the meanings which Empson finds in the poem. It needs little
reflection to see that precisely the same could be said of the way in which
a psychiatrist makes sense of and thus gives unity to the ramblings of a
patient. The unity of a poem is of a different order.

The tendency of Empson's word 'scheme' is clear enough: a poem
becomes an item to be generalised and fitted into whatever arrangement
the critic has in mind: in this case the framework of the seven types of
ambiguity. That the poem has its own uniquely valuable mode of
generalising, without losing the immediate particularity of the experience,
is ignored. The tendency is far more marked now than it was in the
twenties, and it is inevitably generated by any critical approach which
ignores the elements of poetry considered as 'realisation'. It is worthwhile
examining briefly a typical instance.

4. Literary evaluation and linguistic analysis

Reductivism is always a danger in literary criticism; the kind now in
question is that which is generally associated with such phrases as 'a poem
is a complex linguistic entity'. That sort of language is not necessarily
misleading, but one of its common abuses is exemplified in Roger

Fowler's 'The Structure of Criticism and the Languages of Poetry', which is a convenient piece for discussion since it offers itself, in an introductory anthology of contemporary critical approaches, as an argument for the 'approach through language'. The initial step (Empson's name is adduced as a support for taking it) is to say that there is no essential difference between the language of poetry and language in other uses. The following statement is characteristic:

> the communicative activities of a society are . . . split again and again and again with great delicacy and complexity into perhaps thousands of functional adaptations – commercials, sonnets, workshop manuals, recipes, odes, metaphysical lyrics . . ., dirty jokes, classical plays, Mozartian libretti, meteorological reports, epics, sports commentaries . . . (*Stratford on Avon Studies*, xii, 187)

The step is facilitated by emphasising the importance of *all* language: it is 'creative' (as Chomsky says); it determines the nature of its speaker's 'world'; it carries with it, in each of its numerous registers, an attendant cultural complex; and so on.

Having argued that poetry is amenable to the kind of analysis employed by linguists on other language uses, Fowler gives some brief examples of his method in practice. Typical of these is a general commentary on Pope's *Essay on Man*. Pope's style, it is said, full of antithesis, oxymoron, paradox, and so on, exhibits the same sort of tensions as does man's focal position on the Chain of Being. Fowler touches on this only briefly and in general terms, but it is easy to imagine the connection between linguistic features and cultural elements being demonstrated in great detail and at great length, with an exposition of the significance of the Chain of Being for neo-classical civilisation.

There is, however, an essential and obvious omission in Fowler's scheme. In the discussion in Chapter 14 of *Biographia Literaria*, Coleridge acknowledges the obvious sense in which Fowler's basic contention is true. A poem, Coleridge confesses, 'contains the same elements as a prose composition'. But he then devotes himself to explaining the difference in *effect*, which hinges on the presence in poetry of the realising imagination. The way in which that presence shows itself in the *language* of poetry has already been touched upon. All language may be 'creative' in Chomsky's sense, but it is certainly not 'creative' in Coleridge's sense, which is the sense that matters when we are speaking of poetry.

In any linguistic community it is, as Fowler says, important to be able to distinguish between an epic and a dirty joke (and that, even granting the great delicacy and complexity of the socio-linguistic structure, is not after all a very difficult procedure): to be a literary critic or theorist it is also necessary to be able to distinguish between a *good* epic and a *bad* one, between, say, one by Milton and one by Blackmore. Since Fowler's analytic method takes no account of the poetic imagination it is unable to do this.

To put it in a slightly different way, an essential part of our feeling that we are in the presence of a poem is a sense of its value. This is not a matter of measuring ('*a* is better than *b*', and so forth) but of what Pope, for instance, had in mind when he described 'wit' as 'something whose truth convinced at sight we find / That gives us back the image of our mind.' That 'shock of recognition' is obviously by no means infallible; we all sometimes have it when we shouldn't and fail to have it when we should; but it remains an indispensable criterion. It is not as mysterious in origin as prickling sensations at the back of the neck or other similar tokens of conviction. It is, as Pope's phrasing indicates, a sign that we are in the presence of 'realised' art and is therefore amenable to an analytic approach though of a suggestive not a demonstrative kind.

To return to Fowler's example, it is clear that *any* Augustan couplets about the Chain of Being could be described in the same way as he describes *An Essay on Man*. His claim, therefore, that his approach can 'specify what kind of object' a poem *is* ('Structure of Criticism', 179) and consequently produce a general theory of poetry, has to be rejected. This is no mere theoretical quibble. It is a sad irony of much current literary criticism that a subtle analytic technique, divorced from the broader and 'unscientific' principles that have traditionally both justified analysis and kept it within due bounds, actively inhibits students from recognising, not theoretically but in their imaginations, the nature of poetry.

Having commented on that critical line and noted its relation with Empson, it is important to distinguish between it and a related line, which owes more to Richards and which, though more subtle, is open to similar objections. An instructive example is an essay by Michael Riffaterre which was part of a celebrated structuralist exegetic orgy, started by Jakobson and Levi-Strauss, over Baudelaire's sonnet, 'Les Chats'. This essay is particularly useful for our purposes for several reasons; Riffaterre is a sensitive and sensible critic, so that one isn't attacking merely a man of straw; the essay states with great clarity the theory and the method which it exemplifies; and the discussion of which it formed a part occurred at the heart of the structuralist movement.

Riffaterre's theory differs from Fowler's in two important respects announced at the beginning of his essay; he believes that the language of poetry is different from everyday language, and that his method of analysing it can indicate poetic value. The connection with Richards can be briefly registered by quoting Riffaterre's statement of the central principle, which he shares with Jakobson: 'the recurrence of equivalent forms, *parallelism*, is the basic relationship underlying poetry' (*Yale French Studies*, xxxvii/xxxviii, 201). W.K.Wimsatt has noted the connection between this principle and some suggestions made by Richards, developing the theory of interinanimation, in *The Philosophy of Rhetoric* (see *Stratford on Avon Studies*, xii, 77). Richards points out that the evocative force of words like 'flash', for example, comes from their calling up, in the background, a group of associated words ('flame', 'flare', 'flicker', and so on). It is easy to see the connection between this and alliteration, except that alliteration works not in the implicit background of words but explicitly along the line of the syntax. Jakobson generalises Richards' observation into the theory that the power of poetry is a matter of numerous patterns of recurrence of that type. The recurrences may be obvious, as in the case of rhyme, or of great subtlety and delicacy.

A commentator armed with this theory and possessing some skill in phonetic, syntactic, and semantic description, has an analytic machine of great power; seeing it at work on a poem is rather like watching a combine harvester going through a field of wheat. Riffaterre's analysis of 'Les Chats' need not be described in detail; it is sufficient to make two points about the theory, disregarding the validity of this particular application of it. First, Riffaterre criticises the Jakobson/Levi-Strauss analysis of the poem, on the grounds that they have been sometimes misled by recurrences which have nothing to do with the poetic structure but which spring merely from the fact that all language, particularly at the phonetic and syntactic levels, naturally exhibits patterns of recurrence. This is obviously true and will be referred to again later. Riffaterre's sensible safeguard is to let analysis be guided, from the start, by some well-attested opinions, from poets and critics, about the broad structure of the poem.

Second, Riffaterre (and this is where the weakness of his theory lies) in claiming to demonstrate the value of the poem, *equates* value with a high degree of coherence. Like Richards, that is, he translates the idea of imaginative fusion into one of multiple interconnection; but he lacks Richards' awareness that this is only an analytic device. The deficiency is immediately clear if we move from theory to practice; one can find any amount of critical exposition of subtle coherence in poems of no more than competent quality; conversely, there are poems of the first rank, such as *The Waste Land*, the over-all coherence of which has been seriously questioned. There is always a leap from the demonstration of coherence to the claim that a work is imaginatively realised, and the leap is always a real one, not a formality. Riffaterre, as one would expect, seems to be half-aware of this, since, after his long analytic commentary, he does not repeat his claim to have shown that the poem has high value, but contents himself with saying that he has given a complete interpretation. That is true, and a useful thing to have done, so long as its limitations are not forgotten.

That they *are* easily forgotten, and in influential quarters, is inadvertently shown by the essay by Wimsatt referred to above. It quotes Jakobson's 'structural' analysis of the slogan used in Eisenhower's presidential compaign: 'I like Ike'. The analysis shows, convincingly, that the phonetic and syntactic pattern is close, subtle, and in connection with the deeper reverberations of the words; it is, indeed, a very clever bit of public relations rhetoric. Wimsatt then notes that the analysis is merely a 'humorous capsule' which shows what the method can do if applied to more worthy matter. But how can the reader know that it *is* only a 'humorous capsule', except by exercising his literary judgement? And here one has to refer again to the point made by Riffaterre that Jakobson's approach, being essentially uncritical, is likely to discover 'patterns' which are merely accidental, having nothing to do with the particular structure of the poem. The element in Wimsatt's argument that is particularly dangerous, and characteristic, is that he claims to be taking a moderate stance. The literary critic, he feels, can make use of the analytic method in order to 'locate poetic objects' without succumbing to the grammarians' totalitarian claim that they can account for *everything* in a poem. But, as we have seen, all that the method can locate is a high degree of coherence; the poem is somewhere else.

The question of the inevitable gap between analysis and response can be usefully discussed a little further by referring again to Leavis' dictum that analysis can only 'point to' or 'draw a line around'. In Leavis' later work the belief implied in that dictum is developed with reference to the thinking of Polanyi. The extent to which Polanyi's doctrine that 'we know more than we can tell', with its attendant critique of the ideal of objectivity, will, or should, influence the philosophy of science, is, of course, far beyond the scope of this enquiry, but its applicability to literary criticism is cardinal.

To recall it very briefly, Polanyi's account of knowledge emphasises the function of 'attending to' the details of something felt to be a whole, and also the way in which the details disappear into the background when we are 'attending *from*' them to the whole itself. This is evidently one way in which one can speak of our 'leap', and it correctly indicates both the value and the limitations of the analysis of poetry. To have a steady grasp of this should lead to a critical style which doesn't try to escape from its responsibilities by fleeing either into attempts at demonstration or into claims that 'it is all a matter of taste'.

It will by now be apparent that my sketch of English literary criticism is essentially normative. It should, therefore, also be made clear that to speak of a 'common core of principles' and 'distinctive features' is not to suggest that the latter ought to be removed, yielding some ideally pure critical theory. 'Distinctive features' are evidently related, in ways we shall consider when we look at particular critics, to changes of taste and sensibility. Such changes are the forces which drive critics to necessary, and varying, restatements of essentials, and there is no danger of imagining that literature and criticism could continue without them. The opposite danger – of mistaking such changes for radical changes of principle – is, however, one to which the history of English criticism frequently succumbs. One of the aims of the following chapters is to make this less likely to happen.

PART ONE

I. A. RICHARDS

Chapter One

Towards a General Theory of Complexity

Chapter Two

Interinanimation and Activity

CHAPTER ONE

TOWARDS A GENERAL THEORY
OF COMPLEXITY

The Meaning of Meaning

1. Richards' context theory

Ogden & Richards' *The Meaning of Meaning*, first published in 1923, is a foray into the general problem of language and reality, but we need isolate from it only a few cardinal features which are in various ways important for an understanding of Richards' later development. The villain of the book is 'verbal superstition'; the confusion of verbal fabrication and real world. Its burden is that we must consistently distinguish between two uses of language, the referential and the emotive. The former points to the world, the latter arouses or expresses feelings.

The *context theory* of meaning, used to explain the operation of referential language, recurs at later points in Richards' work. The theory is an associationist one, presented in causal terms. In *Principles of Literary Criticism* (1926) it is summarised thus:

> On a number of occasions [a] word is heard in connection with objects of a certain kind. Later the word is heard in the absence of any such object. In accordance with one of the few fundamental laws known about mental process, something then happens in the mind which is like what would happen if such an object were actually present and engaging the attention. The word has become a sign of an object of that kind. (PLC, 127)

As the phrasing implies, this account is part of a general theory of signs, which Hotopf (1965) summarises as follows:

> whenever an object, which has been experienced together with or just before another object, causes us to think of that other, then it acts as a *sign* of the other. These objects are then said to form a context; supply one part of the *context*, and thought of the other follows. (*Language, Thought and Comprehension*, 21)

In *The Meaning of Meaning* (52–4) this is illustrated by saying that a match-scrape may become a sign of the ensuing flame.

The context theory insists that there is no direct relation between words and things. The triangle of meaning is offered as a diagrammatic model of referential meaning (see Fig. 1). In referential language-uses, the word (symbol) occasions a thought (reference) of an object of a certain kind (referent). Such an occurrence is called a 'symbol-situation'. But in most verbal utterances two kinds of sign-situation are involved:

> One is interpreted from symbols to reference and so to referent; the

thought or reference

causal   causal
relation   relation

symbol – – – – – – – – – – imputed – – – – – – – – – – referent
relation

other is interpreted from verbal signs to the attitude, mood, interest, purpose, desire, and so forth of the speaker, and thence to the situation, circumstances and conditions in which the utterance is made.
The first of these is a symbol situation . . ., the second is merely a verbal sign-situation like the sign-situations involved in all ordinary perception. (MM, 223–4)

The words 'attitude', 'mood', 'interest', 'purpose', 'desire' link directly with the division of meaning into a number of different aspects, or functions. Five functions are enumerated (MM, 226–7):

(i) symbolisation of reference; (ii) the expression of attitude to listener; (iii) the expression of attitude to referent; (iv) the promotion of effects intended; (v) support of reference

The fifth function is little used after *The Meaning of Meaning*. It is described as follows:

Besides their truth, or falsity, references have a character which may be called, from the accompanying feelings, Ease or Difficulty. Two references to the same referent may be true but differ widely in this ease, a fact which may be reflected in their symbols. (MM, 225)

The first four functions are commonly referred to, in Richards' subsequent writing, as sense, tone, feeling and intention (PC, 181ff). In a later essay, 'Towards a Theory of Comprehending' (SI, 26), a scheme of seven functions appears, which correspond to the earlier five, approximately as follows:

sense $\left\{\begin{array}{l}\text{indicating}\\\text{characterising}\end{array}\right.$

tone
feeling $\left\{\begin{array}{l}\text{valuing}\\\text{influencing}\end{array}\right.$

intention $\left\{\begin{array}{l}\text{controlling}\\\text{proposing}\end{array}\right.$

support of
reference $\left\{\text{realising}\right.$

This suggestion of correspondence is not intended to be exact, but merely to show that there is, in the later schema, nothing essentially new.

The only other important point to be remembered at present from *The Meaning of Meaning* is that, from the basic account of meaning, a number of rules are derived from determining whether or not a given statement is emotive or referential and, as far as is possible, what sign-situations its references actually involve. These rules are called 'Canons of Symbolism' (MM 87–108). By reference to them a word or statement is translated into the various sign-situations which it might possibly involve. The relevance of this procedure to modern analysis of poetry may be judged by thinking again of the Empsonian analysis of 'Bare ruined choirs where late the sweet birds sang'. It can be said to consist of an enumeration of the sign-situations that may lie behind the words, together with an assertion that the line involves all of them. Thus, although 'ambiguity', or multiple-meaning is, in *The Meaning of Meaning*, regarded as one of the villains of the piece, the insistence upon its ubiquity opens a way for a demonstration of the part it plays in poetic language.

2. Referential and emotive language

This brief outline raises questions in psychology and philosophy which go beyond the scope and competence of this account, but there are several points to note.

The first concerns the aspect of meaning called 'intention'. In general this is heavily stressed and the supplement by Malinowski gives it a central place in an account of language as a tool by which we achieve our ends rather than as a picture of reality (MM, 312) but there is no psychological account of it in the language model which is the keystone of the book. In *Practical Criticism* (1929) and *Coleridge on Imagination* (1934), Richards is able, though with some hesitancy, to discuss the relations between 'sense' and 'tone', or 'sense' and 'feeling', but he is unable to deal with 'intention' in the same way. 'Intention', in fact, is not in the same category as 'tone' and 'feeling'. It may well be a function of reference rather than emotion. Something as purely referential as a railway time-table has an 'intention'. Richards was to realise this and, in an appendix to *Practical Criticism*, says that 'intention' has the function of controlling the relations between the other three aspects. Later, in *Speculative Instruments* (1955), he says: 'Purposing, if you ask for a theory about it . . . can hardly be made more than a puzzle. It is too central' (172–3). This point becomes of importance in a discussion of Schiller's interpretation of Richards' ideas about poetic language, which lays great stress on 'purposing'.

The second point concerns the widespread misunderstanding of what Richards meant by calling the language of poetry 'emotive' rather than 'referential'. Krieger in *The New Apologists for Poetry*, for instance, says that Richards made a 'complete denial to poetry of the rational and meaningful' (142). It is important to clarify both what Richards *was* saying, and what he was *not*. He was not saying that poetry does not employ referential language. A summarised version of the point, from *Principles of Literary Criticism*, offers itself for convenient quotation:

A statement may be used for the sake of the *reference*, true or false, which it causes. This is the *scientific* use of language. But it may also

be used for the sake of the effects in emotion and attitude produced
by the reference it occasions. This is the *emotive* use of language.
(PLC, 267)

What Richards *was* saying may be illustrated by the following:

> Only occasionally will a symbolisation be available which, without
> loss of its symbolic *accuracy*, is also *suitable* (to the author's attitude
> to his public), *appropriate* (to his referent), *judicious* (likely to
> produce the desired effects) and *personal* (indicative of the stability
> or instability of his references). The odds are very strongly against
> there being many symbols able to do so much. (MM, 234)

Put another way, the differences between 'referential' and 'emotive' uses,
'are due simply to the fact that an arrangement of symbols which will
re-instate a situation by evoking emotions similar to those originally involved will, as things happen, very rarely be an adequate symbol for it'
(MM, 239). Richards was, in fact, noting no more than Johnson, in his
discussion of the 'familiar' style, which he thought should be the staple
of epistolary literature:

> But it is natural to depart from familiarity of language upon occa-
> sions not familiar. Whatever elevates the sentiments will con-
> sequently raise the expression; whatever fills us with hope or terror
> will produce some perturbation of images, and some figurative
> distortions of phrase. (*Rambler*, 152)

Johnson's phrase 'raising of the expression' is equivalent to Richards'
'emotive aspects of language', and his 'perturbation of images' is equivalent to Richards' 'loss of symbolic accuracy'. Both Richards and Johnson
are noting an obvious truth: obvious, that it, if one has in mind a rigorous
notion of symbolic adequacy.

3. Underplaying meaning, and overplaying language

Those who have attacked Richards' insistence that the language of
poetry is emotive have therefore commonly misunderstood him, as
Hotopf claimed. There is, however, a weakness in Richards' early formulations which may have lent colour to the misunderstanding.

This weakness is describable as an implicit assumption that Swinburne
is the standard for discussing the language of poetry, and it involves a
heavy stress on what Richards was later to call 'tied imagery', which consists of 'articulatory imagery' and 'auditory imagery', produced by the
physical process of speaking and hearing the words, both of these effects
being heightened by metrical arrangement (PLC 118–21). In *The
Meaning of Meaning* it is said, for instance:

> One of the chief distinctions . . . between poetry and strict scientific
> prose is that in poetry we must consciously attend to the sensory
> characters of the words, whereas in prose we need not do so. This
> conscious attention to words as sounds does, however, tend to
> impede our further interpretations. (MM, 210)

The theme is later repeated in the remark that the 'means by which words may evoke feelings and attitudes are many', followed by a list of means headed by tied imagery and rhythm. He adds that 'rhythms, and especially metres, have to a small degree an hypnotic effect' (MM, 239). Emotionality, exaggeration of belief-feelings, the occulting of the critical faculties, the suppression of the questioning – 'Is this so as a matter of fact?' – attitude, all these are characteristics of metrical experiences and fit in well with a hypnosis assumption. (MM, 240) These remarks involve more than a view that strictly referential truth is irrelevant to poetry. They suggest a general relaxing of the mind, of the kind that some modern critics have seen to be deleteriously inculcated by poetry like Swinburne's.

The underplaying of mental activity in the reading of poetry may partly spring from the concept of two sign-situations being involved in verbal utterance, as described above. It seems likely that this view of the emotive aspect, as different in kind from the referential, inhibited interest in the relations between them. These relations were to interest Richards more, as his thinking developed, and his ponderings on them in *Practical Criticism* are an important step on the way to the ideas expressed in *Coleridge on Imagination*.

The separation of referential and emotive is further apparent in the comments on metaphor in *The Meaning of Meaning*. Metaphor is divided into two broad kinds: 'emotive' and 'symbolic'. Richards says of the former:

> [it is] used not, as in strict symbolising, to bring out . . . a structural feature in a reference, but rather to provide, often under cover of a pretence of this elucidation, new, sudden and striking collocations of references for the sake of the compound effects of contrast, conflict, harmony, inter-inanimation and equilibrium which may be so attained. (MM, 240)

The latter involves 'the use of one reference to a group of things between which a given relation holds, for the purpose of facilitating the discrimination of an analogous relation in another group' (MM, 213).

Principles of Literary Criticism uses the same formulation as *The Meaning of Meaning*. A symbolic metaphor is 'illustrative or diagrammatical, providing a concrete instance of a relation which would otherwise have to be stated in abstract terms' (PLC, 239). An emotive metaphor is a 'semi-surreptitious method by which a greater variety of elements can be wrought into the fabric of the experience'. In *Practical Criticism*, however, the emphasis is changed. The distinction between the two modes is drawn, but Richards now claims that one usually finds a combination of the two and that most 'descriptions of feelings, and nearly all subtle descriptions, are metaphorical and of the combined type' (PC, 222). By this time, having become more interested in the interweaving of the two aspects, he was unable to separate them.

There is a further weakness in *The Meaning of Meaning*, which runs through Richards' work, and will be discussed in more detail in relation to his thought after *Coleridge on Imagination*. This weakness is an excessive faith in the powerful knowledge released by a mastery of the laws of language, and it is one of the central topics of Hotopf's critique. Hotopf contends that Richards overestimates the benefit to be derived from a heightened awareness of how language works, and neglects such obvious ways of increasing understanding as, for instance, a growing familiarity with a given subject. In so far as the study of literature is concerned, Richards' procedure, and his high ambitions, are clearly stated in *The Philosophy of Rhetoric*. Here he defines 'rhetoric', which he sees as the central discipline of the humanities, as 'a philosophic discipline aiming at a mastery of the fundamental laws of the use of language', and adds that 'the whole business of Rhetoric comes down to comparisons between the meanings of words'. English literature, as a subject for study, was always of interest for Richards primarily as a source of material for enquiry into 'the fundamental laws of the use of language'. It is hard to think of any other English critic who might be described as 'major', whose interest in literature is so peripheral. His dominating pursuit of an understanding of language that would provide the key to literature and to life, and the corresponding absence of any deep or prolonged study of a given body of literature, have two consequences for Richards' thinking about the analysis of poetic language. First, it leads him to exaggerate the scope of the analysis of linguistic complexity. This happens, as we shall see, in *Coleridge on Imagination*. Later, however, a certain disillusionment appears, for example in the extreme modesty of his commentary on a poem by Empson (see Chapter 6 below). Although Richards developed a satisfactory idea of complexity in the language of poetry, and a satisfactory method of analysis, he was less sure of their proper scope, at one moment holding out fantastic hopes, at another advocating excessive caution. In his more optimistic moments he affords support to the ambitious side of contemporary analytical criticism.

Principles of Literary Criticism

1. Richards' general theory of complexity: impersonality, irony, and vigilance

In *Principles of Literary Criticism*, Richards turns aside from his concern with language to develop a general notion of *complexity*. This notion requires an extended quotation:

> The extent to which any activity is conscious seems to depend very largely upon how complex and how novel it is. The primitive and in a sense natural outcome of stimulus is action; the more simple the situation with which the mind is engaged, the closer is the connection between the stimulus and some overt response in action, and in general the less rich and full is the consciousness attendant. A man walking over uneven ground, for example, makes without reflection or emotion a continuous adjustment of his steps to his footing; but

let the ground become precipitous and, unless he is used to such places, both reflection and emotion will appear. The increased complexity of the situation and the greater delicacy and appropriateness of the movements required for convenience and safety, call forth far more complicated goings on in the mind. Besides his perception of the nature of the ground, the thought may occur that a false move would be perilous and difficult to retrieve. This, when accompanied by emotion, is called a 'realisation' of his situation. The adjustment to one another of varied impulses – to go forward carefully, to lie down and grasp something with the hands, to go back, and so forth – and their co-ordination into useful behaviour alters the whole character of his experience. (PLC, 109)

Richards was an enthusiastic climber, and the spectacular nature of the example is perhaps a little distracting, but the main features are clear. The complexity of response produced by unfamiliarity creates a richer consciousness; when this is accompanied by emotion, a realisation of the experience occurs. This point lies behind Richards' elaboration of 'stock-responses'. The 'stock-response' is that of the man unthinkingly walking over uneven ground. Conversely, the description of the unfamiliar situation employs words which are recurrent in the school of criticism that Richards helped to found: 'complexity', 'realisation', 'delicacy', 'rich and full ... consciousness', and so on. Richards' essential point is commonplace enough. His stress on the importance of novelty is like that which appears, for example, in Johnson's definition of 'wit' or Coleridge's definition of the imagination. As Richards himself says in the preface, 'one does not expect novel cards when playing so traditional a game' (PLC, I).

Two further points about that account should be made. First, it supposes a high level of discrimination of stimuli; and, second, neither here, nor at any other point in *Principles of Literary Criticism*, is there an account of the complexity of poetic *language*. The first is important because Richards, at certain points, argues a view of poetry that involves a low level of discrimination. This, as we have seen, is prominent in *The Meaning of Meaning*; it will be referred to henceforth, for the sake of convenience, as Richards' 'hypnotic theory' of poetry. The second is important because Richards' essential achievement, in *Coleridge on Imagination*, was the formulation of a general idea of complexity in such a way that it could be conveniently harnessed to his ideas about the complexity of poetic language.

The above account of 'complexity' has bearings on some other key ideas in *Principles of Literary Criticism*. First, *impersonality*, which is defined in terms of complexity of response. Richards describes our reaction to certain poems as follows:

We cease to be oriented in one definite direction; more facets of the mind are exposed and, what is the same thing, more aspects of things are able to affect us. To respond, not through one narrow

channel of interest, but simultaneously and coherently through
many, is to be *disinterested* in the only sense of the word which
concerns us here . . . And to say that we are *impersonal* is merely a
curious way of saying that our personality is more *completely*
involved. (PLC, 251-2)

Such poems, in this way, make us feel that we are in close touch with
actuality. In responding to things or experiences in the complex way just
described, 'we seem to see "all round them", to see them as they really
are; we see them apart from any one particular interest which they may
have for us. (PLC, 252).

'Impersonality', thus defined, is closely related to Richards' well-
known definition of *irony*. He offers this in terms of two contrasted
groups of poems:

A poem of the first group is built out of sets of impulses which run
parallel, which have the same direction. In a poem of the second
group the most obvious feature is the extraordinarily [sic] heterogeneity of the distinguishable impulses. But they are more than
heterogeneous, they are opposed. They are such that in ordinary,
non-poetic, non-imaginative experience, one or other set would be
suppressed to give as it might appear freer development to the
others. (PLC, 250)

The quality which the second group possesses is called 'irony', a somewhat technical term, having only a tenuous link with the ordinary use of
the word. Richards is overtly describing the 'equilibrium' resulting from
the resolution of such opposed impulses, but in terms of a feeling of
increased awareness of actuality, and the account of 'irony' blends with
the account of 'impersonality' already described. The same is true of the
account of 'synaesthesis' in Ogden & Richards' *The Foundations of
Aesthetics* of which the closing words are:

In conclusion, the reason why equilibrium is a justification for the
preference of one experience before another, is the fact that it
brings into play all our faculties. In virtue of what we have called the
synaesthetic character of the experience, we are enabled, as we have
seen, to appreciate relationships in a way which would not be possible under normal circumstances. Through no other experience
can the full richness and complexity of our environment be realised.
The ultimate value of equilibrium is that it is better to be fully than
partially alive. (91)

Thus, both 'impersonality' and 'irony' are defined in terms of a complex
response which produces a heightened consciousness of actuality.

The idea of a complex response through many channels is elaborated
in Richards' account of the poet's memory. Memory is described as 'that
apparent revival of past experience to which the richness and complexity
of experience is due' (PLC, 103). As a model of the working of memory
Richards gives, instead of metaphors from telephone exchanges or
stores of records, this:

an energy system of prodigious complexity and extreme delicacy of organisation, which has an indefinitely large number of stable poises. Imagine it thrown from one poise to another with great facility, each poise being the resultant of all the energies of the system. Suppose now that the *partial* return of a situation which has formerly caused it to assume a stable poise, throws it into an unstable condition from which it most easily returns to equilibrium by reassuming the former poise. Such a system would exhibit the phenomena of memory; but it would keep no records though appearing to do so. (PLC, 104)

We are invited, as an aid to comprehension, to think of this system as a polyhedron 'with a large number of facets upon any one of which it can rest' (PLC, 105).

This model is put to use in Chapter XXII, 'The Poet's Experience'. The argument is as follows. The poet's experience is unusually rich and complex, because he is unusually able to connect disparate areas of experience. He can do so because his past experience is at easier recall. Richards quotes Dryden's description of Shakespeare as a man to whom 'all the images of nature were still present' (PLC, 181). One might also remember Boswell's account of Johnson's mind, which Leavis quotes in *The Common Pursuit* while describing the vitality of Johnson's poetry:

> As he was general and unconfined in his studies, he cannot be considered as a master of any one particular science; but he had accumulated a vast and various collection of learning and knowledge, which was so arranged in his mind, as to be ever in readiness to be brought forth. (163)

Or one may equally well recall Eliot's description of the poet's mind as 'a receptacle for seizing and storing up numberless feelings, phrases, images, which remain there until all the particles which can unite to form a new compound are present together'.

In Richards' scheme, recall of a complex structure of impulses will be more frequent than that of a simple structure. In terms of the imaginary polyhedron, 'the broader the facet the more numerous are the positions from which the polyhedron will settle down on that facet' (PLC, 182).

But the complex structure must be *organised*: 'Experience which has this organised character, it is reasonable to suppose, has more chance of revival, is more available as a whole and in parts, than more confused experience' (PLC, 183). This organisation depends on *vigilance*, which term describes a state in which 'the nervous system reacts to stimuli with highly adapted, discriminating and ordered responses' (PLC, 184). In summary the 'point as regards revival can be put conveniently by saying that experiences of high vigilance are the most likely to be available' (PLC, 184).

An example is given, worth noting in relation to a similar passage by Eliot:

> The wheeling of the pigeons in Trafalgar Square may seem to have

no relation to the colour of the water in the basins, or to the tones of a
speaker's voice or to the drift of his remarks. A narrow field of
stimulation is all that [people less vigilant than the artist] can
manage, and we overlook the rest. But the artist does not, and when
he needs it, he has it at his disposal. (PLC, 183)

Eliot writes:

When a poet's mind is perfectly equipped for its work, it is constantly amalgamating disparate experience; the ordinary man's experience is chaotic, irregular, fragmentary. The latter falls in love,
or reads Spinoza, and these two experiences have nothing to do with
each other, or with the noise of the typewriter or the smell of cooking;
in the mind of the poet these experiences are always forming new
wholes.

In his insistence upon vigilance as the condition of the complexity of the
poet's experience, Richards is offering a picture of the poet directly
opposed to the stereotype of poet as dreamer. In this respect he is of that
period in which the idea of the poet as 'wit' was vigorously revived.

The ideas of 'complexity', 'impersonality', 'irony', and 'vigilance',
emphasise a high level of discrimination of stimuli. Richards remarks that
the poet is 'pre-eminently accessible to external influences and discriminating with regard to them' (PLC, 181) and (from the reader's point
of view) in reading poetry 'we seem to see things as they really are'
(PLC, 252). This is not, for Richards, peripheral; many of his key
statements depend upon it.

There are, however, important elements in *Principles of Literary
Criticism* which appear to work in a contrary direction. These are contained in the 'hypnotic theory', which involves a low level of discrimination of stimuli or a reduction of 'vigilance'.

2. Richards' hypnotic theory of poetry

The 'hypnotic theory', as developed in *Principles of Literary
Criticism*, postulates an equilibrium of impulses. This involves, and
conflicts with, the view which supposes a high level of vigilance.

Consider some points at which a low level of discrimination is discussed, and how this relates to the 'hypnotic theory', and to the idea of
equilibrium of opposed impulses.

In Chapter XI, 'A Sketch for a Psychology', Richards says that 'experience has two sources which in different cases have very different
importance' (PLC, 87). When we are responding to things in the outside
world 'our behaviour in all probability will only be appropriate . . . in so
far as it is determined by the nature of the present and past stimuli that we
have received from those things and things like them' (PLC, 87). When,
however, we are 'satisfying our needs and desires a much less strict connection between stimulus and response is sufficient' (PLC, 87).

We are given some examples of this less strict connection:

A baby howls at first in much the same way, whatever the cause of his unrest, and older persons behave not unlike him. Any occasion may be sufficient for taking exercise, or for a quarrel, for falling in love or having a drink. (PLC, 87)

This is indeed a low level of discrimination, and Richards clearly has in mind our conduct during our less aware moments. Yet this idea of a loose connection between stimulus and response, this inhibition of awareness for satisfaction of a need, heavily colours some areas of his discussion of poetry.

This can be seen in his disagreement with Coleridge about the action of metre. He quotes Coleridge's description of the effect of metrical rhythm:

> It tends to increase the vivacity and susceptibility both of the general feelings and of the attention. This effect it produces by the continued excitement of surprise, and by the quick reciprocations of curiosity still gratified and still re-excited, which are too slight indeed to be at any one moment objects of distinct consciousness, yet become considerable in their aggregate influence. As a medicated atmosphere, or as wine during animated conversation, they act powerfully, though themselves unnoticed. (PLC, 143)

Richards praises this description but with such reservations as to seem odd that he should have singled it out in the first place. Coleridge is saying, specifically of metre, what he had said of imaginative poetry in general; that it heightens both thought and feeling in the reader. That it does *both* is crucial to Coleridge's claims for poetry. But Richards argues:

> [metre works] not as Coleridge suggests, through the surprise element . . . but through the absence of surprise, through the lulling effects more than through the awakening. Many of the most characteristic symptoms of incipient hypnosis are present in a slight degree. Among these [are] susceptibility and vivacity of emotion, suggestibility, limitations of the field of attention and marked differences in the incidence of belief-feelings closely analogous to those which alcohol and nitrous oxide can induce . . . (PLC, 143)

To alcohol and nitrous oxide one might, among poets, add Swinburne. The lulling process contrasts with the vigilance stressed elsewhere, unless one is to argue that what is produced by the poet's heightened vigilance in turn decreases the reader's vigilance.

This treatment of Coleridge on metre may be compared with Richards' treatment of Coleridge on imagination. Richards gives an edited quotation from Coleridge:

> imagination . . . reveals itself in the balance or reconciliation of opposite or discordant qualities . . . the sense of novelty and freshness, with old and familiar objects; a more than usual state of emotion, with more than usual order; judgment over awake and steady self-possession with enthusiasm and feeling profound or vehement. (PLC, 242)

He uses this to buttress his claim that the essential significance of poetry lies in its reconciliation of opposed *feelings*. Here too he is neglecting Coleridge's stress on *awareness*, on mental activity.

The connection between the account of metre, and that of situations where there is a low level of discrimination of stimuli is suggested in another quotation from Chapter XI:

> To this partial independence of behaviour (from stimulus) is due the sometimes distressing fact that views, opinions and beliefs vary so much with our differing moods. Such variation shows that the view, belief or opinion is not a purely intellectual product, is not due to thinking in the narrower sense, of response that is governed by stimuli, present or past, but is an attitude adopted to satisfy some desire, temporary or lasting. (PLC, 87–8)

The 'hypnotic theory' is linked to the idea of equilibrium of opposed impulses and hence is promoted to a central place in *Principles of Literary Criticism*. This is done by asserting that the equilibrium, or reconciliation, is primarily brought about by the 'tied imagery', heightened by rhythm. 'Tied imagery', which we have already briefly mentioned, is described as follows: 'The chief of these [the tied images] are the auditory image – the sound of the word in the mind's ear – and the image of articulation – the feel in the lips, mouth, and throat, of what the words would be like to speak' (PLC, 118–9). It is further said that these 'forms of tied imagery might also be called verbal images, and supply the elements of what is called the "formal structure" of poetry' (PLC, 121). They form, that is, the material upon which metre operates.

Tied imagery is inaccessible to inspection. Richards, attacking a crudely representational theory, insists that the 'tied imagery' does not operate by any *resemblance* to sensation:

> What gives an image efficacy is less its vividness as an image than its character as a mental event peculiarly connected with sensation. It is, in a way which no one yet knows how to explain, a relict of sensation and our intellectual and emotional response to it depends far more upon its being, through this fact, a representative of a sensation, than upon its sensory resemblance to one. (PLC, 119–20)

The relation between image and sensation is 'at present hidden from us in the jungles of neurology' (PLC, 120). Richards is making the same sort of point as Johnson when he denied Pope's claim that metrical effects are capable, in themselves, of subtle expressiveness. Richards' thinking is also in line with that of *The Meaning of Meaning*; there he denied any direct relation between word and thing, so here he says out that there is no direct relation between 'tied image' and sensation.

This account of the 'tied imagery' looks to the key chapter on the 'imagination'. Richards discusses the experiences occasioned by the resolution of opposed impulses, and adds:

> These opposed impulses from the resolution of which such experiences spring cannot usually be analysed. When, as is most often the

case, they are aroused through formal means, it is evidently impossible to do so. (PLC, 250–1)

The 'formal means' are the tied imagery and the metre, and Richards is here attributing to them what he sees as the most crucial effect of poetry. At this point he adduces Coleridge: 'To point out that "the sense of musical delight is a gift of the imagination" was one of Coleridge's most brilliant feats' (PLC, 245). This gift, translated into Richards' language, is the 'power of combining all the several effects of formal elements into a single response', and the mode of operation is 'most intricate and most inaccessible to observation' (PLC, 245).

Both Richards and Coleridge claim a central place for metre, but the difference is that for Coleridge metre heightens vigilance, whereas for Richards it has an hypnotic effect: a very large difference, as Richards came to realise.

3. Richards' interest in a hypnotic theory

An analysis of the central place of the 'hypnotic theory' in *Principles of Literary Criticism* raises the question why Richards wished so heavily to emphasise the importance of tied imagery and its inaccessibility to observation.

The chief reason is that, wishing to deny that poetry uses language referentially (in itself a fair denial), he attempts to emphasise those elements farthest from reference. He wants to defeat those who go to poetry looking for a 'message'; a thought, idea, belief or opinion, which may be extracted from it. Hotopf rightly regards this as the chief motive in Richards' insistence that poetry is composed of 'pseudo-statements', or that it is non-referential (*Language, Thought and Comprehension*, 173). Richards always wanted to insist, in varying formulations, that the 'meaning' of a poem is what one goes through in reading it, not something that can be extracted and contemplated in separation. In *Principles of Literary Criticism* message-hunting is called the 'substitution of an intellectual formula for the poem or work of art' (PLC, 275).

Richards attacks the message-hunters by asserting that poetry does not make statements but arouses 'attitudes': 'it is in terms of attitudes, the resolution, inter-inanimation, and balancing of impulses – Aristotle's definition of Tragedy is an instance – that all the most valuable effects of poetry must be described' (PLC, 113). In *Science and Poetry* (which is largely a popularisation of *Principles of Literary Criticism*) the terms 'attitudes' and 'pseudo-statements' occur together:

> A pseudo-statement is a form of words which is justified entirely by its effect in releasing or organising our impulses and attitudes (due regard being had for the better or worse organisations of these *inter se*); a statement, on the other hand, is justified by its truth, i.e. its correspondence, in a highly technical sense, with the fact to which it points. (59)

In denying that poetry is referential, Richards consistently uses a rigorous notion of reference.

The formal definition of 'attitudes' occurs in *Principles of Literary Criticism*. They are 'imaginal and incipient activities or tendencies to action' (PLC, 112). This accent upon bodily response rests on Richards' suggestion that 'every perception probably includes a response in the form of incipient action. We constantly overlook the extent to which all the while we are making preliminary adjustments, getting ready to act in one way or another' (PLC, 107). This is illustrated by a brief account of how Richards was caused to leap out of his chair by a leaf falling on his head, as he sat out of doors reading of a centipede that bit Captain Slocum as he was sailing across the Atlantic. The stress on bodily response appears also in *Science and Poetry*, where it is said, for instance: 'Emotions are what the reaction [to a poem], with its reverberation in bodily changes, feels like. Attitudes are the impulses towards one kind of behaviour or another which are set ready by the response' (19).

Such is the key motive for Richards' giving the 'tied imagery' (the direct effects of sound, articulation and metre) a central place in his account of the functioning of poetry. The primacy of direct effects is the basis of the 'hypnotic theory', which lies in uneasy relation to the view that poetry involves a high level of awareness.

We are not directly concerned with the ultimate motives for the doctrine of 'pseudo-statements', since our business is with Richards' enquiries into the complexity of poetic language, but obvious factors may be mentioned. Richards is attempting to cope, in the field of aesthetics, with the problems occasioned by the general collapse of belief in Christian dogma. In *Principles of Literary Criticism* this attempt appears as the following proposition:

> clear and impartial awareness of the nature of the world in which we live and the development of attitudes which will enable us to live in it finely are both necessities, and neither can be subordinated to the other. They are almost independent, such connections as exist in well-organised individuals being adventitious. (PLC, 282)

Poetry is important because it 'conclusively shows that even the most important among our attitudes can be aroused and maintained without any belief entering in at all' (*Science and Poetry*, 61). The theological beliefs which once, for many people, buttressed the Christian ethic, may have been undermined, but the ethic may, Richards suggests, be fully justified on experiential grounds. At many points this may be persuasive but Richards refuses to face squarely up to the difficulties. To say, for instance, that someone can, without 'believing' in the immortality of the soul, adopt the 'attitude' which accompanies such a belief, seems a somewhat unreal claim. No matter how subtly one translates a statement such as 'the soul is immortal' into a series of 'pseudo-statements' designed to express or arouse an 'attitude', it still, ultimately, claims to say something about the nature of reality; something which one may accept, reject, or remain undecided about, but which one cannot simply wish away.

4. Richards' failure to reconcile complex and hypnotic

Having described the 'hypnotic theory', noted its central place in *Principles of Literary Criticism*, and suggested the motives for its appearance there, let us see how Richards manages to gloss over its odd contrast with the view of poetry as heightened vigilance.

He does so by a consistently ambiguous use of one of his basic terms: *impulse*. This ambiguity has been described at length by Hotopf, who calls the two uses of the word the microscopic use and the macroscopic (*Language, Thought and Comprehension*, 43–4). The macroscopic is that which appears, to take examples from ordinary usage, in phrases like 'an impulse to laugh' or 'an impulse to flee'. Hotopf calls it macroscopic as involving far more than is covered by the microscopic use, which means a passage of electrical and chemical change along a nerve fibre. Hotopf criticises this ambiguity on the grounds that Richards, by unfair use of it, manages 'to refer to "large abstractions" and minute events, [and] so . . . is able to combine large theoretical significance with a stress on actual experience as the touchstone of value' (45).

For our purposes, the upshot of the ambiguity is that when Richards is talking of the 'realising' power of poetry, its power to make the reader feel in touch with actuality, he needs the microscopic sense, but when he is propounding the doctrine of equilibrium of opposed impulses, he shifts the emphasis to the macroscopic.

The microscopic use is relevant to the illustrative situations already quoted. The poet, listening to the speaker in Trafalgar Square, observed not only the drift of the speech, but the flight of the pigeons, the colour of the water in the fountains, the tone of the speaker's voice, and so on. His vigilance enabled him to receive an unusually wide variety of stimuli, or, in plain language, he was unusually attentive and receptive. This, it will be recalled, made him, also, unusually retentive of experience. That the response should be minute and detailed, and not automatic, is also the basis of the general account of complexity which opened our discussion of *Principles of Literary Criticism*. The poet is open to a large number of incoming 'impulses' (microscopic sense).

In the doctrine of equilibrium the emphasis is on the macroscopic sense, as is evident in Richards' most memorable example, Aristotle's account of tragedy. Here, Richards claims, are reconciled two elemental 'impulses': Pity, the 'impulse' to approach, and Fear, the 'impulse' to turn away (PLC, 245–6).

Richards' definition of the term 'impulse' makes it clear how this ambiguity arises. An 'impulse' is the 'process in the course of which a mental event may occur, a process apparently beginning in a stimulus and ending in an act' (PLC, 86). The microscopic sense concentrates on the receiving part of the process, the macroscopic on the reacting part.

This ambiguity allows Richards to combine the 'hypnotic theory' with that which pre-supposes a high degree of awareness in poet and in reader, and to harness to poetry the general theory of value set forth in *Principles of Literary Criticism.*

The simple basis of this theory of value is contained in the remark that anything 'is valuable which will satisfy an appetency without involving the frustration of some equal or *more important* appetency' (PLC, 48). Throughout the chapter called 'A Psychological Theory of Value' in which this remark occurs, 'impulse' is used synonymously with 'appetency'. The last quotation, for instance, is followed by a sentence beginning, 'There are certain evident priorities among impulses . . .' (PLC, 48). 'Satisfaction' is a key word. The highest values, for instance, are said to be attained by 'those fortunate people . . . whose free, untrammelled activity gains for them a maximum of varied satisfactions and involves a minimum of suppression and sacrifice' (PLC, 53).

To this macroscopic use of 'impulse' Richards then attaches the claim that poetry arouses 'attitudes'. From this junction it follows that poetry affords opportunities of attaining the highest values, because it can satisfy a greater number of simultaneous, and even opposed, impulses. It can do so because 'the different impulses which have to be reconciled are still at an incipient or imaginal stage', and the poetic situation is not 'complicated by the irrelevant accidents which attend overt responses' (PLC, 112).

5. Two theories: two kinds of poetry

There are, in effect, two theories of poetry in *Principles of Literary Criticism.* Richards postulates two kinds of poetry which correspond to the two theories. Their representatives are Swinburne and Hardy.

In a discussion (PLC, 129) of the varying importance of the sense of words in poetry, Swinburne is quoted:

> There glowing ghosts of flowers
> Draw down, draw nigh;
> And wings of swift spent hours
>   Take flight and fly;
> She sees by formless gleams
> She hears across cold streams
>   Dead mouths of many dreams that sing and sigh.

Richards comments: 'Little beyond vague thoughts of the things the words stand for is here required. They do not have to be brought into intelligible connection with each other' (PLC, 129). In contrast, a few lines of Hardy are quoted:

> 'Who's in the next room? – who?
>   I seemed to see
> Somebody in the dawning passing through
>   Unknown to me.'
> 'Nay: you saw nought. He passed invisibly.'

Generalising from this, Richards suggests that Hardy 'would rarely reach his full effect through sound and sense alone' (PLC, 129), and that, in his case, more 'important are the further thoughts caused by the sense, the network of interpretation and conjecture'. The kind of poetry which operates through a minimal action of the sense and a maximal action of the direct effects gradually disappeared from Richards' field of serious interest. This relates to the general change in poetic taste that was being effected by Eliot.

The two different kinds of poetry correspond to a similar division in Richards' account of metre. He stresses the hypnotic action of metre, in which respect he takes issue with Coleridge. This action is, in terms of the structure of *Principles of Literary Criticism*, by far the more important because of its connections with the doctrine of equilibrium and with the general theory of value. But, Richards adds, in his chapter on 'Rhythm and Metre', 'metre has another mode of action not hitherto mentioned' (PLC, 144). He uses the term 'movement' to describe this mode of action, and speculates about primitive connections between metre and dancing. As an example he gives:

> And now the numerous tramplings quiver lightly
> Along a huge cloud's ridge; and now with sprightly
> Wheel downward come they into fresher skies.

Here, there is said to be 'a very close connection between the sense and the metrical movement'. Further examples of this type of connection are given and Richards then adds:

> Nor is it always the case that the movement takes its cue from the sense. It is often a commentary on the sense and sometimes may qualify it, as when the resistless strength of Coriolanus in battle is given an appearance of dreadful ease by the leisureliness of the description.
>
> Death, that dark spirit, in's nervy arm doth lie
> Which being advanc'd declines, and then men die.
>
> Movement in poetry deserves at least as much study as onomatopoeia. (PLC, 145)

In Richards' account of this second mode of action of metre, the emphasis is very far from anything suggested by the idea that metre has a 'lulling' incipiently hypnotic tendency. In suggesting that a profitable area of study is the interweaving of emotive aspects with the sense, it shows the same tendency as the comment on Hardy. Yet the fact that Richards classes it, in importance, only with onomatopoeia, while giving the hypnotic effect the central place, shows that his position is still very different from that in the account of metre, in *Coleridge on Imagination*.

These comments on metre afford a convenient opportunity to point a distinction already made. That Richards, in his remarks on Hardy, and on that action of metre which may be called 'movement', is opening the way towards a greater emphasis on the importance of sense, and its relations with other aspects of meaning, does not infer that he is abandoning the claim that poetry is non-referential. In the lines quoted above, words like 'tramplings', 'quiver' and 'sprightly' are not used referentially. There are, in Johnson's words, 'figurative distortions of phrase' and there is 'some perturbation of images'. Richards never abandons this position. What is open to change is his view of the role played by 'sense'.

The imminence of such a change is indicated by the following remark from *Science and Poetry* (22–3)

> A good deal of poetry and even some great poetry exists (e.g. some of Shakespeare's Songs, and, in a different way, much of the best of Swinburne), in which the sense of the words can be *almost* entirely missed or neglected without loss.

Here the word 'even' confesses that this is, at least, an exceptional state of affairs. But *Science and Poetry* also permits us to recapitulate those features of Richards' thinking which encourage the lingering on of the 'hypnotic theory', and a consequent neglect of the mental activity which poetry involves. An intrinsically loose connection between sense and the emotive aspects of meaning is implied by the idea that poetic experience has two streams, an 'intellectual' and an 'active, or emotional' stream. Richards says that our 'thoughts are pointers and it is the other, the active, stream which deals with the things which thoughts reflect or point to' (*Ibid.*, 14). This separation of reference and emotion corresponds with the similar separation which we have noted in *The Meaning of Meaning*, where the referential and the emotive functions of language are said to involve two different kinds of sign-situation. It also corresponds to the general fact, elaborated by Hotopf, that Richards employs the two different psychological theories for the referential and the emotive functions (Hotopf, *Language, Thought and Comprehension*, 47).

To anticipate, we can see how much Richards was to change, by comparing his above comment on the two 'streams' with the following, from *Coleridge on Imagination*, which stresses the primacy of sense: 'The patterns of our thought *represent*, in various ways, the world we live in. The patterns of our feelings represent only a few special forms of our commerce with it' (89). And, to anticipate still further, in Richards' re-issue of *Science and Poetry*, there is an acknowledgement of the difficulties caused by the basic separation of the referential and the emotive aspects:

> The author [i.e. Richards] does, it is true, mention 'innumerable connections' between his 'intellectual' and his 'active or emotional' streams and speak of their separation as no more than 'an expositor's artifice'. But the whole layout of the account fights against a sufficient recognition of these mutual influences; and it is this I must now try to redress. (3)

6. Unsatisfactory features of the hypnotic theory

To this point, *Principles of Literary Criticism* has been studied both in regard to a theory of poetry which supposes complexity, produced by a high level of awareness, and in regard to the 'hypnotic theory', which has contrary tendencies. The relation between them has been shown to be uneasy, with some potential for a change of emphasis. It is intended to show why changes were necessary, with particular reference to those required by a theory of the complexity of poetic language, and a technique for its analysis. But first, obvious general objections to the 'hypnotic theory' may be mentioned.

The 'hypnotic theory' is, through the assertion of the central importance of tied imagery, connected with the doctrine of equilibrium, and hence with the general theory of value. It is a weakness that the general theory of value is, in its application to poetry, fundamentally suspect. The point is decisively made by Hotopf, who points out the dubiety of claiming that 'impulses', in the sense of needs and desires, may be 'satisfied' by the kind of incipient or imaginal action involved, in Richards' view, in the reading of poetry (Hotopf, *Language, Thought and Comprehension*, 48–9). To take an obvious instance, a sexual 'impulse' may well be aroused by a poem, but it can scarcely be 'satisfied' by one.

Richards himself seems to be implicitly aware of the difficulty, because when he is presenting his general theory of value he talks straightforwardly of the 'satisfaction of appetencies', but when he is applying it to poetry he uses, not 'satisfaction', but words like 'balancing', 'reconciliation', 'adjustment', 'resolution', and so on (PLC, 112, 113, 251).

That weakness, important as it is, is not of direct concern, since this enquiry is not into the theory of the value of poetry as presented in *Principles of Literary Criticism*. But as it involves the ambiguous use of the word 'impulse', discussed earlier, it relates to a general weakness of more concern. This is the awkwardness of the language of 'stimulus' and 'response', of 'actuality' and 'desire', of 'perceived' and 'perceiver', which colours the whole of the book. 'Impulse', as he defines it, is a useful term for Richards because it enables him, albeit unjustifiably, to slide from stimulus to response and back again as the needs of the moment dictate; but it brings him intolerable difficulties. As his insights into the complexity of poetic *language* develop, he has to re-formulate the general theory of complexity in terms of a creative account of the mind, rather than a stimulus–response account. Only by doing so is he able to bring the general theory and the theory of language usefully together.

A further factor for change is that Richards' stress on the importance of the tied imagery, and his account of how it functions, puts the chief way in which poetry works beneath the scope of analysis. It is only, he suggests, through an 'accident', that the 'ironic' group of poems listed in his chapter 'The Imagination', reveal for inspection their complex action (PLC, 250–1). In the majority of cases this complex action is supposed to go on in the neurological jungle of the tied imagery.

An inspection of the poems, however, produces no reason to believe them in any way peculiar, nor does Richards give any such reason. A

brief consideration of some of them will show this, as also the path along
which Richards' hint that they are complex ('ironic') leads.

Richards' essential statement about the two groups of poems runs as
follows:

> A poem of the first group is built out of sets of impulses which run
> parallel, which have the same direction. In a poem of the second
> group the most obvious feature is the extraordinary heterogeneity
> of the distinguishable impulses. But they are more than hetero-
> geneous, they are opposed. (PLC, 250)

The second group offers itself very readily for analysis as exemplifying
that complexity of meaning which Richards pointed out in his contrast of
Hardy with Swinburne; the 'network of interpretation and conjecture'
caused by the sense of the words.

One such is Marvell's *The Definition of Love*:

> My Love is of a birth as rare
> As 'tis for object strange and high:
> It was begotten by Despair
> Upon Impossibility.
>
> Magnanimous Despair alone
> Could show me so divine a thing,
> Where feeble Hope could ne'r have flown
> But vainly flapt its tinsel wing.
>
> And yet I quickly might arrive
> Where my extended Soul is fixt,
> But Fate does iron wedges drive,
> And always crowds it self betwixt.
>
> For Fate with jealous eye does see
> Two perfect Loves; nor lets them close:
> Their union would her ruin be,
> And her Tyrannic pow'r depose.
>
> And therefore her Decrees of Steel
> Us as the distant Poles have plac'd,
> (Though Love's whole World on us doth wheel)
> Not by themselves to be embrac'd.
>
> Unless the giddy Heaven fall,
> And Earth some new Convulsion tear;
> And, us to join, the World should all
> Be cramp'd into a *Planisphere*.
>
> As Lines so Loves *oblique* may well
> Themselves in every Angle greet:
> But ours so truly *Parallel*,
> Though infinite can never meet.

Therefore the Love which us doth bind
But Fate so enviously debars,
In the Conjunction of the Mind,
And Opposition of the Stars.

Here, it is noticeable that Richards' term 'irony' might easily be extended into its normal sense. This immediately leads to a feeling that his term, therefore, could apply to any poem in what Leavis calls 'the line of wit'; and Eliot had produced his well-known definition of 'wit', which resembles Richards' definition of 'irony', before *Principles of Literary Criticism* was written.

The irony of Marvell's poem hinges on the fact that the exalted nature of the love described is not entirely a matter of inclination, it is necessity which bars it from a more earthy fruition. While, therefore, giving its exalted nature due recognition, Marvell is acknowledging that it is not quite as simple as that. The situation, in general, is common and readily recognisable, and it is no defect in the poem that Marvell does not explicitly state the nature of the barriers between the woman and himself. The point about their inclinations is made clear in,

And yet I quickly might arrive
Where my extended Soul is fixt.

But for the accidents of fate there would soon be a meeting of more than minds. This theme is carried on through stanza seven where the geometrical metaphors are also puns on the language of clandestine assignation ('oblique', 'angle'), and these puns prepare the way for a similar activity in the final stanza:

Therefore the love which us doth bind,
But Fate so enviously debars,
Is the conjunction of the mind,
And opposition of the stars.

'Conjunction', in the ordinary sense of 'union', may have two meanings. First: 'We both have a mind to make love, but, unfortunately, can't.' Second: 'Ours is a case of a marriage of true minds.' These two meanings echo the central irony of the poem. Further, especially in view of the slightly rakish feel of the puns in stanza seven, it seems likely that 'conjunction' also carries the meaning 'sexual union', common at the time. In this case, 'of the mind' takes on a slightly different sense and the meaning of the line is, 'We are compelled to restrict ourselves to merely *imagining* making love.' The movement of sense is complicated, but it is managed with a fine ease. The same is true of 'rare' in the first stanza. It easily carried, at the time, the derogatory sense of 'precious', so that again there is reference to the basic irony; Marvell is glancing at the possibility that, in making such high claims for his love, he may be partly indulging in 'precious-ness'.

Richards' list makes it clear that the reflection of 'irony', in his meaning of the word, into complexity of sense is by no means restricted to 'metaphysical poetry'; Scott's *Proud Maisie* shows similar features:

Proud Maisie is in the wood,
Walking so early,
Sweet Robin sits on the bush,
Singing so rarely.

'Tell me, thou bonny bird.
When shall I marry me?'
'When six braw gentlemen
Kirkward shall carry ye.'

'Who makes the bridal bed,
Birdie, say truly?'
'The gray-headed sexton
That delves the grave duly.'

'The glow-worm o'er grave and stone
Shall light thee steady;
The owl from the steeple sing,
"Welcome, proud lady".'

The complex of feelings here is more peculiar, and therefore more difficult to describe in general terms, than that in Marvell's poem. It involves the fact that though the prophecy is deadly, it is made by a sweet robin singing on a bush. To look at the verbal details, the owl also 'sings', an odd word to use of an owl's cry, but completely justified. The complexity may best be described by spelling out the attitude to Maisie adopted by both robin and owl: 'We sing because we are indifferent to your fate; we do not particularly care for you. We are also singing because your pride is not sufficiently important to us to provoke our anger; we have seen many such, and remain serene. None the less, we are also singing because your pettiness does offer a justifiable opportunity for a sad smile over your inevitable downfall.' The owl also sings as part of the funeral rite, in which the glow-worm also figures, and implies: 'Although not particularly concerned for you as an individual, we do that which common humanity requires we should do for anyone; to that extent we are saddened by your death.' The total attitude, though it sounds intolerably complicated when an attempt is made to describe it in detail, is easily recognisable. It is an attitude often aimed at by moralists, and is compounded of detachment, a slight touch of contempt, absence of animus, and a steadiness free from any preaching note. Judgement is made without any of the unpleasant emotional concomitants that usually attend it, and made, therefore, with a touch of sadness.

That is a clumsy attempt to spell out what Scott suggests so economically and deftly. The important point is that it is a matter of complexity of meaning of a kind that one would expect in any good dramatic poem.

It is evident that, having given the essential clue, Richards would have to turn his attention increasingly to complexity of meaning and that, in doing so, he would have to abandon the 'hypnotic theory', with its stress on the primacy of the tied imagery. This process may have been accelerated by the experience that lies behind the next book that we shall examine, *Practical Criticism*, where Richards was disturbed, and with good reason, by the low level of vigilance of the average poetry reader of the time. The effect of poetry on many of his 'protocol' writers appears to have been more than incipiently hypnotic.

Practical Criticism

1. Developments of complexity theory

In this chapter I shall discuss *Practical Criticism* (1929) under three aspects; first, the development of the view that sees poetry as involving a high degree of vigilance; second, Richards' work on the language of poetry, which, though incomplete in comparison with the account given in *Coleridge on Imagination*, constitutes an important advance; third, the retention of unhelpful elements from the earlier work.

The development of the view of poetry as postulating an unusual degree of awareness involves discussions of 'stock-responses' and of 'sentimentality'. Richards claims that 'good poetry owes its value in a large measure to the closeness of its contact with reality and . . . may thereby become a powerful weapon for breaking up unreal ideas and responses' (PC, 251).

The subject of stock-responses had already been broached in *Principles of Literary Criticism*. In that work, Richards says:

> The normal child under the age of ten is probably free from them, or at least with him they have no fixity or privileged standing. But as general reflection develops the place of the free direct play of experience is taken by the deliberate organisation of attitudes, a clumsy and crude substitute. 'Ideas', as they are commonly called, arise. A boy's 'Idea' of Friendship or of Summer or of his Country is not, though the name would seem to imply it, primarily an intellectual affair. It is rather an attitude, or set of attitudes, of tendencies to act in certain fashions rather than others. Now reflection, unless very prolonged and very arduous, tends to fix the attitude by making us dwell in it, by *removing us from experience*. (PLC, 202)

By way of illustration Richards analyses a sonnet by Ella Wheeler Wilcox:

> After the fierce midsummer all ablaze
>   Has burned itself to ashes and expires
>   In the intensity of its own fires,
> Then come the mellow, mild, St Martin days
> Crowned with the calm of peace, but sad with haze.
>   So after Love has led us, till he tires
>   Of his own throes and torments, and desires,

Comes large-eyed Friendship: with a restful gaze
He beckons us to follow, and across
Cool, verdant vales we wander free from care.
Is it a touch of frost lies in the air?
Why are we haunted with a sense of loss?
We do not wish the pain back, or the heat;
And yet, and yet, these days are incomplete.

One may accept Richards' description of stock-responses, and agree
with his dismissive comment on the poem, and yet find his commentary
less than satisfactory. Its unsatisfactoriness springs from Richards'
preoccupation with the doctrine of equilibrium. He asks why the poem is
popular and replies:

> The explanation is, probably, in the soothing effect of aligning the
> very active Love–Friendship groups of impulses with so settled yet
> so rich a group as the Summer–Autumn simile brings in. The mind
> finds for a moment an attitude in which to contemplate a pair of
> situations (Love and Friendship) together, situations which are for
> many minds, particularly difficult to see together. (PLC, 201)

This seems less than fair to the poem. Whatever one may feel about its
defects, its last four lines do not aim to soothe. Nor are the love and
friendship situations put *together*; one follows the other, and neither is
seen by the poet to be entirely satisfactory. Richards has been somewhat
unfair to the poem because he wishes to claim that it is merely a *superficial* 'reconciliation of opposed impulses' (PLC, 201). The second feature
of his commentary is more satisfactory but, in the context of *Principles of
Literary Criticism*, it seems almost an accident:

> The heavy regular rhythm, the dead stamp of the rimes, the obvious-
> ness of the descriptions ('mellow, mild, St Martin'; 'cool verdant
> vales') their alliteration, the triteness of the close, all these accen-
> tuate the impression of conclusiveness. (PLC, 201)

It is more satisfactory, because Richards' comments on the triteness of
the language would elicit general agreement, but it has an accidental air
because there is, in *Principles of Literary Criticism*, no enquiry into poetic
language. There is not even a hint of a connection between complexity of
language and the defeat of stock-responses, which was to become the
basis of *Coleridge on Imagination*. How much connection there is between
the two in *Practical Criticism* will be explored later, but it is convenient
first to illustrate how stock-responses and sentimentality are, in *Practical
Criticism*, more firmly elaborated in terms of the general idea of complexity. As in the earlier book, the 'chief cause of ill-appropriate, stereo-
typed reactions' is said to be *'withdrawal from experience'* (PC, 246).
There are, according to Richards, several ways in which this might
happen, but the ones he wishes to remark are, first, 'through convention
and inculcation, as when a child, being too easily persuaded what to
think and to feel, develops parasitically'; second, 'intellectually, as when

insufficient experience is theoretically elaborated into a system that hides the real world from us' (PC, 246).

In both cases the basic process is similar, and defined in terms of simplification as against complexity. Substitute ideas for experience and 'even the most elaborate idea falls short of the complexity of its object'. Further, 'we may call up our idea by the mere use of a word' (PC, 246-7). This is in direct descent from the emphasis, in *The Meaning of Meaning*, on the dangers of 'word-magic': the substitution of symbolic phantoms for reality.

The danger is to be avoided in one of two ways: either by 'scientific' thinking:

> a thorough attempt to compare all the aspects of an object or situation, to analyse its parts, to reconcile one with another all its various implications, to order it in one coherent intellectual fabric with everything else we know about everything connected with it . . . (PC, 249);

or by having at our disposal 'a wide available background of relevant experience', which enables us to unite 'aspects of experience that ordinarily remain unconnected'. On this view, 'the secret of genius is perhaps nothing else than this greater availability of all experience coupled with larger stores of experience to draw upon' (PC, 249-50). This clearly rests upon the cluster of ideas that have been seen in *Principles of Literary Criticism*, and which are there drawn together in the account of the poet's memory.

Sentimentality, as discussed in *Practical Criticism*, has a similar relation with the general idea of complexity.

Richards begins with various possible senses of the word 'sentimental' and then offers the remark that a 'response is sentimental if it is too great for the occasion' (PC, 258). This does not lead very far, and Richards develops a more complex definition which employs the psychologists' use of the word 'sentiment', meaning 'a more or less permanent arrangement in the mind: a group of tendencies towards certain thoughts and emotions organised around a central object' (PC, 260). Two kinds of inappropriateness in such groups of tendencies are outlined. First, when the object changes but the tendencies persist, as when a man continues 'living in a certain house although increase in motor traffic has made life there almost insupportable'; second, when the situation remains the same but the sentiment changes, as when a man turns painful war-time experiences into a subject for nostalgic reverie. These two forms of distortion are used to offer the following definition:

> A response is sentimental when, either through the over-persistence of tendencies or through the inter-action of sentiments, it is inappropriate to the situation that calls it forth. It becomes inappropriate, as a rule, either by confining itself to one aspect only of the many that the situation can present, or by substituting for it a factitious, illusory situation that may, in extreme cases, have hardly

anything to do with it. We can study these extreme cases in dreams and in asylums. (PC, 261)

The less extreme and more common simplification, by confinement to one aspect, is the more important. It is clearly a type of stock-response, and like the victims of stock-responses, the 'sentimentalist, in brief, is not distributing his interest widely enough' (PC, 270). Again the root idea is that of complexity, of the heightened and enriched consciousness produced by receptivity to a wide variety of stimuli.

Richards' concern with multiplicity of response is important because his recurrent dwelling upon it enables him, eventually, to translate Coleridge's key term 'fusion' into the idea of multiple interconnection. This is the most important single move in Richards' bringing together of the general idea of complexity and his account of linguistic complexity.

2. Interconnection between 'parts' of words

Richards' work on poetic language, in *Practical Criticism*, shows certain hesitancies. One reason for this is his suspicion of analysis, which may be illustrated briefly before we look at the work itself.

The views of poetry in *The Meaning of Meaning* and, to a lesser extent, in *Principles of Literary Criticism*, inevitably generate suspicion of analysis, because they suppose that the essential action of poetry lies beneath the level of observation. In *Practical Criticism* there is increased emphasis on the importance of meaning which is open to analysis, yet there is still a cautionary strain, of which the following is representative. Richards sees analysis as cure for insensitive reading, but remarks of the cure:

[it] might be worse than the disease. The risk of supposing that the feelings which the logical expansion of a poetic phrase excites must be those which the phrase was created to convey is very great. We easily substitute a bad piece of prose for the poem. (PC, 216)

This cautionary strain is also present in *Coleridge on Imagination*, where, for instance, it is remarked that no amount of analysis can convey the precise feel of a poem and that we always run the risk of mistaking our analytical instrument for the phenomena that it is attempting to describe (97). In later books, especially *Speculative Instruments* and *So Much Nearer*, it is noticeable that references to Empson tend to be sceptical, while those to his imitators are disparaging. The following is typical:

Within my lifetime – I seem almost to recall a specific beginning – a practice of expressing whatever a line of passage could possibly yield under squeezing has grown up. At first the practitioners were few and some of them (Laura Riding and William Empson, for example) early became renowned for powerful grasp; but competition soon jacks up standards. There are fashions in reading as well as in writing. Perhaps questions of relevance are now due for more searching discussion.

There is, of course, truth in this. But it also recalls that feature of Richards' work touched upon at the close of the first section of this chapter. When carried away by the feeling that the key to the laws of language is within reach, Richards can throw caution to the winds and embark upon projects beyond the scope of his analytical technique. When not in this mood he tends to be overcome by the multitude of difficulties in the way of analysis. This is probably because he never himself used analysis in extended literary work, with the consequences that he undervalues its usefulness.

Other hesitancies in Richards' work on language in *Practical Criticism* will be dealt with as they arise. His work itself is based on four aspects of meaning: *sense, tone, feeling* and *intention*. 'Intention' is neglected because of its centrality and, therefore, its difficulty; its function is to control 'the relations among themselves of the other three functions'. Hotopf has adversely commented on Richards' reliance on these few basic terms: 'One misses very much the illumination that the distinguishing of varied uses by linguistic philosophers has given to language. Richards' "uses" are a few old flags set above a mass of percipience.' (*Language, Thought and Comprehension*, 250) This is not entirely fair, since all depends on what the purpose of the analysis is.

Take, first, Richards' discussion in the chapter 'Figurative Language'. In comparison with the earlier books, the greater emphasis on the importance of *sense* is apparent:

> In most poetry the sense is as important as anything else; it is quite as subtle, and as dependent on the syntax, as in prose; it is the poet's chief instrument to other aims when it is not itself his aim. His control of our thoughts is ordinarily his chief means to the control of our feelings, and in the immense majority of instances we miss nearly everything of value if we misread his sense.
>
> But to say this – and here is the distinction we have to note – is not to say that we can wrench the sense free from the poem, screw it down in a prose paraphrase, and then take the doctrine of our prose passage, and the feelings this doctrine excites in us, as the burden of the poem. (PC, 191)

Here again is that feature of Richards' work that was correctly described by Hotopf; the chief motive in the doctrine of 'pseudo-statements' was to defeat those who seek messages or ideas from poetry. Richards' thinking did not, in this respect, undergo any basic change. But Hotopf neglects the change that went on *within* the basic framework of ideas, a change that might be described as a movement away from Swinburne; and it is around Swinburne that a large part of the discussion of sense, in *Practical Criticism*, revolves.

The context is a discussion of Poem IX and of comments on it by the protocol-writers, one of whom, annoyed by the slack way in which the senses of the words are handled, sharply describes it as 'Swinburne-cum-water'. Richards takes up the defence on Swinburne's behalf:

> He is indeed a very suitable poet in whom to study the subordination, distortion and occultation of sense through the domination of verbal

feeling. But the lapses of sense are very rarely so flagrant, so un-
disguised, that the reader, swept on by the swift and splendid
round-about of the verse, is forced to notice them. (PC, 195).

It is noticeable that even the defence presents Swinburne as a good
source of case-material for the analyst, rather than as a poet. By way of
illustration Richards quotes from *Atalanta in Calydon*:

> Before the beginning of years
>   There came to the making of man
> Time, with a gift of tears;
>   Grief, with a glass that ran.

Richards does not mention Eliot, but he is, whether intentionally or not,
defending Swinburne against Eliot's criticism. In his essay upon
Swinburne, (*Selected Essays*, 326) which is a part of his whole early
critical programme, Eliot had said of the same chorus:

> This is not merely 'music'; it is effective because it appears to be a
> tremendous statement, like statements made in our dreams; when
> we wake up we find that the 'glass that ran' would do better for time
> than for grief, and that the gift of tears would be as appropriately
> bestowed by grief as by time. (1)

It is, in fact, possible to argue that the transposition is not entirely point-
less (man's subjection to time, for instance, is an essential source of
tears, and grief makes time hang heavily) and Richards does so (PC, 196).
But his general comment has an apologetic sound:

> Some connection [between the words], though it may be tenuous or
> extravagant, can almost always be found in Swinburne, perhaps
> because of his predilection for the abstract and the vague. Vague
> thoughts articulate one with another more readily than precise
> thoughts.

The phrasing of that may be used to make the obvious point that Richards
himself, in the same chapter, gives the soundest possible general grounds
for *agreeing* with Eliot's view that Swinburne's use of language is less than
satisfactory:

> The enjoyment and understanding of *the best poetry* requires a
> sensitiveness and discrimination with words, a nicety, imaginative-
> ness and deftness in taking their sense which will prevent Poem
> IX ... from receiving the approval of the most attentive readers. To
> set aside this fine capacity too often may be a damaging indulgence.
> (PC, 198)

The reader of Swinburne, by Richards' own account, 'swept on by the
swift and splendid roundabout of the verse', neglects such niceties. And
this comment on the rhythm serves to recall that Richards is rapidly, in
Practical Criticism, moving away from a hypnotic account of metre. This
is clear in his remark on Poem XII, a rather empty and inflated description
of clouds. When, Richards says, there is,

> high-sounding grandiloquent diction and a very capably handled

march of verse, when, above all, the movement is familiar and 'hypnotic', when there is nothing to force the reader to work at it, we feel safe in going ahead, the poetic function slips loose and private poems result. (PC, 160)

The defence of Swinburne is a rather desperate rear-guard action, which may easily be defeated by Richards' own arguments.

In general, then, subtlety of sense receives more attention in *Practical Criticism* than Richards has given it hitherto. Of more particular interest than this, however, are some other points that are made in the discussion of Poem IX. These occur in regard to the metaphor in:

Unless the sea were harp, each mirthful string
Woven of the lightning of the nights of Spring.

Among other objections, the protocol writers had criticised 'woven', on the grounds that strings are *not* 'woven', and the whole on the grounds that it is a mixed metaphor, since the harp is said to be made of sea and lightning (PC, 127). With regard to the latter point, Richards attempts a rule: 'Mixtures in metaphors (and in other figures) may work well enough when the ingredients that are mixed preserve this efficacy, but not when such a fusion is invited that the several parts cancel one another.' (PC, 196) Richards' account is condensed, and he does not explain what he means by 'parts', but the implication is clear enough. As a bare possibility the metaphor is not nonsense; the lines of waves on the sea are most visible near a shore, and a curving shore may be thought of as resembling the shape of a harp. Lightning may readily be thought of as a line in the sky and, hence, not ridiculously, as a string. But the metaphorical action is very bare and single, since none of the usual further implications of the words are employed. The context cancels out the implications of rapidity, explosiveness, brightness and so on which are part of the 'meaning' of 'lightning'. The same is the case with 'sea'. Richards then applies the rule to 'woven', and arrives at a similar conclusion. The power to generate certain feelings,

that 'woven' in a proper context certainly possesses, is damped and cancelled as it blends with the sea and lightning ingredients, nor is there anything else in the passage that it can seek help from in preserving an independent existence. (PC, 197)

Richards is appealing to that principle which eighteenth century critics called 'propriety': that words in poetry should fit in, or interconnect, as richly as possible with the other words in the context. It is a principle open to abuse and, in discussing the doctrine of 'propriety', the extent that it was abused by Johnson will be considered. But it is no accident that Richards should comment, while discussing his protocol-writers' objections to the sea-harp metaphor: 'It is clear that the spirit of Dr Johnson has happily not altogether vanished from literary criticism' (PC, 127). Unfortunately, it *had* vanished to the extent that Richards, in *The Philosophy of Rhetoric*, could see only the eighteenth century *abuses* of the doctrine of 'propriety', failing to point out its similarity with his own theory. Richards makes the following generalisation from his discussion of 'sense' in poetry:

> Is the pull exerted by the context (and in these cases the whole of the rest of the poem is the context) sufficient to overcome what may be described as the normal separate feeling of the questionable word? . . . Or does the word resist, stay outside, or wrench the rest of the poem into crudity or confusion? To triumph over the resistances of words may sometimes be considered the measure of a poet's power (Shakespeare being the obvious example), but more often it is the measure of his discretion. (PC, 212-3)

Johnson's notes on Shakespeare are an extended enquiry into the points at which Shakespeare's triumphs in this respect are questionable.

In the discussion of sense, what is valuable for Richards' further thinking is the notion of interconnection of 'parts' of words. His use of the word 'fusion', in his rule about mixed metaphor, indicates that he does not yet think in terms of multiplicity of interconnection, but that he has moved a long way from the view expressed, in the following, from *The Meaning of Meaning*:

> the use of metaphor involves the same kind of context as abstract thought, the important point being that the members shall only possess the relevant feature in common, and that irrelevant or accidental features shall cancel one another. (MM, 214)

Richards now stresses the function of the *several* parts. Further, these are parts of meaning and, therefore, accessible to analysis.

A closer look at Richards' work on language in *Practical Criticism* suggests why it was difficult for him to arrive at the idea of *multiplicity* of interconnection. The section most rewarding to examine (his discussion of the relations between sense and feeling) is also of intrinsic interest.

His intention here, as in the bulk of *Practical Criticism*, is primarily pedagogic:

> the most curious and puzzling cases of mutual dependence between different kinds of meaning occur with sense and feeling. They are, as a rule, interlinked and combined very closely, and the exact dissection of the one from the other is sometimes an impossible and always an extremely delicate and perilous operation. But the effort to separate these forms of meaning is instructive, and can help us both to see why misunderstandings of all kinds are so frequent, and to devise educational methods that will make them less common. (PC, 209)

Richards seems in fact to be pursuing literary critical rather than pedagogic aims, and this division of intention may partly explain the confusion that hangs over some parts of his discussion of the problem.

Richards says there are three broad types of relation between sense and feeling in poetic language: (1) 'where the feeling is generated by and governed by the sense'; (2) where 'the word first expresses a feeling, and such sense as it conveys is derived from the feeling'; (3) where 'sense and feeling are less closely knit: their alliance comes about through the context'. The third type is said to be 'the usual condition in poetry', and Richards devotes most of his attention to it (PC, 210–12).

A source of difficulty throughout the discussion is the vague way in which Richards uses the word 'feeling': 'Under "Feeling" I group for convenience the whole conative–affective aspect of life-emotions, emotional attitudes, the will, desire, pleasure–unpleasure, and the rest.' (PC, 181n) This is more inconvenient than convenient, because Richards ought to have distinguished between 'feeling' as in, say, 'This feels smooth', and as in 'I feel pity for him'. The situation is similar to that produced by the ambiguous 'micro' and 'macro' uses of 'impulse', and has a similar consequence; Richards carelessly bundles together the idea of a heightened awareness through receptivity to a multiplicity of stimuli and the idea of an equilibrium of opposed feelings.

The way in which this is done, and its implications, emerge clearly in Richards' discussion of the third type of relation between sense and feeling, with reference to the final stanza of Poem x, a pleasantly whimsical account, by G. H. Luce, of the triumph, decline and fall of a cloud on a summer's day:

O sprawling domes, O tottering towers,
O frail steel tissue of the sun –
What! Have ye numbered all your hours
And is your empire all fordone?

Richards' analysis concentrates on the second line, and is worth reproducing not only for the purpose of the argument but also to recall the nature of his contribution to modern criticism; insistence on the close scrutiny of what the words in a poem are doing and how such a scrutiny might proceed. His analysis here is excellent, and runs as follows:

'Tissue', to begin with the noun, has a double sense; firstly, 'cloth of steel' in extension from 'cloth of gold' or 'cloth of silver', the cold, metallic, inorganic quality of the fabric being perhaps important; secondly, 'thin, soft, semi-transparent' as with tissue-paper. 'Steel' is also present as a sense-metaphor of Aristotle's second kind, when the transference is from *species* to *genus*, steel a particular kind of strong material being used to stand for any material strong enough to hold together, as it appears, the immensity of the cloud-structure. The colour suggestion of 'steel' is also relevant. 'Frail' echoes the semi-transparency of 'tissue', the diaphanousness, and the impending dissolution too. 'Of the sun' it may be added runs parallel to 'of the silk-worm', i.e., produced by the sun. (PC, 215)

This is an analysis of the senses of the words: the 'fibrillar articulations and correspondences of the sense', as Richards calls them. He restricts his attention to the sense because, when we attempt to analyse words in poetry, we 'can track down their equivocations of sense to some extent, but we are comparatively helpless with their ambiguities of feeling' (PC, 213). The analysis, that is, is something of a second-best; we cannot analyse feelings in complex language, therefore we must be content with an analysis of the sense. The relative importance of sense and feeling appears in the following comment on 'frail steel tissue of the sun': 'the sense here is intricate, and . . . when it is analysed out it shows a rational correspondence with the feeling which those readers who accept the line as one of the felicities of the poem may be supposed to have experienced'. 'Feelings' are still of great importance.

Although complexity of sense is receiving much more attention, Richards is still far from the position indicated by the quotation already cited from *Coleridge on Imagination*: 'The patterns of our thought *represent*, in various ways, the world we live in. The patterns of our feelings represent only a few special forms of our commerce with it.'

The reason why so much emphasis, in the analysis of Luce's poem, remains on feelings, is that Richards' loose employment of the word permits a lingering trace of the doctrine of equilibrium.

This is indicated by his comment on 'sprawling' in the stanza quoted above, which he takes as his initial example when giving his general account of the third type of relationship between sense and feeling:

> Its sense (in *Poem X*) may be indicated as an absence of symmetry, regularity, poise, and coherence, and a stretched and loose disposition of parts . . . The feeling of 'sprawling' here is a mixture of good-mockery and affected commiserations. (PC, 211)

'Feeling' here means 'attitude to subject', and Richards seems to be referring to the idea of a reconciliation of opposed impulses; in this case mockery and pity. The suggestion that the doctrine of equilibrium is still at the back of his mind may be supported by looking at his comment, elsewhere, on the line of Luce's poem in which the shadow of the cloud, moving in the wind, is said to 'sidle up the garden stair'. Richards remarks:

> 'sidle' gives the accidental, oblique quality of the movement of the shadow, and gives it in a single word by means of a single particularising scene. Condensation and economy are so often necessary in poetry – *in order that emotional impulses shall not dissipate themselves* – that all means to it are worth study. (PC, 200–1)

Since the tone of Luce's poem is lightly whimsical or ironical, this reinforces Richards' appeal to the doctrine of equilibrium. The quality conducive to equilibrium is called, it will be remembered, 'irony', and its technical sense easily overlaps with the ordinary sense, as noted in respect of Marvell's *The Definition of Love*.

However, in the analysis of 'frail steel tissue of the sun', 'feeling' does not mean 'attitude to subject'. Richards' analysis of the complexity of the *senses* of the words does nothing to explain their *feeling*, if we take 'feeling' to mean 'attitude to subject'. It is only in the word 'frail' that the feeling of 'good-humoured mockery and affected commiseration' appears – the cloud is something of a back-slider, failing to live up to its promises – and Richards does not even mention this function of the word. What his analysis brings out so well is the way in which the multiplicity of meaning 'realises' the object by calling up a vivid impression of the cloud. 'Feeling', in this case, means no more than it does in phrases like 'I've really got the feel of it now', implying a grasp which is surer than any given by merely abstract understanding. This is what 'feeling' means in the generalisation that Richards draws from his analysis: 'most readers will admit that, *as a rule*, the full sense, analysed and clearly articulated, never comes to the consciousness; yet they may get the feeling perfectly' (P C, 214). That situation is also described in the remark that when a 'phrase strikes us as particularly happy, or particularly unfortunate, we can usually contrive, by examining the fabric of the sense into which it fits, to find rational grounds for our approval or dislike'. 'Frail steel tissue of the sun', *as analysed by Richards*, is simply a 'happy phrase', and it contains no 'feelings' of the kind which could come under the head of 'attitude to subject' and so find a place in the doctrine of equilibrium.

The line contains oppositions, or contrast-effects, which sharpen the impact, as Richard brings out when he notes the inorganic, metallic nature of 'steel' and the organic quality of 'tissue of the sun'; this is of some importance, and the point eventually finds a place in Richards' account of the function of disparity between tenor and vehicle, in *The Philosophy of Rhetoric*. But such contrasts are not of the kind needed for the doctrine of equilibrium.

Richards uses the term 'sense' as loosely as the term 'feeling'. That 'steel' is strong, metallic, inorganic, of a certain colour; that 'tissue' is thin, soft, semi-transparent; that 'steel tissue' reminds one of cloth-of-gold; that 'tissue' reminds one of tissue-paper, and so on, may all be said to be a matter of the 'senses' of the words. But 'feeling' is also intimately involved, in that the words evoke a high degree of sensory detail; Richards' analysis seems to be almost an enumeration of the properties of the objects. Richards thinks that his analysis is merely of the 'senses' of the words, because he takes 'feeling' to mean 'attitude to subject', and he seems to be unaware that he has in fact given a convincing analysis not merely of the 'senses' (which are in some vague correspondence with the overall 'feeling') but of the total effect of the line. In *Coleridge on Imagination* he drops the doctrine of equilibrium with its accompanying stress on 'feeling', and is consequently able to offer similar analyses not merely as pedagogic devices or as substitutes for a more preferable but impossible analysis of 'feeling', but as a central feature of his theory of poetry. In *Practical Criticism* the doctrine of equilibrium inhibits a fruitful development of Richards' work on poetic language.

A more important general point is that this confusion tends to conceal the fact that there are, in Richards' work as a whole, two distinct versions of complexity. The first version, which takes 'feeling' to mean 'attitude to subject', involves the notion of 'irony', or complexity of attitude. The second version, which Richards describes in the phrase 'fibrillar articulations and correspondences of the sense', does not necessarily involve complexity of attitude. In this second version the words bring heightened awareness of, or realise, their objects through multiplicity of meaning.

That this two-fold division is important may be illustrated by referring again to Empson's *Seven Types of Ambiguity*. Empson's first two types correspond with the second version above, while his remaining five types all involve, at varying levels of consciousness, 'complexity of attitude'. Further, the first type 'covers almost everything of literary importance'. However, the types involving complexity of attitude occupy the bulk of the book, and this is a fair indication of the preoccupation of an important line of modern criticism, with its heavy emphasis on complexity of attitude and its relative neglect of the other, and (as Empson confesses) more important, type of complexity. This preoccupation and neglect corresponded with the increased interest in the 'poetry of wit', since it is obviously in the work of Donne and his followers that complexity of attitude is most readily found. It has been easy to make the assumption that complexity of language which 'realises' objects and experiences *must* be accompanied by visible 'complexity of attitude', and that poetry of simple attitudes can only attain a low degree of realisation. This has been especially so where the simple attitude happens to be one which the dominant modern taste finds uncongenial, as in the case of that which used to go under the name of 'the sublime'. This particularly involves Milton and his eighteenth century followers.

It seems unlikely that books on critical theory have much effect on taste – they follow it rather than dictate it – but *Practical Criticism* has been an influential work and it may be that the failure to distinguish between the two distinct versions of complexity that have just been described, helped to reinforce assumptions that were already congenial. The stress on the importance of 'complexity of attitude' disappears from Richards' thinking in *Coleridge on Imagination*, but that book never seems to have had the currency of his earlier work.

To close this account of Richards' thinking about sense and feeling at this stage, it is worth pondering on a remark from *Mencius on the Mind* (1932), (105) which makes clear why he thought that 'feeling' in the sense of 'attitude to subject', may remain relatively untouched by an analysis of the 'sense'. Discussing the relations between sense and feeling in words, Richards says:

> When a word has been much used with a sense that is naturally associated with a strong and rich emotive reverberation, it frequently carries this gesture over to senses that give no natural support for any such stirrings . . . The chief danger . . . is that we may insist upon giving a word a far more elaborate sense than it really has, in order to justify its gesture, because we have not noticed what other

senses it may have on other occasions from which the stirring qualities derive.

Whatever else may be said about this, it clearly implies a relatively low level of language-use, a level involving little 'vigilance'. Because of his interest in linguistic duplicity, Empson, in *The Structure of Complex Words* (56–7) rejects Richards' point, insisting that the feeling smuggled in by a different sense must also bring that sense along with it and that, consequently, such uses *do* involve complexity of sense. Empson's argument is convincing but that does not, of course, raise the level of this use of language. Richards is still giving high praise to Swinburne in this part of *Mencius on the Mind*, and recalls his postulation of two kinds of poetry in *Principles of Literary Criticism*. In Swinburne's poetry 'little beyond vague thoughts of the things the words stand for is . . . required. They do not have to be brought into intelligible connection with one another', whereas in Hardy's poetry, 'more important are the further thoughts caused by the sense, the network of interpretation and conjecture which arises therefrom (PLC, 129). Clearly, it is in Swinburnian poetry that the process described in *Mencius on the Mind* may most readily occur. When, as in reading Hardy, the mind is actively engaged in interpretation of interconnections of the sense, there is much less chance of feelings being illicitly brought in. Richards, in short, in *Mencius on the Mind*, is still able to base his discussions of poetic language on Swinburnian poetry.

3. Problems of 'stimulus/response'

Two general features of *Practical Criticism* should be noted; Richards' intention in writing the book, and his continued use in it of the language of stimulus and response. This last can be illustrated from his discussion of stock-responses. He continually implies a situation in which there is a hard-fact world – *given, out there* – to which we respond with varying degrees of appropriateness. This is apparent for instance in his remark that a stock-response 'hides the real world from us', or in his comments on the way in which subjective needs distort reality (PC, 246–7). His claim is that good poetry breaks down stock-responses and thereby attunes us to reality. His evident difficulty is that what is presented in, say, a play by Shakespeare is not, in any normal sense of the word, 'real'. There is nothing unusual about the difficulty, and Richards gives the usual answer: good poetry heightens our *capacity* for appropriate response. This answer assumes an ideal situation; a man may, clearly, read poetry for a life-time without any discernible improvement in his response to 'reality', and nobody improves as much as they might, but the ideal is a valid one. What is unsatisfactory is that Richards' language of stimulus and response leads him to make his answer in terms of the doctrine of equilibrium, at a time when it was being undermined by other important elements in his thinking.

His account of appropriate responsiveness is conducted with reference to Confucius' concept of 'sincerity' (PC, 283–91). For Confucius, as translated by Legge, sincerity 'is that whereby self-completion is effected, and its way is that by which man must direct himself', and in 'self-completion the superior man completes other men and things also . . . and this is the way by which a union is effected of the external and the internal'. Richards glosses this with: 'Being more at one within itself the mind thereby becomes more appropriately responsive to the outer world.' (PC, 287). This is in direct descent from *The Foundations of Aesthetics* (79) where it is said of synaesthetic experiences (i.e. experiences characterised by equilibrium of impulses):

> our individuality becomes differentiated or isolated from the individualities of things around us. We become less 'mixed into' other things. As we become more ourselves they become more themselves, because we are less dependent upon the particular impulses which they each arouse in us.

The discussion of Confucius revolves around the same ideas: 'The completed mind would be that perfect mind . . . in which no disorder, no mutual frustration of impulses remained', and, that being the ideal, the human organism must effect a 're-ordering of its impulses so as to reduce their interferences with one another to a minimum' (PC, 285–6). As moral exhortation this would elicit general agreement, though, no doubt, disagreement would quickly arise as to the order of priority of 'impulses', in cases of 'interference'; but in its application to poetry it is open to the objections already raised against the doctrine of equilibrium.

One of the striking things, about Richards' quotations from Confucius is the suggestion of an account of the mind in creative terms, rather than in terms of appropriate response to stimuli: 'In self-completion the superior man completes other men and things also.' In *Coleridge on Imagination* Richards employs a 'creative' account, which enables him to abandon the doctrine of equilibrium, and offers an opportunity for bringing neatly together his work on language and his view of poetry as heightener of awareness. In *Practical Criticism* this aspect of Legge's version of Confucius simply fails to interest him.

The over-all intention of *Practical Criticism* engenders some confusion as to the way in which poetry may be said to heighten awareness. Richards' avowed aim in analysing the relations between sense and feeling in words is pedagogic. He thinks that training in such analysis might, if cautiously undertaken, lead to improved reading, and this is a reflection of one of the chief ambitions of the book. In the introduction he says: 'It is as a step towards . . . training and technique in discussion that I would best like this book to be regarded.' What he has in mind may be summarised as follows. The various opinions of the students who expressed views on the poems in *Practical Criticism* illustrate a variety of possible approaches to the poems, and also show these approaches at varying levels of sophistication. This array of views constitutes material for the study of the genesis and development of opinions in what Richards calls the 'middle' subjects. These are the subjects (such as ethics, metaphysics and religion) which resemble literary criticism in that they are neither, on the one hand, like mathematics, nor, on the other hand, like commerce and law. Of the benefit to be derived from such an array of views, Richards says:

> When the first dizzy bewilderment has worn off, as it very soon does, it is as though we were strolling through and about a building that hitherto we were only able to see from one or two distant standpoints. We gain a much more intimate understanding both of the poem and of the opinions it provokes. Something like a plan of the most usual approaches can be sketched and we learn what to expect when a new object, a new poem, comes up for discussion. (P C, 9)

The intention, as with the analysis of the relations between sense and feeling in words, is to increase understanding of the ways in which language works. Richards' argument by analogy will not bear close scrutiny. His procedure may well increase understanding of each *view* of the poem, but is as likely to damage our own understanding of the poem as to improve it. To read a poem while holding in mind the various other reactions that it might provoke seems a certain way of destroying the fullness and genuineness of one's own response. The process in the reading of poetry which provides a more accurate analogy with viewing a building from a number of points, is that of understanding the relation between the parts of the poem; of understanding its coherence.

Richards' approach is typical of those modern approaches which regard poetry as material for illustrating theories in other fields: linguistic, anthropological, and so on; approaches which are valid only in so far as they recognise that they have lost what makes the poem a poem.

The kind of awareness involved in an attempt to understand how a poem provokes a variety of opinions is different from the kind of awareness involved in the reading of poetry as poetry, and Richards is in danger of confusing the two. At some points in his later work, because of his tendency to treat poetry primarily as case material for the study of language, he does confuse them. *Coleridge on Imagination*, though arguably Richards' most interesting contribution to literary criticism, is not entirely free from this confusion.

CHAPTER TWO

INTERINANIMATION AND ACTIVITY

Coleridge on Imagination

1. Richards' 'stimulus / response' account replaced by a creative one

In *Coleridge on Imagination* (1950, 1st edn 1935) Richards gives an account of the mind in terms of creativity, or activity, in Chapter 3. This is the first real chapter, the previous two consisting mostly of castigations of those who failed to perceive how penetrating a *psychologist* Coleridge was. Coleridge, says Richards, was ahead of his time, yet the key psychological ideas in his account of the mind contain 'little . . . which a modern psychologist . . . will treat now as other than a commonplace' (ci, 60). These ideas are familiar and may be briefly stated. There are no sense *data*, only *facta*; our perceptions are creations. In these acts of creation we are also creating *ourselves*, because the 'subject [the self] has gone in to what it perceives, and what it perceives is, in this sense, itself'; hence 'the subject is what it is through the objects it has been' (ci, 57). This equates with the assumption of the 'modern psychologist', which is 'the governing condition of his science', that 'the activities of the self . . . are results of past activities' (ci, 61).

Coleridge further proposed that we should become aware of this creative process by an act of 'realising intuition'; aware, also, by means of 'inner sense', of our awareness. This act of self-knowledge is the first postulate of philosophy.

The creative process itself is the 'primary imagination', which creates the everyday world with which we are all familiar. The 'secondary imagination' is also creative, since it breaks down, reforms and unifies the products of the 'primary imagination'. The 'fancy' works, through the agency of memory, with the products of the 'primary imagination', but merely arranges them differently, without essentially modifying them.

The importance of the 'secondary imagination' is that:

> it gives us not only poetry in the limited sense in which literary critics concern themselves with it – but every aspect of the routine world in which it is invested with other values than these necessary for our bare continuance as living beings: all objects for which we can feel love, awe, admiration; every quality beyond the account of physics, chemistry and the physiology of sense-perception, nutrition, reproduction and locomotion; every awareness for which a civilised life is preferred by us to an uncivilised. (ci, 58–9)

The essential mark of genius is a high degree of 'secondary imagination', or '"an unusual intensity of the modifying power"' (CI, 74). Richards illustrates this power with a quotation from Coleridge:

> The Heaven lifts up my soul, the sight of the ocean seems to widen it. We feel the same force at work, but the difference, whether in mind or body that we should feel in actually travelling, horizontally or in direct ascent, *that* we feel in FANCY.
>
> For what are our feelings of this kind but a motion IMAGINED, with the feelings that would accompany that motion, less distinguished, more blended, more rapid, more confused, and, thereby, co-adunated.

In effect, the 'secondary imagination' reformulates his earlier version of the poet's memory; it reforms the products of the 'primary imagination' in such a way that they are freely available for transfer to other experiences, and consequently the poet is peculiarly able to find connections between disparate areas of experience. This is evident in the poet's gift for metaphor, of which, 'The Heaven lifts up my soul' is an example. Here lies the force of Coleridge's remark that '"association depends in a much greater degree on the recurrence of resembling states of feeling than on trains of ideas"'.

Here also lies Coleridge's insistence on increased liveliness of thought in the imaginative process: the co-presence of 'judgement ever awake and steady self-possession with enthusiasm and feeling profound or vehement' (*Biographia Literaria*, ii, 12). The consequences of relaxing one's thought are made clear in the following distinction between 'fancy' and 'imagination':

> You may conceive the difference in kind between the Fancy and the Imagination in this way, that if the check of the senses and the reason were withdrawn, the first would become delirium, and the last mania. (CI, 74)

In the first the consequence would be incoherent recall of past experience, in the second, extreme distortion of reality by an emotion that has run out of control. In one of Coleridge's examples, '"an unusual intensity of the modifying power, ... detached from the discriminative power, might conjure a platted straw into a royal diadem"'.

Richards believes that Coleridge's 'views of the mind as an activity are a new charter of liberties' (CI, 56). Coleridge does not introduce a 'split between the ingredients of the mind':

> In his best analyses he transposes feelings, thoughts, ideas, desires, images and passions with a freedom which descriptive psychology has only recently regained. He treats all these elements in the psychological inventory as forms of the activity of mind – different, of course, and with different functions – but not to be set over against one another in two groups either as products to be opposed to the processes which bring them into being, or as presentations to be set against the reverberations they arouse and which shift them about. (CI, 56)

This 'charter of liberties' is very welcome to Richards because it frees him
from feeling that in order to progress with a theory of complexity in poetic
language he has first to settle such problems as the relations between
sense and feeling in words. In elaborating his theory, he can simply treat
the interconnection between the various aspects of meaning as part of the
creative activity which a poem induces in the reader.

2. 'Interinanimation'

In his account of the complexity of poetic language, Richards' key
move is to translate Coleridge's idea of 'co-adunation' into multiplicity of
interconnection, or, as he terms it, *interinanimation*. With respect to
language, the distinction between 'fancy' and 'imagination' is rephrased
as follows:

> the structure or *constitution* of poetic meanings may vary from
> extreme federalism . . . to the strictest centrality – from a case . . .
> where the meanings of the separate words are almost completely
> autonomous (and their grouping is for a purpose which does not
> concern them) to the case . . . where the several units of meaning
> surrender almost all their local independence in a common co-
> operative purpose. (CI, 81)

Richards is using the notion, noted in *Practical Criticism*, of 'transactions
between the parts of the sense', but it now takes a central place in a general
account of poetry, instead of being an incidental pedagogic device.

The distinction, as regards complexity of language, between 'fancy'
and 'imagination' is illustrated by discussion of two passages from *Venus
and Adonis* which Coleridge himself had used as examples.

> Full gently now she takes him by the hand,
> A lily prison'd in a gaol of snow,
> Or ivory in an alabaster band;
> So white a friend engirts so white a foe.
>
> . . .
>
> Look! how a bright star shooteth from the sky
> So glides he in the night from Venus' eye.

In 'prison'd' and 'gaol of snow' Richards notes an 'absence of interaction
between the parts of the comparison', and expands the point as follows:

> In contrast to the implied efforts or will to escape of the *prison'd*
> hand, a lily would be the most patient of captives. And anything *less*
> resembling a gaol of snow than Venus' hand could hardly be chosen –
> except in *two* uncombined 'points of likeness distinguished', two
> accidental coincidences, namely that the gaol and the hand are both
> enclosures and both white. But Venus' hand is not a static enclosure,
> and the whitenesses will seem less compatible the more we consider
> them. (CI, 78–9)

This bears a striking resemblance to the style of analysis one finds in
eighteenth-century editions of Shakespeare; as will be illustrated later.

In contrast, in the second passage 'the more the image is followed up, the more links of relevance between the units are discovered':

> The separable meanings of each word, *Look!* (our surprise at the meteor, her's at his flight), *star* (a light-giver, an influence, a remote and uncontrollable thing), *shooteth* (the sudden, irremediable, portentous fall or death of what had been a guide, a destiny), *the sky* (the source of light and now of ruin), *glides* (not rapidity only, but fatal ease too), *in the night* (the darkness of the scene and of Venus' world now) – all these separable meanings are here brought into one. (CI, 83)

The analysis resembles that of 'frail steel tissue of the sun' in *Practical Criticism*, with the important difference that Richards is no longer worrying about the relations between sense and feeling. The various 'meanings' listed in his commentary could be called 'feelings' as much as 'senses'. Most of them are not 'senses' listed in any dictionary.

The relation between the 'interinanimation' of the meanings, and the creative account of the mind, is contained in the following:

> as the reader's mind finds cross-connexion after cross-connexion between [the meanings], he seems, in becoming more aware of them, to be discovering not only Shakespeare's meaning, but something which he, the reader, is himself making. His understanding of Shakespeare is sanctioned by his own activity in it. As Coleridge says: 'You feel him to be a poet, inasmuch as for a time he has made you one – an active creative being'. (CI, 83–4)

A further summarising by Richards may be added:

> Shakespeare is realising, and making the reader realise – not by any intensity of effort, but by the fulness and self-completing growth of the response – Adonis' flight as it was to Venus, and the sense of loss, of increased darkness, that invades her. (CI, 83)

This reformulates the view expressed in *Principles of Literary Criticism* and *Practical Criticism*, where the value of poetry is found in its heightened awareness through complexity of response. It is noticeable that in the example, and in its analysis, there is no mention, implicit or explicit, of complexity of *attitude*. Richards talks simply in terms of 'activity' or 'creativity' or 'interinanimation' and drops the doctrine of equilibrium. He has brought together his work on language and his theory of the value of poetry, with neatness and simplicity.

In his account of poetic language he emphasises the importance of sense. Here in full is the quotation earlier given in part:

> the peculiar reference of thoughts to the things-they-are-of gives them modes of interaction with one another which are lacking in the case of feelings. And this interplay is studied as their logical compatibility or incompatibility, and other relations. The patterns of our thought *represent*, in various ways, the world we live in. The patterns of our feelings represent only a few special forms of our commerce with it. (CI, 89)

Richards' later reissue of *Science and Poetry*, under the new title *Poetries and Sciences*, recognises that a defect of the original had been failure to stress the importance of the *sense* in poetic language. This does not mean that he abandons the essential point of his doctrine of 'pseudo-statements'. He continues to insist that poetry does not present extractable ideas, or beliefs, but the process which *is* the poem is now seen to be largely an activity of thought, whereas previously it was chiefly emotional.

His position may be further described with reference to his views on metre. He accepts, indeed accentuates, Coleridge's account of metre, with which he was in disagreement in *Principles of Literary Criticism*. The central idea is that the 'movement of the verse becomes the movement of the meaning' (CI, 119)

Practical Criticism contained anticipations of this:

> The movement or plot of the word-by-word development of the poem, as a structure of the intellect and emotions, is always, in good poetry, in the closest possible relation to the movement of the metre, not only giving it its tempo, but even distorting it – sometimes violently. (PC, 230)

In *Coleridge on Imagination* the position is essentially the same, as is clear in such remarks as: 'The perceived relations between temporal parts of an utterance, which seem to the ear to constitute good metre, derive from relations between parts of its meaning.' (CI, 120) But 'movement' is now given greater significance and precision by reference to the idea of 'inter-inanimation'; rhythm is a moving pattern of subtly interconnected aspects of meaning. It is also, of course, now very neatly tied-in with Richards' general theory of poetry. How far Richards has travelled may be shown by setting the statement that 'the movement of the verse becomes the movement of the meaning', alongside his earlier view that 'movement in poetry deserves at least as much study as onomatopoeia'.

The nature of the impressiveness of Richards' achievement in *Coleridge on Imagination* can be indicated by a quotation from the closing paragraphs of Empson's *Seven Types of Ambiguity*, published four years earlier:

> I suppose that all present-day readers of poetry would agree that some modern poets are charlatans, though different people would attach this floating suspicion to different poets: but they have no positive machinery, such as Dr Johnson thought he had, to a great extent rightly, by which such a fact could be proved . . . The result is a certain lack of positive satisfaction in the reading of any poetry: doubt becomes a permanent background of the mind, both as to whether the thing is being interpreted rightly and as to whether, if it is, one ought to allow oneself to feel pleased. Evidently, in the lack of any machinery of analysis, such as can be thought moderately reliable, to decide whether one's attitude is right, this leads to a sterility of emotion such as makes it hardly worth while to read the poetry at all. (255–6)

This focusses the need felt at the time. Richards indeed developed a 'machinery of analysis, such as can be thought moderately reliable', which has much in common with the analysis employed by Dr Johnson, with the addition that it is more comprehensive, more subtle, more firmly based in a general theory of poetry, and without the excesses which characterised the eighteenth-century doctrine of propriety. The idea of interinanimation resembles the doctrine of propriety in its concern with the ways in which words in a poem fit together. A further point by Empson comes aptly:

> It is not that such machinery is unknown so much that it is unpopular; people feel that, because it must always be inadequate, it must always be unfair.

Richards' contribution was a recall to what seems elementary, a reminder rather than a discovery; but it was a timely reminder, and to re-state in modern terms a 'machinery of analysis' of the Johnsonian type required a great and sustained effort of enquiry.

Before considering some problems raised by *Coleridge on Imagination*, it may be helpful to look at examples other than the brief ones given by Richards. This may clarify the implications of the ideas, especially since Richards himself is parsimonious with examples. What is to be illustrated is, first, Coleridge's remark, quoted earlier:

> The Heaven lifts up my soul, the sight of the ocean seems to widen it... For what are our feelings of this kind but a motion IMAGINED, with the feelings that would accompany that motion, less distinguished, more blended, more rapid, more confused, and, thereby, co-adunated.

Second, Richards' idea that this action of the imagination, at the level of language, produces a great degree of 'interinanimation'.

Here is the description of the Brangwen farm at the beginning of Lawrence's *The Rainbow*:

> The farmers knew the intercourse between heaven and earth, sunshine drawn into the breast and bowels. The rain sucked up in the day-time, nakedness that comes under the wind in autumn, showing the birds' nests no longer worth hiding. Their life and inter-relations were such; feeling the pulse and body of the soil that opened to their furrow for the grain, and became smooth and supple after their ploughing, and clung to their feet with a weight that pulled like desire, lying hard and unresponsive when the crops were to be shorn away. The young corn waved and was silken, and the lustre slid along the limbs of the men who saw it.

The imaginative process is particularly clear in words like 'sucked up', 'slid', and 'desire'. The feelings immanent in the experiences pointed to by the words are present, but are 'more blended, more rapid, more confused, and, thereby, co-adunated'. The life of the farm is 'realised' by an 'unusual intensity of the modifying power'. 'Interinanimation' is prominent in, for instance, 'the lustre slid'. The reader begins by taking 'lustre' as the sheen of the corn; with 'slid' he feels that *touch* is involved, and so takes 'lustre' as 'smoothness to the touch', and this is re-inforced by 'along the limbs'. At 'who saw it' he has to interpret back again in visual terms, and the net result is a blending of visual and tactile effects; the men see the corn so keenly that they feel it, and this gives 'slid along the limbs' the sense of a tremor running along the muscles. There is, to generalise, a varying exploitation of the possibilities of the words as the reader moves through the sentence, and it is a case, to use Richards' political analogy which we have already quoted, of extreme centralism. This is one instance of the way in which sexual feelings are, in the description, transformed and transferred, and the description exemplifies the way in which the imagination humanises the world, investing it with all the qualities for which we can feel 'love, awe, admiration'.

As a less obvious example, consider a stanza which has a widely attested power to move and which does not *feel* particularly complex:

> My love is like a red red rose
>   That's newly sprung in June:
> My love is like a melodie
>   That's sweetly play'd in tune.

The second-person mode of address in the next stanza ('As fair art thou, my bonny lass') leads the reader to take 'love' in the first stanza as referring, primarily, not to the woman but to the poet's feeling, because it seems natural to assume that he is talking to her throughout the poem and therefore would not refer to her in the first stanza in the third person. In the comparison of the rose with the feeling of love 'the more the image is followed up the more links of relevance between the units are discovered'. Its unfolding is the heart opening, and its redness is that of blood; the general sense of beauty and naturalness are obviously relevant, and, more particularly, the sense of surprise at the sudden appearance ('newly sprung') of this beauty, which implies something spontaneous and outside the man's control. It is here that 'June', which otherwise might appear an inert rhyme-word, is effective; it cancels any feeling of frailty in the newly sprung flower. The summer strength of this flower might be brought out by a comparison with Perdita's,

> pale primroses,
> That die unmarried, ere they can behold
> Bright Phoebus in his strength (a malady
> Most incident to maids).
>   (*The Winter's Tale*, Act iv, Scene iv)

There is, however, a strong natural pull towards taking 'my love' as referring to the woman, as well as to the poet's feeling, and it is, in fact, a case of Empson's second type of ambiguity, in which there are two different senses but one resultant meaning. Here, the implications of unfolding, blood, beauty, naturalness, spontaneity, spring freshness with summer strength, are as relevant to the woman as to the feeling. One might say that the woman matches the poet's feeling. Such, then, is the complex activity which lies behind this apparently simple song, the remarkable vividness and vitality of which familiarity never seems to dull. The activity of the imagination which is the condition of the verbal complexity, lies in the 'co-adunation' of the poet's feelings about the woman and about the flower.

To repeat a point made earlier, neither in the passage from Lawrence nor in the stanza from Burns, is there any complexity of *attitude*.

3. Richards' philosophical uses of interinanimation

Richards' further use of his theory and method raises difficulties which can be hinted at by noting his claim that 'the study of the modes of language becomes, as it attempts to be thorough, the most fundamental and extensive of all enquiries' (c1, 231). This development of the intention of *Practical Criticism* is illustrated by Richards' remark that it is 'as a step towards . . . training and technique in discussion that I would best like this book to be regarded'. This preoccupation will be called Richards' 'philosophical' interest, as opposed to his literary interest. The upshot, for our purposes, is confusion of two kinds of reading; first, the reading of poetry as poetry; second, the reading of poetry as material for a study of the modes of language.

Examination of Richards' intention best begins with his discussion of a couplet from Coleridge's *Dejection* Ode:

> To thee do all things live from pole to pole,
> Their life the eddying of thy living soul.

Richards calls this 'a concrete example of that self-knowledge, which . . . was for Coleridge, both 'speculatively and practically', the principle of all his thinking' (c1, 152). Coleridge is not only aware of the creativity of the mind, but also aware of his awareness. Richards admires the metaphor of the eddy because it presents a 'fact of mind', and avoids falling into either of the doctrines derivable from that 'fact of mind', each being only a partial representation. This is an example of Richards' insistence that poetry does not deal in ideas or doctrines. The 'fact of mind' is what is generally described as a relation between a subject and an object, perceiver and perceived, and the metaphor of the eddy presents this relation with great subtlety, imaging concretely the 'co-alescence' of the subject with the object.

The two seemingly opposed doctrines into which this 'fact of mind' may be translated are the 'realist' and the 'projective'. The first says:

> The mind of the poet at moments, penetrating 'the film of familiarity and selfish solicitude', gains an insight into reality, reads Nature as a symbol of something behind or within Nature not ordinarily perceived. (c1, 145)

The second says that the 'mind of the poet creates a Nature into which his own feelings, his aspirations and apprehensions, are projected' (CI, 145).
To refer back to the passage from *The Rainbow*, the 'realist' view would be, 'The Brangwen farm is like that; Lawrence has penetrated to the deeper reality'. The 'projective' view would be, 'The Brangwens are merely projecting their own sexual feelings onto the farm'. For Richards, the two views would be distortions, effected for different ends, of the 'fact of mind' which is conveyed by the imaginative complexity of Lawrence's language.

The language in which 'facts of mind' are presented must be complex, and the final import of poetry, for Richards, is: 'to preserve us from mistaking our notions either for things or for ourselves. Poetry is the completest mode of utterance' (CI, 163). The function of his analytic method is to increase our sensitivity to that mode of language which conveys 'facts of mind' rather than doctrines:

> The study of this wrenching, of the translation of imaginative acts into doctrines, is that mode of tracing the source of philosophy in 'facts of mind', which, in Coleridge's view of 1801, was to make the theory of poetry 'supersede all the books of metaphysics and all the books of morals too'. (CI, 143)

Richards is not without Coleridgean ambition, and one of Hotopf's main themes is his exaggeration of ambiguity in philosophical writing, springing from his desire to show that various central philosophical insights are 'imaginative', and that translations of them into doctrines are distortions.

Richards' ambition is connected with the decline of religious belief. If a man says, 'The soul is immortal', the 'realist' view sees it as true, while the 'projective' view sees it as merely a projection of certain obvious needs and desires. If, however, he says it in the 'imaginative' mode, Richards can see it as a 'fact of mind', of which both 'realist' and 'projective' views are distortions. In describing this particular function of the 'imaginative' mode, Richards uses 'projective' language, but claims that he does so only because one has to use the language of one view or the other, unless one is to write poetry oneself (CI, 18-19). A quotation from *The Philosophy of Rhetoric* (134) is convenient:

> Does the Divine Comedy, or the Bible tell us something which we must accept as true if we are to read it aright? These are questions that we cannot possibly answer satisfactorily unless we are clear as to the ways in which metaphoric utterances may say or tell us something. Mr Eliot remarks somewhere of the Divine Comedy that the whole poem is one vast metaphor. It is. And, if so, what is it that we might believe in it? Is it the tenor or the vehicle or their joint presentation; or is it 'that tenor and vehicle are thus and thus related there'.

The alternative ('that tenor and vehicle are thus and thus related') refers, evidently, to 'interinanimation', or the lack of it. In this view, the important question is not 'is it true?' but 'is it realised?' The drift of Richards' argument is towards the identification of 'beauty' and 'truth'; and the last sentence of the following, from *Coleridge on Imagination*, shows that 'goodness' is very ready to be added:

> The saner and greater mythologies are not fancies; they are the utterance of the whole soul of man and, as such, inexhaustible to meditation. They are no amusement or diversion to be sought as a relaxation and an escape from the hard realities of life. They are these hard realities in projection, their symbolic recognition, co-ordination and acceptance. Through such mythologies our will is collected, our powers unified, our growth controlled. (CI, 171)

Richards' use of the word 'mythology' is not intended to be slighting, since he claims that 'scientific' views of the world are also 'mythologies', in that they are produced by the creativity of mind, and not by perceptions of a given, hard-fact, reality (CI, 177).

Such delicate areas as Dante and the Bible apart, the problem of faith disappears, and Richards' views are such as most students of literature would find easily acceptable. To say of, for instance, *Anna Karenina*, that its 'truth' is not literal but one of 'realisation'; that it is a 'projection' of the 'hard realities of life', rather than an escapist fancy, and that through reading it 'our will is collected, our powers unified, our growth controlled', is only what is usually said.

Such are the applications which Richards envisages for his theory of complexity, and he hopes that if his views are accepted, criticism will be 'freed for the inexhaustible enquiry into the modes of mythology and their integration "according to their relative worth and dignity" in the growth of our lives' (CI, 184).

In their accounts of the response evoked by 'imaginative' poetry, Coleridge and Richards emphasise 'ease' as a feature of the process. The 'realising' activity is characterised 'not by any intensity of effort, but by the fulness and self-completing growth of the response' (CI, 83). The point is further developed in Richards' attack on the 'cross-word puzzler's' approach to poetry:

> the detective intelligence, or the Cross-word Puzzler's Technique, are not proper methods in reading poetry . . .; there is another way of 'looking into' abstruse poetry – a receptive submission which will perhaps *be reflected* in conjectures but into which inferences among these conjectures do not enter. (CI, 215–6)

Hotopf (*Language, Thought and Comprehension*, 71) has noted this element in Richards' thinking: 'Many times Richards refers to a sort of effortless, exhilarating, continuing activity of the mind, which is set off by some instance of another's imagination. He seems to take it as hallmark of the Imagination'. 'Ease' is likewise central in Coleridge's views because it is intimately linked with the *pleasure* which poetry gives:

> that sort of pleasurable emotion; which the exertion of all our faculties gives in a certain degree; but which can only be felt in per-

fection under the full play of those powers of mind which are spontaneous rather than voluntary, and in which the effort required bears no proportion to the activity enjoyed. (CI, 113)

In Richards' case the emphasis upon the 'ease' of response to poetry is a modification of his account of the 'instantaneity' of response, in *Practical Criticism*, where it is said that the reader's apprehension of a complex meaning takes place in a flash, whereas the conscious analysis of that meaning may be a laborious process (PC, 214). In *Coleridge on Imagination*, Richards puts more emphasis upon the interpreting activity.

This activity is very different from that required by Richards' philosophic interest, to which poetry is merely material for an enquiry into the modes of language. In *Speculative Instruments*, he gives a convenient description of the kind of attention required for this enterprise. The first need is for 'an abundant provision of examples of skilled and less skilled interpretations, specimens of minds at work in the interactions of words' (SI, 51). *Practical Criticism* is, in fact, a collection of such examples from poetry; *Interpretation in Teaching* is an equivalent collection from prose. Study of this material requires the following:

> Vigilant field observation; responsive immersion in the actual, in its full concreteness, before, during, and after the passage of the abstractive processes which yield perception; endlessly returning, self-correcting care for the *how* as well as for the *what* and the *why* and the *whither* of the concern . . .; an unwinking lookout for analogues in all respects however remote, and avid curiosity about all modes of analogy and parallelism; . . . and, above all perhaps, an itch to see how things look from other angles. (SI, 51)

The striking feature here is the conspicuous absence of 'ease', of any kind.

Richards tends to confuse these two kinds of reading. One consequence of this is Schiller's misinterpretation, which relates particularly to Richards' reference to 'an itch to see how things look from other angles', and which will be described later. The consequence that immediately concerns us is that Richards is led into stating an important part of his theory of poetry, in *Coleridge on Imagination*, in terms of the kind of reading required by the philosophic interest, and this has exposed him to valid criticism from Hotopf.

It seems surprising that Richards *should* confuse the two kinds of reading. Not only are the differing degrees of difficulty evident even to cursory examination, but they also seem to correspond to the two levels of awareness' sketched in Richards' initial account of the creative activity of the mind. Further, the necessary distinction seems to be virtually made in the quotation above from *Speculative Instruments*, where 'responsive immersion' seems to correspond to the phrase 'receptive submission' in *Coleridge on Imagination* (CI, 216)

The point of confusion lies in the importance which Richards attaches to Coleridge's lines,

To thee do all things live from pole to pole
Their life the eddying of thy living soul.

The peculiarity of these lines is that their *subject-matter* is philosophical
(the relation between subject and object), and they consequently compel
the reader to that second level of awareness which, according to Coleridge,
is 'the first postulate of philosophy', and which constitutes self-knowledge.

Richards claims that this self-knowledge is also self-creation, and that
self-creation is the final end of poetry. His emphasis upon these particular
lines makes him appear to be claiming that *all* poetry achieves that end in
the same way.

Hotopf (89) however points out that 'the self-forming, that comes from
the self's awareness of itself embroiled in its experience, is limited only to
poems specifically dealing with this', and adds:

clearly Coleridge's emphasis upon being aware of what one is doing
at the moment one is doing it, is relevant [to the study of philosophy]
in a way it does not seem to be relevant in connection with poetry.

Hotopf's point seems valid; the awareness involved in realisation of the
'what' of the poem (an awareness produced by imaginative activity) does
not in itself involve awareness of the 'how' of the poem, unless the 'how'
happens also to be the subject of the poem. Hotopf's criticism appears
seriously to invalidate Richards' claim that poetry gives self-knowledge
and, thereby, self-creation.

However, Richards' confusion is incidental rather than radical. To say
that the reading of poetry brings self-knowledge, and self-creation, is a
traditional claim which could be illustrated from many critics, and some
versions of it will be discussed in our examination of eighteenth-century
criticism. One of the most memorable brief formulations appears in
George Herbert's lines on the reading of the Scriptures:

Such are thy secrets, which my life makes good,
And comments on thee: for in ev'ry thing
Thy words do find me out, and parallels bring,
And in another make me understood.

The context makes secondary any accusatory implications in 'find me
out', the main implication being that which appears in such phrases as
'He has found himself'. Herbert's lines do not necessarily imply a formal
account of the mind in creative terms, but they contain the essential point
that Richards' theory needs: the most important understanding to be
derived from poetry is that self-understanding which seems to be a finding
of the self. This understanding involves awareness of the 'what' but not
of the 'how' of a poem, and it readily accommodates itself to Richards'
account of the realising powers of complex language.

4. Richards' literary uses of interinanimation

Richards also wishes to use his theory for making large propositions
about the history of English poetry, and this involves the claim that,

roughly speaking, eighteenth-century poetry is radically unpoetic. Examination reveals that it is an unjustifiable *use*, whatever the final merits of the view which it is buttressing. The question merits illustration because this view of eighteenth-century poetry constitutes something of an orthodoxy in the school of criticism which Richards helped to establish.

Richards compares passages by Gray and Blake, and attempts 'comparative studies of poetic structures' (CI, 200). From Gray he takes the opening of the *Elegy*:

> The Curfew tolls the knell of parting day,
>   The lowing herd winds slowly o'er the lea,
> The plowman homeward plods his weary way,
>   And leaves the world to darkness and to me.

From Blake:

> Memory, hither come,
>   And tune your merry notes:
> And, while upon the wind
>   Your music floats,
> I'll pore upon the stream,
> Where sighing lovers dream,
> And fish for fancies as they pass
> Within the watery glass.

He describes the difference between them as follows: in Gray's lines 'it is clear that almost all the rest can be properly regarded as dependent from and controlled by the prose-sense'; in Blake, the words have senses, but 'this is not to say that the whole poem derives simply from the articulation of these senses (as was almost the case with Gray)' (CI, 205). Blake's language exhibits a greater degree of 'interinanimation', or interaction between the different aspects of meaning; the 'senses of the words here come to them as much from their feelings (to use this term as a convenient abbreviation for "the rest of their powers upon us") as their feelings come from their senses'.

There are two objections to this account. The theoretical one is that Richards is again beginning to puzzle about the *relations* between sense and feeling. One of the advantages that using Coleridge had for Richards, was the removal of this puzzle, needing one only to describe the interweaving of the parts of the meaning, without establishing questions of *precedence* between the parts. To ascribe a greater degree of interinanimation to an equality of precedence between sense and feeling is to bring back the old puzzle.

The practical objection is that Richards ignores the complexity of Gray's language. Of Blake he says:

> For example, *tune* may be read as 'sing, utter' or as 'accord, bring into order', *the stream* may be the 'mere river' or 'the stream of life, or time, or desire', and *glass* may show merely the translucency of the

water or turn it into an image-making reflection of things, as a crystal we gaze into. (CI, 204)

It is not that Richards exaggerates complexity in Blake, though 'utter' and 'accord' are redundant, and the further meanings of 'stream' and 'glass' are merely those which might feature in *any* allegorical or metaphorical use of the words. Further, it is not possible to examine Richards' claim that there is, in Blake's lines, equality of precedence between sense and feeling, because there is no evidence given to support it.

More important is his failure to analyse Gray's lines. The 'lowing herd', for instance, is also a funeral procession, attending the death of the day, so that 'slowly' means 'sadly' as well as 'tiredly', and the 'lowing' takes on a mournful note. But the herd, like the ploughman, are returning *home* for the night, hence the feeling of sadness is modified. With the ploughman, similarly, the feeling of homecoming is blended with the feeling of dreariness carried by the phrase 'weary way'. This dreariness relates to the monotony of the peasant life, which is dwelt upon at length later in the poem. In view of that later development, and in connection with the death of the day, the 'weary way' is 'the journey of life' and 'homeward', therefore, also means' death'. This touches upon the complex of feelings that appears in the final stanza of the poem, where death is not only the 'abode' of the young poet, but also 'the bosom of his Father', and where there is, consequently, the same link between death and homecoming. This complexity readily lends itself to description in Coleridgean terms; the scene of the opening of the poem is 'realised' in terms of a set of feelings about death, and thus shows 'an unusual intensity of the modifying power'.

The difference between the poems is in technique, not in radical poetic power, and therefore cannot be explained or described by Richards' method of analysis. In terms of complexity, or interinanimation, Gray in this poem, is to be set *with* Blake, not against him. Further, the assertion that in Blake sense and feeling have a different order of precedence is not supported. Richards later confesses as much when he renames the old 'aspects of meaning' 'respects' and says: 'It seems to me unlikely that the participations of the respects have, in poetry, any fixed precedence' (SI, 42n).

The view of eighteenth-century poetry implicit in the comparison of Gray with Blake is explicitly stated in Richards' postulation of a national decline in the ability to use language:

> With the eighteenth century, the variety of the modes of metaphor in speech and in writing rapidly declined. Dr Johnson, for example, can show, at times, strange obtuseness in distinguishing between degrees of metaphor. It was this which made Donne seem artificial, absurd, unimpassioned and bewildering to him. (CI, 194)

Further, the bulk of the examples of 'fancy' with which Richards illustrates his account of 'interinanimation' are taken from Dryden's *Annus Mirabilis*, and this re-inforces the general attitude he takes to eighteenth-century poetry in *Coleridge on Imagination*.

The theme is resumed on Richards' comparison of Donne with Dryden, in an essay entitled 'The Interaction of Words' in *The Language of Poetry* (ed. A. Tate) and it is convenient to look at this here.

Of some lines from Donne's *First Anniversary*, Richards says:

there is prodigious activity between the words as we read them. Following, exploring, realising, *becoming* that activity is, I suggest, the essential thing in reading the poem. Understanding it is not a preparation for reading the poem. It is itself the poem. And it is a constructive, hazardous, free creative process, a process of conception through which a new being is growing in the mind. (*Language of Poetry*, 76)

On the other hand, of some lines from Dryden's *Anne Killigrew*:

No doubt there are interactions between the words but they are on a different level. The words are in routine conventional relations like peaceful diplomatic communications between nations. They do not induce revolutions in one another and are not thereby attempting to form a new order. Any mutual adjustments they have to make are preparatory, and they are no important part of the poetic activity. (*Language of Poetry*, 76)

One reason for this, Richards says, is that: 'Public declamation – the style of reading which the *Ode* suggests as right – does not invite close attention to the meaning'. Richards' comments on the Dryden lines are all adverse, though offered as limiting criticisms, not outright condemnations. He has no doubt that Dryden succeeded in doing what he was trying to do, but that his attempt is of intrinsically limited interest. As with the earlier comparison of Gray and Blake, Richards sees here 'two very different types of the interactions of words in poetry'.

Dryden's poem is not like Donne's, but Richards' analysis shows similar inadequacies to those in the comparison of Gray with Blake. He exaggerates Donne's complexity:

For who is sure he hath a Soule, unlesse
It see, and judge, and follow worthiness;

'sure' is more than 'confident, without doubts about it'; it means 'safe, firm, immovable', because seeing, judging and following worthiness are themselves the very possession of a soul, not merely signs of having one. (*Language of Poetry*, 82)

'Sure', I think, means no more here than it does in almost any occurrence; 'I am sure of it', in reply to a query, exhibits the same 'activity'.

More important is Richards' neglect of the complexity of Dryden's lines:

Thou youngest virgin-daughter of the skies,
Made in the last promotion of the blest;
Whose palms, new pluck'd from Paradise,
In spreading branches more sublimely rise,

Rich with immortal green above the rest:
Whether, adopted to some neighbouring star,
Thou roll'st above us, in thy wandering race,
Or, in procession fixt and regular,
Mov'd with the heaven's majestic pace;
Or, call'd to more superior bliss,
Thou tread'st with seraphims the vast abyss:
Whatever happy region is thy place
Cease thy celestial song a little space.

This *is* 'declamatory', but it is more than merely so. The movement is closely attuned to the meaning, as is particularly evident in the fourth and eleventh lines. Here one may profitably recollect Richards' own account of metre, in *Coleridge on Imagination*, as a movement among meanings. The more important point, however, is the interaction between the different kinds of motion described in the lines; the words from which the long sentence springs are 'rise', 'roll'st', 'wandering', 'procession', 'mov'd', 'pace', and 'tread'st', and there is a climax in the eleventh line, where the movement described is both stately and magical. The impressiveness of this line depends partly on the local effect, which is somewhat like Marvell's description of the fawn, in his *Nymph Complaining for the Death of her Fawn*, which 'trod as on the four winds', but much of its power comes from its relations with the movements described in the other key words. That the movement in this line is stately and magical relates also to the word 'sublimely' in the fourth line, since the feeling which informs the whole passage comes under the head of the 'sublime'. The lines, like Gray's, exhibit an 'unusual intensity of the modifying power', and to see them as merely 'declamatory' is to miss the point; the sound and rhythm are in the closest relation with the interactions of meaning.

As in the comparison of Gray with Blake, the natural use of Richards' analytic method would be to place Donne and Dryden, for all their differences, together. If it were to be used for making distinctions, they would be between Donne and Dryden on the one hand, and inferior poets of the metaphysical and neo-classical schools on the other. Richards is attempting to use the theory for work which falls outside its scope.

5. Richards' views on the analysis of poetic language

An examination of Richards' misuses of his theory highlights a general feature of his approach to analysis: a combination of hesitancy about what can be done at present, combined with high hopes of what may be accomplished in the future. The hesitancy and the hopes are both exaggerated.

Richards' hope is that, inconclusive as his analyses may be, they point the direction in which a spectacular development might occur. He feels that 'in view of the immense improvement in our powers that we owe here to Coleridge, it would be idle to set bounds *now* to what may be possible'

(CI, 127). At the same time, he points out that if we are asked 'whether the doctrine of Imagination can supply conclusive arguments' about the status of a given poem our answer 'must be a firm No'.

It is imaginable that the degree of realisation, or the status as a mode of language, of a given poem might, eventually, be conclusively demonstrated. However, even if it could be demonstrated with mathematical certainty, what would have been achieved? It is universally agreed that Shakespeare is a supreme writer in the imaginative mode. The demonstration of it is not mathematical, but no one has any doubt of it. But to *understand* that it is so, as against merely knowing it, is a different matter, and one in which there is no place for short-cuts. The reader will know nothing worth knowing about *King Lear* until he has been thoroughly engaged in a reading of that play. Essentially Richards' high hopes embody a desire to arrive without having travelled. To recollect, say, Keats' lines, from *On Sitting Down to Read 'King Lear' Once Again*:

> for, once again, the fierce dispute
> Betwixt damnation and impassioned clay
> Must I burn through

is sufficient to make the point. What conclusive arguments about the linguistic mode of *King Lear* would serve any useful purpose without this essential prerequisite? Richards *assumes* this prerequisite, and the conclusive arguments about the linguistic mode are additional; but for a man who had read *King Lear* as Keats read it such arguments, though interesting, would be marginal.

What is faulty in Richards' procedure is the over-estimation of what refinement of the analytic method might accomplish. No one would deny that such a refinement, if accompanied by sufficient literary experience, would be valuable.

In Richards' case, it is difficult to resist the conclusion that there is insufficient literary experience, and here lies the paradoxical reverse of the coin of his high hopes; his underestimation of what analysis can do now. One does not find in Richards that deliberateness of judgement, enforced by analysis, that one finds in, say, Johnson's Shakespeare criticism, where the analytic method, though in itself less refined than Richards', is more effective because it is in the service of prolonged literary experience.

Richards' cautiousness, on the other hand, appears in his calling his analytical method a 'speculative instrument', a phrase that anticipates the title of his later collection of essays, *Speculative Instruments*. The point of so calling it is to prevent us from forgetting 'that we are not trying, in our descriptions, to say *what happens*, but framing a speculative apparatus to assist us in observing a difference': the difference being between 'fancy' and 'imagination'.

There are general factors behind Richards' cautiousness, but there is also a more specific motive. Richards' own summary of his key move in his account of complexity in *Coleridge on Imagination* runs as follows:

In place of 'the power by which one image or feeling is made to modify many others and by a sort of *fusion to force many into one*', I have used phrases which suggest that it is the number of connexions between [the meanings], he seems, in becoming more aware of them, that give the unity – in brief, that the co-adunation is the inter-relationship of the parts. (CI, 84–5)

In Coleridge's thinking, no justification is offered for translating the idea of 'fusion' into the idea of multiplicity of interconnection, and Richards' insistence that we are not claiming to describe what actually happens is a counter to this objection. He particularly needs the counter, because his idea of multiplicity of interconnection reduces the distinction between 'fancy' and 'imagination' to one of *degree*, whereas Coleridge had insisted that it is a distinction in *kind*. The distinction has to be reduced to one of degree, because, evidently, there will be *some* interconnection between the words in *any* piece of writing.

It is important for Richards to counter the objection, because, as we have seen, he wants the analytic method for distinguishing between different 'modes' of language, and therefore wishes to preserve the idea of a distinction in kind. But his insistence that the analytic method does not pretend to describe 'what happens', when we are reading complex language, hardly squares with his commentary on the lines from *Venus and Adonis*, in his initial account. There, as we have seen, Richards says:

as the reader's mind finds cross-connexion after cross-connexion between the meanings, he seems, in becoming more aware of them, to be discovering not only Shakespeare's meaning, but something which he, the reader, is himself making. His understanding of Shakespeare is sanctioned by his own activity in it. (CI, 83–4)

It is hard to see this as anything other than a description of 'what happens', even if one concedes, as is necessary, that spelling out the process in detail inevitably distorts, to some extent, the nature of the actual experience.

The problems which Richards' cautiousness is trying to counter, however, disappear if one sees the analytic method simply as a tool for cultivating close attention to the functioning of words in poetry, and as an attempt, admittedly inexact, to point to places where the functioning seems significantly successful or unsuccessful. This use seems humbler than the ones envisaged by Richards, but, in fact, the kind of attentive reading inculcated and illustrated by it, is the fundamental art which those engaged in the study of literature are primarily attempting to develop, in themselves and in others. A reader whose habit of response to language has developed at the level required by the complexity of Shakespeare or Pope, will have little difficulty in detecting slackness, inertness, or failure to exploit the full powers of language, in his reading of literature in general. Whether a given degree of slackness is in the mode of 'fancy' is a question which will not be of over-riding interest to him, since he will already possess that soundness of judgement which is the most important outcome of deliberate literary study.

Richards' development has involved an increasing emphasis on the role of *sense* in poetry, and here, it seems, lies the reason for his preference of Donne's lines over Dryden's. A plain man might say, having been asked to compare the two passages, that Dryden deals in 'images', whereas Donne deals in 'ideas', and this rough and ready distinction would have a large element of truth in it. Richards' taste is now at the opposite pole from that which involved a high estimate of Swinburne. This tendency may be readily highlighted by noting that, in the two collections of essays, *Speculative Instruments* and *So Much Nearer*, the only essay which concerns itself with examination of a literary work, is called '*Troilus and Cressida* and Plato'; and it is amply confirmed by Richards' own poetry, which is intellectually strenuous, by any standards.

This taste is intimately connected with the theoretical tendencies of Richards' later work. These tendencies are implicitly in the idea of 'activity', in *Coleridge on Imagination*, and appear more fully in *The Philosophy of Rhetoric*, which will now be examined, along with Richards' subsequent work. The argument is that the later development of the idea of 'activity' is an exaggeration, in the opposite direction from those earlier tendencies which underestimated the role of sense in poetry.

The Philosophy of Rhetoric

1. Interinanimation as 'activity'

The development of Richards' concept of 'activity', and a related attack on accounts of poetry which stress the importance of images, are central to *The Philosophy of Rhetoric*. The attack begins in the first chapter. Lord Kames is shown pondering on a speech by Williams, one of the private soldiers in *Henry V*. The topic of conversation is what 'a poor and private displeasure can do against a monarch' (Act IV, Scene i), and Williams remarks that a subject, seeking redress for an injury inflicted by a king, 'may as well go about to turn the sun to ice with fanning in his face with a peacock's feather'. Richards quotes Kames' comment:

> The peacock's feather, not to mention the beauty of the object, completes the image: an accurate image cannot be formed of that fanciful operation without conceiving a particular feather: and one is at a loss when this is neglected in the description.

Richards has fun contemplating Kames 'blandly enjoying the beauty and completeness of the lively and distinct and accurate image of the feather he has produced for himself'; though it would in fact have been easy to pick out far less absurd examples of Kames' 'imagist' doctrine. The example Richards selects may well have been the kind of thing Johnson had in mind when he remarked that much of Kames' work is 'chimerical'.

Richards' attack on Kames' assumptions is pursued in the fourth chapter, where he makes the following general point:

> We cannot too firmly recognize that how a figure of speech works has

nothing necessarily to do with how any images, as copies or dupli-
plicates of sense-perceptions, may, for reader or writer, be backing
up his words. (PR, 98)
This distrust of 'images', here coming to the fore in Richards' thinking,
had always been an element in his work. It expressed itself in the theory
of meaning in *The Meaning of Meaning*, and in, for instance, the remark,
in *Principles of Literary Criticism*, that 'too much importance has always
been attached to the sensory qualities of images'.

In the sixth chapter the attack turns towards Hulme, who is quoted as
saying of the language of poetry:

> [it] is not a language of counters, but ... a visual concrete one. It is
> a compromise for a language of intuition which would hand over
> sensations bodily. It always endeavours to arrest you, and make you
> continuously see a physical thing, to prevent you gliding through an
> abstract process.

To this Richards opposes his own view:

> So far from verbal language being a 'compromise for a language of
> intuition' – a thin, but better-than-nothing, substitute for real
> experience, – language, well-used, is a *completion* and does what the
> intuitions of sensation by themselves cannot do. Words are the
> meeting points at which regions of experience which can never com-
> bine in sensation or intuition, come together. They are the occasion
> and the means of that growth which is the mind's endless endeavour
> to order itself. (PR, 130–1)

Language is not simply a tool for recording or reflecting experience, but
an intimate part of experience, with an organising function. Richards'
point is similar to that vividly recorded by Eliot in *The Dry Salvages*:

> We had the experience but missed the meaning,
> And approach to the meaning restores the experience
> In a different form ...
> ... the past experience revived in the meaning
> Is not the experience of one life only
> But of many generations.

Eliot's lines also indicate that for the poet a language is, amongst other
things, a record of similar past struggles. Richards illustrates this by
quoting Shelley:

> Language is vitally metaphorical; that is, it marks the before un-
> apprehended relations of things and perpetuates their apprehension,
> until words, which represent them, become, through time, signs for
> portions or classes of thought instead of pictures of integral thoughts;
> and then, if no new poets should arise to create afresh the associations
> which have been thus disorganised, language will be dead to all the
> nobler purposes of human intercourse. (PR, 90–1)

Richards not only points out the omissions in the 'imagist' doctrine but
also offers a theory of poetic language in which the key term is 'activity'.

Fundamentally, this is the theory found in *Coleridge on Imagination*, but the element of 'activity' is further stressed by a reformulation of the context theory of meaning. 'Activity' is now geared for an attack on 'imagism', in that it is at the furthest possible remove from the idea that words represent things.

In *The Philosophy of Rhetoric* meaning is defined as '*delegated efficacy*', and 'what a sign or word means is the missing parts of the context' (32). 'Context' had already been defined in *The Meaning of Meaning*. To offer our own example, the word 'book', in a particular occurrence, 'means' the parts of its 'contexts' in previous occurrences, which are relevant to the new occurrence. To define 'meaning' in this way may well arouse indignation in some quarters. The reason why Richards wants so to define it may be illustrated from *Interpretation in Teaching* (48):

> The multiplicity and interdependance of the meaning of words, so much insisted upon here, becomes obvious and necessary as soon as we conceive of interpretation in terms of sign-situations.

The context theory lays great emphasis on the interpreting *activity*. 'Multiplicity' arises from the large number of past contexts involved in the recurrence of a word, and 'interdependence' from the fact that the present context determines the relevant selection from the past contexts.

Harnessed to the context theory is the idea that a 'perception is never just of an *it*; perception takes whatever it perceives as a thing of a certain sort. All thinking from the lowest to the highest – whatever else it may be – is sorting' (PR, 30). This idea had always been present in Richards' thinking, but it now occupies a more important place. A simple illustration of the idea might run as follows: a child has a category – a 'sort' – which it thinks of as 'hard things'; a chair may be in this category. As it grows, 'chair' becomes more specifically defined by partaking of a number of sorts, and may, eventually, in a given situation, become 'an interesting example of the work of Sheraton'. As Richards says, a perception is 'the more concrete as we take it as of more sorts' (PR, 31).

This position is re-stated in *Interpretation in Teaching* (49):

> To think of anything is to take it *as* of a sort (as a such and such) and that 'as' brings in (openly or in disguise) the analogy, the parallel, the metaphoric grapple or ground or grasp or draw by which alone the mind takes its hold. It takes no hold if there is nothing for it to haul from, for its thinking is the haul, the attraction of likes.

For Richards, all language works in the same way as metaphor: 'a word is normally a substitute for (or means) not one discrete past impression but a combination of general aspects. Now that is itself a summary account of the principle of metaphor.' (PR, 93)

The chief objection to this is that in metaphor proper the 'aspects' to be combined are from so much more widely different areas of experience than those involved in the mere recurrence of a word, that the process must contain an important additional factor. In Hotopf's view, the importing of the principle of metaphor into the theory of meaning is one of the unjustifiable strategies by which Richards suggests that philosophy is like poetry; if *all* meaning is metaphoric, the most apparently technical and dry piece of philosophic prose is riddled with metaphor. This point is not so important for Richards' thinking about poetry, the highly metaphoric nature of which no one would want to deny, but it shows how hard he is pushing.

It would be easy, for instance, to translate Empson's list of comparisons in 'bare ruined choirs' into terms of the 'sorts' which constitute Shakespeare's perception of the tree and the ruined monastery, to note the part played by them in the metaphorical process, and to suggest how the context here dictates the relevant selection of features of past contexts. Such a translation would not affect any increase in descriptive power, but it would tend to prevent any talk about the 'vivid particularly' of the 'image', which might easily arise if the analysis were put in terms of 'associations', 'qualities' or 'properties' of the objects in the 'image': it would emphasise the intensity of the interpreting activity.

2. Uses of the idea of activity

The above account of meaning has some valuable features, partly connected with its role as a 'policeman' theory, as Richards puts it, whose function is to keep out the simplifying distortions involved in a crudely 'imagist' view. The justice of this point comes out in Richards' common-sensical remark that the words in poetry act as follows:

> [they] make us apprehend, understand, gain a realizing sense of, take in, whatever it is that is being meant – which is not necessarily any physical thing. But if we say 'a realizing sense', we must remember that this is not any 'sense' necessarily, such as sense-perception gives, but may be a feeling or a thought. What is essential is that we should really take in and become fully aware of – whatever it is.
> (PR, 130)

A useful analytic procedure that is linked to Richard's stress on 'activity' is the naming of the two parts of a metaphor and the insistence that the relations between them are not entirely a matter of resemblance. This springs directly from the attack on Hulme's view that accuracy of correspondence between the two parts is the sole criterion of metaphor.

The two parts are called 'tenor' and 'vehicle' (PR, 96). If we call a man 'a lion in battle', his courage is the 'tenor' and the lion the 'vehicle'. Richards notes that names for the two principal parts of a metaphor had not been put into general currency, and suggests that one of the important factors in Hulme's mistaken view was the ambiguous use of 'metaphor' to mean sometimes 'vehicle' and sometimes 'vehicle and tenor'. The insistence that the relations between tenor and vehicle are not entirely a matter of resemblance runs as follows:

> In general, there are very few metaphors in which disparities between tenor and vehicle are not as much operative as the similarities. Some similarity will commonly be the ostensive ground of the

shift, but the peculiar modification of the tenor which the vehicle brings about is even more the work of their unlikenesses than of their likenesses. (PR, 127)

The principal example that Richards gives is Hamlet's, 'What should such fellows as I do crawling between earth and heaven?'. Richards comments:

> There is disparity action. . . . When Hamlet uses the word *crawling* its force comes not only from whatever resemblances to vermin it brings in but at least equally from the differences that resist and control the influences of their resemblances. The implication there is that man should not so crawl. (PR, 127)

What a 'disparity action' is doing, and how important it is, in a given case, may be a matter for argument, but Richards' work here is valuable, and its merit, as with the basic doctrine of 'interinamination', with which it is closely connected, is its simplicity.

At the same time, Richards rejects the position which he illustrates by a quotation from the surrealist André Breton:

> To compare two objects, as remote from one another in character as possible, or by any other method put them together in a sudden and striking fashion, this remains the highest task to which poetry can aspire. (PR, 123)

Richards describes the happy medium between this extreme and the Kamesian or Hulmean extreme, by a metaphor from archery:

> As the two things put together are more remote, the tension created is, of course, greater. That tension is the spring of the bow, the source of the energy of the shot, but we ought not to mistake the strength of the bow for the excellence of the shooting; or the strain for the aim (PR, 125)

This commonsense view is similar to that held by Johnson, although Johnson did not explicitly formulate the idea of 'disparity action'.

The nature and usefulness of this feature of *The Philosophy of Rhetoric* need neither explanation nor comment, except to note that disparity action, which is a type of complexity or 'interinanimation', will be more prominent in dramatic poetry than in descriptive, narrative, or reflective poetry. Compare Hamlet's remark with Richards' own metaphor from archery. In the latter case it is much more difficult to see what the disparity action is doing, other than giving pleasure through surprise. For instance, the disparity between physical strength in the vehicle and mental strength in the tenor is merely irrelevant. There is a direct link between this and the tendency of the critical school which Richards helped to inspire, to prefer dramatic poetry: poetry which keeps close to actual speech. This is clear in Leavis' comment on Donne's line 'Call country ants to harvest offices': 'It is the fact that farm-labourers are not ants, but very different, that, equally with the likeness, gives the metaphor its force.' Leavis associates this process with 'the tone of sublimely, contemptuous good humour' that marks the opening of the poem (an article in *Scrutiny*, xiii). Disparity will be even more apparent when irony as well as a dramatic quality is present.

The idea of disparity action is closely related to Richards' suggestive discussion of Eliot's lines:

> Well, that Sunday Albert was home, they had a hot gammon,
> And they asked me in to get the beauty of it hot.

Richards says that when 'people talk of "beautiful food" some are apt to shudder' at such gross use of the word 'beauty', and adds of Eliot's line:

> [it uses] that shudder, and all the pathetic reverberations from its occasion and its contrasts. That is the full use of the language – which dramatic writing more than any other, of course, requires. It takes its word, not as the repository of a single constant power but as a means by which the different powers it may exert in different situations are brought together . . . with an interinanimating opposition. (PR, 85)

3. Dangers of the idea of activity

That Richards, nevertheless, is in danger of moving to an opposite extreme from that occupied by Hulme and Kames, appears in the remark that the 'language of the greatest poetry is frequently abstract in the extreme and its aim is precisely to send us "gliding through an abstract process".' (PR, 129) The last phrase describes what Hulme thought poetry should, above all, avoid. To illustrate his point Richards quotes from *Troilus and Cressida*.

> This she ? No, this is Diomed's Cressida.
> If beauty have a soul, this is not she,
> If souls guide vows, if vows be sanctimony,
> If sanctimony be the gods' delight,
> If there be rule in unity itself,
> This is not she.

Richards comments: 'We are not asked by Shakespeare here to perceive beauty, but to understand it through a metaphoric argument as the "rule in unity itself" and to understand its place in the soul's growth' (PR, 129). With regard to this particular instance, Richards' use of the word 'abstract' is rather misleading. In these lines Shakespeare is not primarily asking us to understand 'beauty'; he is depicting a young man whose love has been betrayed. We are not 'gliding through an abstract process', but, if we read aright, grasping a particular moment in a human experience. Admittedly, words like 'abstract' and 'particular' are not very satisfactory here, in any case, but they can fairly serve to make our point.

To take lines like this as the basis of a poetic theory is as potentially misleading as it would be to take, say, a poem by Hulme. Hulme invites description in terms of sharp particularity, so these lines invite description in terms of 'activity'.

4. Dr Schiller's account of Richards as an illustration of these dangers

Does Richards mislead himself by emphasis on poetry which most prominently exhibits 'activity'? In *I. A. Richards' Theory of Literature*, Dr Jerome Schiller takes for his centre the later developments of Richards' thinking, where the idea of 'activity' is most elaborately developed. It will be argued that this account not only distorts beyond recognition Richards' views in *Coleridge on Imagination*, but also is of very limited applicability when tested against its own examples. The advantage of examining Schiller's account lies in the fact that his unifying and clarifying of important elements in Richards' work after *Coleridge on Imagination*, brings their weaknesses to the fore, although to him they seem strengths. The chief weakness is that Richards' stress on poetry of the kind exemplified in Troilus' speech confuses the reading of poetry with the study of philosophy, and thus serves the same purpose as Coleridge's metaphor of the 'eddy' in *Coleridge on Imagination*, but with more noticeable consequences.

According to Schiller, the essential value of poetry lies in the fact that its language demands a special kind of attention. Such language has multiple meanings, behind which there is a multiplicity of conceptual frameworks and, hence, of purposes. The value of this special language is that it compels the reader to become aware of the balancing of various purposes underlying his various interpretations; this results in 'self-knowledge' or 'self-realisation'.

'Frameworks' and the purposes they involve are central to the account, and are elaborated as follows:

> every utterance has the function of purposing because it affirms some framework or organisation of things and events. This framework is rarely established by the utterance in question. But, as intelligible only within such a framework, and thus dependent upon its acceptance, the utterance directly supports the framework and indirectly supports the attitudes which underlie its establishment. (Schiller, *Richards' Theory of Literature*, 66)

The illustrative examples of these 'frameworks' which Schiller gives serve to recall some of the sources which lead to his account:

> A typical example is the contrasted pair of views of nature – realistic and projectionistic – described in *Coleridge on Imagination*, which closely parallels the similar contrast between the 'magical' and 'scientific' views of the universe in *Science and Poetry*. A few of his frameworks are fresh and intriguing, such as the American susceptibility to 'suggestion' as opposed to the English sense of 'tradition'; or the Chinese attitude towards the acceptability of a statement, determined by the way in which the statement fits in with accepted social practice, and not by its meeting intellectual standards. (*Ibid.*, 67)

The emergence of 'purposing', the aspect of meaning which Richards used to call 'intention', into a primary place calls for note. Richards says, for instance, that the various other aspects of meaning may all occasionally lapse in various kinds of writing but that 'without purposing, without the feed-forward which structures all activity, no utterance and no comprehending' (SI, 27). This phrasing conveniently shows how the prominence of purposing' is linked with 'activity' as the key notion in an account of reading. The source of Schiller's idea of balanced conceptual frameworks is evident in his reference to the 'realistic' and 'projectionistic' views, seen in the discussion of *Coleridge on Imagination*; complex language presents the 'fact of mind' in which are 'balanced' the two doctrines which may be derived from it.

Schiller supports these points with material taken from Richards' various investigations into the workings of language. He claims that Richards' *own* tendency to confuse the reading of poetry with the use of poetry as material in such enquiries allows us 'to expect and discover material relevant to the description of one sort of interpretation in works ostensibly devoted to the description of the other' (*Richards' Theory of Literature*, 75). The key word here, is 'relevant', and the justice of the claim should be immediately examined.

All Schiller's key examples are taken from Richards, and the first one is the familiar:

> Look! how a bright star shooteth from the sky,
> So glides he in the night from Venus' eye.

Schiller gives an edited version of Richards' commentary:

> Here . . . the more the image is followed up, the more links of relevance between the units are discovered . . . The separable meanings of each word, Look! [our surprise at the meteor, hers at his flight], *star* [a light-giver, an influence, a remote and uncontrollable thing] . . . *glides* [not rapidity only, but fatal ease, too] . . . – all these separable meanings are here brought into one.

Schiller regards *Coleridge on Imagination* as a transitional work, giving hints about the later, and more satisfactory theory, so he provides his own commentary, the essence of which is the remark that 'each meaning found to be relevant indirectly reflects a purpose governing the entire utterance. Thus the multiplicity of meanings reflects a multiplicity of purposes.' It is, to say the least, difficult to conceive how this might be so. A remarkable feat of ingenuity would be needed to enforce the point, and even that degree of ingenuity would be defeated by the further need to associate the purposes with 'conceptual frameworks'. Coleridge, Richards and Schiller agree that the lines are in the highest poetic mode, so that it ought to be a strong candidate for fulfilling the requirements of Schiller's theory.

The same point may be made of the second of his key examples, which is Richards' analysis of Denham's lines on the Thames:

O could I flow like thee, and make thy stream
My great exemplar, as it is my theme!
Though deep, yet clear: though gentle, yet not dull;
Strong without rage; without o'erflowing full.

Schiller's commentary, in keeping with his theory, runs:
The metaphoric relationship between mind and river forces us to
concentrate on the variety of interpretations that we afford to the
mind. Thus the metaphor does not *say* anything directly about the
mind, but merely provides the occasion for multiple sayings.
(*Richards' Theory of Literature*, 85)
The phrase 'variety of interpretation' can only refer to the fact that
Richards had said that 'deep', applied to 'mind', means 'mysterious' and
'rich in knowledge and power'. The essential point, however, is not that
Schiller distorts and exaggerates Richards' thinking, but that the lines
fail to conform to his theory. What the lines 'realise', so far from affording
a 'variety of interpretations' of the kind that might involve differing
'purposes' and 'conceptual frameworks', is what might, for convenience's
sake, be called 'the Augustan norm'.

This is, in fact, subtly brought out by Richards' own commentary. He
notes that in Denham's sequence of metaphorical adjectives, in some cases
the vehicle-meaning has priority, in others the tenor-meaning, and that
'this alternating movement in the shifts may have not a little to do with
the rather mysterious power of the couplet, the way it exemplifies what it
is describing' (PR, 121). Denham is praising, that is, a controlled and
balanced personality, and the antithetical balance of the shifts, like the
antithetical balance of the couplet movement, is one of the factors in the
realising, as opposed to mere statement, of the meaning. The 'interinanimation', or complexity, of the language leads the reader to a re-
creation of what the lines are about, and the heightened awareness issuing
from this constitutes not only self-knowledge but self-creation. In more
ordinary language, the fit reader of Denham not only gets the idea, he
feels what it is like to have that idea, and, further, that part of himself
which answers to the idea and the feeling, comes into being, and is
recognised. This by no means constitutes a complete account of literary
study, but it describes the essence of it.

So far, the practical inapplicability of the theory which Schiller
attributes to Richards has been outlined. Its weakness hinges on the point
that Hotopf makes about Richards' discussion of Coleridge's presentation
of the relation between perceived and perceiver through the metaphor of
an eddy: 'The self's awareness of itself embroiled in its experience' and
the particular kind of "self-realisation" consequent upon it, are limited
to the reading of poetry which is *about* such "embroilment".' And
Hotopf's words here are, in fact, a condensed summary of Schiller's
theory.

The convenience of Schiller's account is that it draws together the elements in Richards' thinking which spring from the use of poetry as material for investigating the workings of language, and thus makes clear their limited applicability to the reading of poetry.

Schiller's licence in drawing, in the building of his theory, upon Richards' use of poetry as case material, is lent plausibility by Richards' own tendency to confuse this procedure with the reading of poetry as poetry.

5. The extent of Richards' own confusion of these interests

One of the most noticeable, and seemingly persuasive of such confusions occurs in 'Poetry as an Instrument of Research', an essay which is of great importance for Schiller's account (s1, 146–54). Richards writes:

> there is an important use of words – very frequent, I suggest, in poetry – which does not freeze its meanings but leaves them fluid, which does not fix an assertorial clip upon them in the way that scientific prose and factual discourse must. It leaves them free to move about and relate themselves in various ways to one another. (s1, 148)

He adds:

> Let me now use the privilege of a definer and invite you to mean – for this occasion – by ᵗPoetryᵗ (ᵗ . . . ᵗ for technical) words so used that their meanings are free so to dispose themselves : to make up together whatever they can. (s1, 149)

Richards' caution here should be immediately noted; the definition is a special one to be used for a special occasion.

Richards illustrates what he means by 'fluid' language by discussing the title of his own essay, 'Poetry as an Instrument of Research'. He draws attention to its 'fluidity' by noting that if we put 'is' for 'as', we give the phrase 'the solidity' fixity, rigidity of responsible prose, . . . we make the sentence, in short, mean what it says and be ready to take the consequences' (s1, 147). As it stands, however, the title is full of possibilities; the various meanings of 'poetry', 'instrument' and 'research' can be set in a number of different patterns. Richards does not give examples, but they are easily supplied: 'Poetry is a means by which we look into our own hearts and minds'; 'The laws of language are best enquired into by using poetry as case material'; 'We become most intimately acquainted with a past culture by studying its literature'; 'The problems of emotive language can best be discussed *in* emotive language; a rigidly scientific procedure is out of place here'. The phrase is, in short, not a statement but an invitation to speculation, inviting an interpreting activity of the highest possible degree.

But there is an evident danger in transferring this idea to poetry, even in a 'technical' sense. Richards notes that the presence or absence of an 'assertorial clip' should be 'thought of as a matter of degree', but goes on to dismiss the point because 'degree suggests measurement and we are not in sight of measurement here'. This is true, but there is, nevertheless, an important and easily perceptible difference between Richards' phrase 'Poetry as an instrument of research' and *a poem*. A poem, in fact, contains much more of an 'assertorial clip'. A phrase detached from a Shakespeare sonnet might, in itself, resemble Richards' title, but in its context in the poem its interaction with the other words evidently reduces its potential variety of meaning. To say that the kind of interpretation required by Richards' title is 'very frequent' in poetry is to exaggerate the notion of 'activity' to an intolerable degree. One might remind Richards of a point he made, in *Coleridge on Imagination*, about some wilfully cryptic modern poetry: 'it is easy to mistake a mere freedom to interpret as we will for controlling unity of sane purpose' (CI, 91). This serves also to make the general point that what Richards calls an 'assertorial clip' is what is usually called 'unity'. A further relevant comment is that the whole discussion reveals the dangers of Richards' habit of using fragments of poetry rather than whole poems, a habit which will have been evident throughout this account.

The confusion is not, however, of radical importance for Richards' thinking about poetry. In the first place, it is an intermittent confusion. Even in the later work Richards is able to make the distinction between poetry as material for studying language, and poetry as poetry. Secondly, Richards' interest, in his writings after *The Philosophy of Rhetoric*, is primarily in the study of language, so that the main effects of any confusion are chiefly in that direction. Thirdly, Richards never attempts to re-interpret the thinking of *Coleridge on Imagination* in the way that Dr Schiller does.

6. Further developments of the idea of activity

In Richards' later work, there is a tendency to make poetry as open-ended as possible; to insist on the variety of possible interpretations of a poem. This line of thought, however, does not depend on any special feature of poetic language, but springs from a general theory of communication, and the variety of interpretations are not simultaneously held in mind by the reader, as he reads.

Important to this tendency is Richards' rejection of the terminology of 'destination' and 'message', as used in communications engineering, which implies that a message is en-coded by the transmitter and de-coded at the destination. Richards is anxious to deny its applicability to any subtle uses of language, calling it, in its application to poetry, the 'Vulgar Packaging View' (4).

He is once more insisting that poetry is composed of 'pseudo-statements', (SI, 147–8), a view that insists that a poem *is* the activity of interpretation, not an extractable idea. The en-coding and the message are inseparable, as was stressed by Richards' account of the *organising* function of language.

In rejecting the idea of a 'destination' Richards refers to C. S. Pierce. In

a critical discussion (*So Much Nearer*, 159) of the terminology of communications engineering, he turns to his audience and asks:

> Are you the Destination? I should hope not ... How you understand
> me will depend upon what I go on to say but more still on what you
> find (now or later) to say to yourself (or to others) about it all.

> This is what the great theorist of sign-situations, Charles Sanders
> Pierce, meant by his doctrine that every sign needs other succeeding
> signs as its interpretants – and so on and so on.

For Pierce, an 'interpretant' is 'that which interprets a sign', and it can
itself, in his view, be nothing but a further sign, which needs, in turn its
own 'interpretants'. According to Gallie in *Pierce and Pragmatism*, there
are, for Pierce, two escapes from the endless process here envisaged. First
his notion of the 'entire general intended interpretant'; second his view
that for certain purposes one may ignore the fact that words are signs
needing 'interpretants' and treat them *as though* they referred directly to
their objects. Richards mentions neither of these devices, perhaps
because of his desire to make interpretation seem as open-ended as
possible.

There is both truth and interest in Richards' pursuit of this line of
thought. Herbert's lines on reading the Scriptures may be recalled:

> Such are thy secrets, which my life makes good,
> And comments on thee: for in everything
> Thy words do find me out, and parallels bring,
> And in another make me understood.

To say that one's life 'comments' on what is reading is a succinct and
memorable way of putting it. The literary work takes its place in one's
experience, and this place will not quite resemble the place it takes in
someone else's experience. Further, as Richards' phrase 'now or later'
implies, this place will change as the reader's experience develops. A
poem by Donne will not, commonly, mean to a reader what it meant to
him five years earlier, or will mean five years later. The point is touched
upon by Empson, discussing the problem of analysis, at the beginning
of *Seven Types*:

> there is a sort of meaning, the sort that people are thinking of when
> they say 'this poet will mean more to you when you have had more
> experience of life', which is hardly in reach of the analyst at all.

Further, if the point on which Richards is insisting is translated into
literary historical terms it resembles Eliot's view that any genuine new
poem changes the relations between poems written in the past. Pope can
never be to a modern reader exactly what he was to Johnson, because the
modern reader knows Wordsworth, Eliot, and so on.

As to Richards' views on the idea of a 'message' being 'en-coded', these
can conveniently be discussed with reference to *Poetries and Sciences*
(111–12), where we read:

> A vast, recent aberration of concern with poets as subjects for bio-

graphy has led too many to think that poems just express items, incidents, occurrences, crises, and so on, in a poet's experience. Against this he expresses the following view:

The more usual thing – so far as available evidence goes – is for a poem . . . to form at its inception a problem. The minimum problem I said was the finding, or creation, of a situation – a confluence of imaginative possibilities – able to support its growth. The situation, that confluence of possibilities, is a system of oppositions and collaborations among words. In brief, a poem begins by creating a linguistic problem whose solution by language will be the attainment of its end. (112)

The metaphor of 'growth', central to Richards' thinking here, is one that we have met before:

Words are the meeting points at which regions of experience which can never combine in sensation or intuition, come together. They are the occasion and the means of that growth which is the mind's endless endeavour to order itself. (PR, 131)

Richards' drift can be suggested by a comparison with Pierce. Gallie says that, for Pierce, 'all we mean by thought or intelligence, is "a sign developing in accordance with the laws of inference"'. Richards, believing with Coleridge that poetry is the utterance of the whole soul, seems to suggest that all we mean by the soul is a sign developing in accordance with the laws of poetic language. A more emphatic way of rejecting the view that language 'en-codes' an 'experience', could scarcely be conceived.

Behind this thinking lies a motive seen before in Richards' work; the hope of an imminent spectacular development. This is now introduced by using feed-forward and feed-back cycles as the model for talking about a poem's 'growth'. In *Poetries and Sciences*, we are given a clear and simple illustration of such a cycle in the free-hand drawing of a circle:

First comes the feed-forward directive as to the size of the circle. It cannot be begun without that. Then with every inch your chalk travels there is feed-back reporting to your nerve-muscle-tendon-joint executives as to violations of the feed-forward directives and an issuing of new feed-forward as to corrective action if needed. (95)

With regard to poetry, this means that 'interinanimation' is seen now as not merely the central feature but as the controlling agency. Richards does not put it in that way but as follows:

in composing, or in choice between interpretations, we note how we are guided by the extent to which change in one component entails change in others, whenever we 'see' that if x varies, p,g . . . must vary too. The process of composition is indeed a weighing of these entailments, a balancing imposed by the rivalling possibilities of the alternates. (97)

'We', here, Richards suggests, means 'the system of relevant feed-forward, which at the moment is being confirmed by feed-back'. An important feature of the account is that we (in the normal sense) will not be entirely aware of the way in which the cycle is controlling the growth of the poem. To that extent the poem is composed by the language system itself.

The hope held out by this way of describing a poem appears in Richards' following remark:

> Such has been the utterly unexpected rate of advance in these matters in recent years and such the promise of contemporary neurological model designs that new and perhaps liberating, light on human potential may be looked for quite soon. (96)

Richards is still searching for the key which will unlock the laws of poetic language. He concedes that this approach may 'go too far', and it may be said that it has already done so. It will be readily acknowledged that the poet's struggle with language is important, and that the inherent tendencies of the language system will have some shaping influence on the poem, but Richards exaggerates this factor. In composing a poem we may see that if 'x' varies, then 'p' and 'g' must vary too, but the choice of 'x' is dictated not only by its relation to 'p' and 'g', but by its relation to what we want to say. 'What we want to say', or the experience which the poem expresses, corresponds, in Richards' analogy, with the 'size of the circle' from which comes the essential 'feed-forward directive'. No doubt expressions such as 'the experience which the poem expresses' are theoretically unsatisfactory, as Richards' whole point here is to insist, but criticism cannot, in fact, proceed without using them. They might be called 'necessary fictions'.

Richards has always been suspicious of 'fictions'. The point is noted by Hotopf (*Language, Thought and Comprehension*, 25) in his discussion of *The Meaning of Meaning*:

> Ogden and Richards' touchstone – one they were always fingering – was the actual psychological conditions that caused an individual utterance.

When Richards attacks the idea that an 'experience' is 'put into words', he is concerned with the psychological complexity of what actually happens, and is, evidently, justified in insisting that words have a formative, not merely an expressive function. He is, likewise, justified in insisting that the poem is not merely received as a 'destination'; the interpreting activity also is formative and not merely receptive. But, to use the phrase which Gallie uses in discussing Pierce, the critic has to proceed *as though* the poem records an experience and he has received this experience. To proceed in this way is not necessarily to fall, as Richards seems to assume, into a mistaken preoccupation with the poet's biography. A safeguard against this is the familiar notion that a poet *generalises* his experience. In Coleridge's formulation, one of the functions of the 'imagination' is to fuse 'the general, with the concrete; the idea, with the image; the individual, with the representative' (*Biographia Literaria*, ii, 12). A typical modern formulation appears in Leavis' remark, in *D. H. Lawrence, Novelist*, in a dis-

cussion of the similarity between Lawrence's relation with his mother
and Ursula's relation with her father in *The Rainbow*, that in the novel 'the
experience is wholly impersonalised (and in being impersonalised, extended)'. The same ground is covered by the neo-classical doctrine of
'generality', which will be examined in our discussion of Dr Johnson.

7. These developments criticised

The kind of criticism produced by Richards' development of the
idea of 'activity' is well illustrated by his own commentary, in *Poetries and
Sciences*, on Empson's poem *Legal Fiction*. He says of the commentary:

What this sort of gloss should be attempting to bring out is the
dependence of what any word or phrase can do in the poem upon
what its other words and phrases can do there: the degree of their
mutual enablement and mutual control. It is this – not any actions
or agencies, and wishes or hopes or endeavours on the part of the
poet or his readers – that settles what the poem may be and when and
how (and whether) it is finished. (117)

The poem runs:

Law makes long spokes of the short stakes of men.
Your well fenced out real estate of mind
No high flat of the nomad citizen
Looks over, or train leaves behind.

Your rights extend under and above your claim
Without bound; you own land in Heaven and Hell;
Your part of earth's surface and mass the same,
Of all cosmos' volume, and all stars as well.

Your rights reach down where all owners meet, in Hell's
Pointed exclusive conclave, at earth's centre
(Your spun farm's root still on that axis dwells);
And up, through galaxies, a growing sector.

You are nomad yet; the lighthouse beam you own
Flashes, like Lucifer, through the firmament.
Earth's axis varies; your dark central cone
Wavers a candle's shadow, at the end.

The most conspicuous feature of Richards' commentary is its avoidance
of any mention of the tone and feeling of the poem. The nearest that
Richards comes to this is in his comment on 'nomad citizen' in the third
line:

nomad citizen: In contrast to the farmer (cultivating his garden). The
fourth verse 'comforts' this farmer, who may feel rather tied by his
holding. He does a lot of travelling inevitably if his property is
sweeping illimitably about in this fashion. It is a disturbing sort of
comfort however: Lucifer is 'fallen from heaven' (*Isaiah*, 14:12)

and the self itself is shadowed by itself, hidden from whatever light
it may produce. (116–17)

The reason why Richards has to avoid, as far as possible, questions of tone
and feeling, is evident if his earlier definitions of those terms are recalled.
'Tone' (the poet's attitude to his audience) and 'feeling' (his attitude to
his subject) quickly bring in the 'actions of agencies, and wishes or hopes
or endeavors' of the poet, which Richards thinks must be kept out of the
discussion. For the same reason he carefully omits any mention of the
poem's 'intention', or what it is 'about'. Omitting, as far as possible, any
consideration of feeling, tone and intention, Richards has to proceed by
commenting on the senses of the words. Typical of this is his comment on
the first line:

> *short stakes:* Both the stakes the prospector drives in to mark the
> boundaries of his claim (line 5) and the posts of the fence that keeps
> cattle (say) in and trespassers out of the spun farm (line 11). Rights
> in this land include everything under and above (line 5). They are
> *stakes*, too, in the sense in which a landowner is said to have a *stake* in
> the country. He has invested money, time and toil in his property;
> he has something *at stake*. (116)

Here Richards might have added that they are also 'stakes' as in gambling.
The farmer's choice appears to be a gamble merely about life, but it turns
out to be a gamble involving eternity.

As well as inhibiting comment on the feeling, tone and intention of the
poem, Richards' approach forbids any mention of its 'images', because all
must be described in terms of 'activity', or the 'mutual enablement and
mutual control' of the words.

The approach, in short, fails to comment on what appear to the reader
to be the main features of the poem.

A commentary on the tone and feeling aspects of the poem might run
as follows: there is an ironical touch in 'real estate of mind', which comes
from the disparity action in the metaphor; the implication is that a 'mind'
shouldn't be fenced off like a piece of 'real estate'. Such a mind is a closed
mind, and the point is taken up again in 'owners' and 'exclusiveness' in
lines 9 and 10. The first stanza appears to congratulate the person
addressed: 'How competently you have managed your affairs. You have
invested in a property free from the distressing proximity of urban and
industrial development'. The ironical implication is: 'In being exclusive
you have cut yourself off from humanity'. Relevant to this implication,
are the feelings evoked by the 'nomad citizen'; he is, as a 'nomad', un-
afraid, and, as a 'citizen', he takes a place in the community. Also relevant
are the feelings evoked by 'train leaves behind', which implies; 'You have
never had enough human contact to be saddened by someone's departure'.

The feeling of the second stanza is one of immensity, which highlights
the petty and futile neatness of the 'well fenced out real estate of mind'.
The contrast is very clear in 'without bound' as opposed to 'well fenced
out'. The feeling of immensity reaches a climax in,

Of all cosmos' volume, and all stars as well.

Here the effect of the long, open vowel sounds, especially in the repeated 'all', re-inforced by the similar sound of 'well', is particularly noticeable. This feeling of illimitability undermines the neat exclusiveness of the first stanza.

The wit of the third stanza carries on the undermining process. The growth metaphor in 'a growing sector', further released by the word 'farm', is grotesque, and its implication is: 'You thought you were only concerned in growing cash-crops, but your farm is growing something that reaches up past the stars'. In terms of the tenor (the 'mind') this means: 'The organisation of your mind, which you arrived at through merely practical consideration, has moral implications of the most far-reaching kind.' This is touched upon also in the first part of the third stanza. The idea of exclusive farm-owners hints at the local rich-man's club, the meeting place of solid, successful men, which is really a type of hell, because it issues from possessiveness, and all that goes with it. In terms of the mind, the 'owner' is the man who is, as D.H.Lawrence would have said, 'ego-bound'; who refuses to acknowledge that he is a part of something beyond himself. The wit in this part of the stanza is generated partly by the word 'exclusive' (what Hell fences out is God). 'Pointed' has a more obscure effect, but the joke, it may be suggested, is that the mutual hostility, inevitably felt by ego-bound men, is symbolised by the pointed goads of the traditional picture of Hell.

The last stanza completes the undermining, but the feeling now is more sombre and grave. It says: 'For all your apparently organised solidity you are finally as evanescent as a flash of light and insubstantial as a candle's shadow.' Relevant to the feeling are the associations of 'Lucifer', and of the flickering candle, which evokes, passingly, the fear that a candle will go out in a dark cellar. Also implied is the point made by Richards: 'You lack self-knowledge, in that you will not recognise that you are not self-sufficient.'

Such a commentary, clearly, involves making suggestions about the poem's 'intention'. The 'intention' is, to use Richards' terms, the essential 'feed-forward directive'; the intention as to the 'size of the circle', without which nothing can be begun. This must correspond to the poet's 'wishes or hopes or endeavours', which Richards wants to cut out. His procedure is not, that is, justified by his own basic model. Nor is it justified by the event. For instance, it is easy to see the relations between 'Lucifer' and the rest of the poem; it is connected with the imagery of light and darkness, with the references to Hell, and with the pride of the 'owners'. To see this is to see 'the mutual enablement and mutual control' of the words. But the appearance of Lucifer is not *dictated* by the rest of the poem. Empson was free to put it in or leave it out. He might have put 'Mulciber', and alluded to the fact that in *Paradise Lost*, Mulciber,

Dropd from the Zenith like a falling Starr.

The appearance of Lucifer is determined not merely by feed-back from the words already used in the poem, but by feed-forward from what Empson 'wants to say'.

Granted, as Richards insists, the struggle with words in the composition has a formative influence. The poet might only discover what he 'wants to say' during the course of that struggle. But to say that this should prevent us from talking about the feelings and intention of the poem is an extreme and inhibiting position. As Empson himself once said, in the context of a similar discussion: 'If critics are not to put up some pretence of understanding the feelings of the author in hand they must condemn themselves to contempt.' (*Seven Types*, xiii–xiv)

Such a pretence, as we have said, does not necessarily involve writing the poet's biography. A mistaken biographical attempt, with regard to this particular poem, would be to try to trace the person addressed, and his actual relations with Empson at the time. No such person, of course, need have existed. The tendency of mind which Empson is describing exists in everyone, and Empson, in fact, may have been addressing himself: meditating on a weakness; in which case the speaker is not even Empson, but a part of Empson. A more plausible biographical attempt would be to relate the poem, in view of its attitude to 'owners', to Empson's interest in Marxism, but this would add nothing essential, since the poem stands on its own feet.

It was noted that Richards also refuses to talk about 'images'. Perhaps the most striking image in Empson's poem is the wavering tip of the cone, seen as a candle's shadow. The working of this is complex. The 'dark central cone' is itself the vehicle of a metaphor. It is the ground, over which the owner of the fenced-off piece of real-estate has rights, stretching down underneath his property to the earth's centre. The tenor of the metaphor is the mystery, the unknown depths, of the owner's being. The furthermost tip of the cone fades into insubstantiality, which is seen as the insubstantiality of a candle's shadow. But the candle's shadow clearly refers back to the original tenor; beneath the most self-sufficiency ('the fenced out real estate of mind') is not only mystery, but also, finally, insubstantiality.

The success of the metaphor depends partly on the fact that the wavering of a candle's shadow is a vivid vehicle for conveying the kind of wavering that we are to imagine. But, as we have already seen, the success also depends on the presence of a whole complex of further feelings about a flickering candle. As well as fear of the dark, there is a feeling of transience, and this is reinforced by the poem's final phrase, 'at the end', which implies the approach of death. This feeling, in turn, works back upon the candle's shadow, rendering it more vivid and precise; it is a dying candle, and the flaring and sinking of its guttering accentuate the wavering of the shadow.

Much of this may be seen as a support for Richards' refusal to talk about 'images'. The 'activity' which makes the interconnections between the words in the metaphor of the flickering candle is certainly intense. To use the language of *Coleridge on Imagination*, the reader seems to be more than merely reading, he feels as though he is creating and thereby realising. But the activity has an end. To use Coleridge's words again, what he is creating is a fusion of an 'idea' with an 'image' (*Biographia Literaria*, ii, 12). He is not merely seeing pictures but the word 'image' *is* hard to avoid, and there is no urgent reason to avoid it, so long as one isn't misled by it. 'Image' is shorthand, one might say, for the upshot of the creative activity.

In Richards' approach the activity seems to have no upshot. The poem begins with a linguistic problem, the words need further particular words with which to interact, and this process goes on until the needs of the various words are satisfied. The critical method is to describe some features of the interaction. It is as though the critic sees some chemicals thrown into a bowl, and then watches them reacting, but is not allowed to say why they were thrown in, or what the end-result was.

In examining the development of the idea of 'activity' and the sort of approach in which it issues, it has been noted that a scientific ambition is present in the development, and this provides the cue for a final comment on this phase of Richards' work.

Bertrand Russell, to take a safe witness in these matters, was of the belief that 'whatever can be known, can be known by means of science; but things which are legitimately matters of feeling lie outside its province'. Richards' neglect of the feeling in Empson's poem, and his attempt to describe its 'activity' merely in terms of sense is dictated, largely, by his hope that 'contemporary neurological model designs' may be harnessed to the analysis of poetry. His attempt, for the reason given by Russell, is unsatisfactory. Feelings play too large a part in poetry to be so neglected.

The scientific ambition is a hope for *certainty*, and this is connected with Richards' exasperation with the chaos, as he sees it, of current literary studies. Just before his analysis of Empson's poem, for instance, he has disparaging comments about various critical approaches; linguistic analysis, archetypal criticism, comparative and historical studies, literary biography, are all viewed sceptically.

One may have a good deal of sympathy with Richards here. The type of literary liberalism which stresses the possibility of a large variety of 'approaches' to poetry is in many cases mere licensing of irrelevance. But a scientific 'cure' would be worse than the disease. In Richards' pursuit of scientific certainty one misses the atmosphere which springs from seeing criticism as, to use the phrase which Leavis seized upon, 'the common pursuit of true judgement'.

In one sense Richards is well aware of the inadequacies of a scientific approach to poetry. He says, for instance, in 'The Future of the Humanities', that 'the main doctrines and positions which keep man humane are insusceptible, at present, to scientific proof' (s1, 67). One notes, there, however, the qualification 'at present', which is the loophole for the entrance of 'contemporary neurological model designs'. But more important is the fact, which we have noted before, that Richards has not extendedly engaged in 'the common pursuit' with reference to a given body of literature. It is, it may be argued, the absence of this sheet-anchor which permits his occasional waywardness.

Richards' thinking is now at the opposite pole from his earlier work, where, as we have seen, there is neglect of the role of sense in poetic language, and a corresponding overemphasis on feeling. The basis for the earlier view was, it has been suggested, poetry of the kind written by Swinburne. The basis for the later view is 'poetry' of the type represented by Richards' phrase 'poetry as an instrument of research', which, in fact, is not 'poetry', but merely an invitation to unlimited speculation. Its nearest equivalent in poetry is a *fragment* such as Coleridge's metaphor of the eddy, which plays a crucial part in *Coleridge on Imagination*.

This account of Richards has held that the period of his work that resulted in *Coleridge on Imagination* is the most fruitful for literary criticism. Here he avoids the extremes of the doctrine of 'equilibrium', with its overstress on feeling, and the doctrine of 'activity', with its neglect of feeling. An over-all view of Richards' work would, in fact, lead us to expect the essential interest, for a literary critic, to lie where I have placed it. His initial interests were psychological, linguistic and philosophical, and these resume their central position in his later work, in which the other large interest is pedagogy. It is in the period from *Principles of Literary Criticism* to *Coleridge on Imagination* that he works most closely on poetry, and the latter book is the valuable culmination of this period.

PART TWO

SAMUEL JOHNSON

CHAPTER THREE

COMPLEXITY AND THE DOCTRINE
OF PROPRIETY

Complexity and the Doctrine of Propriety

1. Introductory

The following examination of some aspects of analytic method, and accompanying ideas about poetry, in eighteenth-century criticism, is concerned chiefly with Johnson's work on Shakespeare. It is primarily intended to establish similarities with the ideas developed by Richards. Incidentally it is hoped to show the need to modify some current assumptions about eighteenth-century criticism; particularly that its ideas about poetic language were highly peculiar and are now exploded.

There is in current history of criticism a tendency to exaggerate differences between schools. The following account, in stressing similarities, runs the risk of dwelling tediously upon very elementary features of critical theory and practice. That the risk is worth taking may be indicated by Robert M. Ryley's 'William Warburton as New Critic', a representative document in modern discussion of eighteenth-century criticism. Here the following suggestion is made:

whereas the neo-classical critic normally asks whether a word is plain or fancy, high or low, Warburton anticipates the semantic interests of twentieth-century critics by trying to determine precisely the meaning of a word or phrase in its special context. (254)

Warburton is indeed a perceptive and sensitive reader, but his procedure is not exceptional, as a cursory comparison of his edition of Shakespeare with Hanmer's, Theobald's or Johnson's, or with eighteenth-century Shakespearean commentary in general, will show. 'To determine precisely the meaning of a word' is the essence of the enterprise.

Professor Ryley finds Warburton's resemblances to the New Criticism 'interesting' but 'superficial'. Is this occasioned partly by the attitude which the 'New Critics' themselves have taken towards eighteenth-century views on poetic language? A brief recapitulation of that attitude may be useful, especially because it will be further discussed at other points in this account of modern analytical criticism.

Leavis believes that Johnson is inhibited from understanding the essential nature of poetic language by the doctrine of *propriety*. Eighteenth-century poetry and criticism alike, Leavis suggests, assume that the language of poetry should be the 'common currency of terms, put together according to the conventions of grammar and logic'. The point is elaborated as follows:

It is not an age in which the poet feels called to explore further below the public surface than conventional expression takes cognizance of, or to push in any way beyond the frontiers of the charted. He has no impulse to indulge in licentious linguistic creation, nor does it occur to him that such indulgence may with any propriety be countenanced. (*Scrutiny*, xii, 194)

Obsession with 'propriety' blinds Johnson, who is the figure chiefly being discussed, to that 'concrete specificity in the rendering of experience' which is the hallmark of Shakespeare's poetry.

A similar nexus of ideas is apparent in Allen Tate's critique 'Johnson on the Metaphysicals'. Discussing his views on metaphor, Tate says: 'I believe it is fair to say that Johnson liked his tenors straight, without any nonsense from the vehicles' (381). The same point is made by Professor Wellek who remarks (in *A History of Modern Criticism*) that Johnson required that 'the tenor and the vehicle should remain neatly separated'. Tate assumes that the vehicle in a metaphor can be equated with a new access of experience, and that the tenor is an idea or a thought. Thus armed, he interprets Johnson's dislike of devotional poetry as a timid adherence to orthodoxy: 'the imaginative act of returning the paraphrase to the hazards of new experience (new vehicles) is an impiety, even a perversity, which he [Johnson] reproves in the Metaphysical poets' (385). Tate generalises this into a broad view which parallels that of Leavis, suggesting that Johnson's incapacity for the creative and dramatic use of metaphor is 'a defect that seems general in that age, when men assumed a static relation between the mind and its object, between poet and subject'.

Tate and Leavis are attacking that approach to language which tends to issue in the familiar 'clothing' metaphor: the poet finds a thought or idea and then 'dresses' it in elegant language. For Leavis the truly poetic use of language is 'exploratory-creative'. But this imagined eighteenth-century poet who writes with 'a common currency of terms put together according to the conventions and logic' is something of a man-of-straw. Against him one might set, for instance, Pope's description of Homer's language:

Aristotle has reason to say, he [Homer] was the only poet who had found out *living words*; there are in him more daring figures and metaphors than in any good author whatever . . . Yet his expression is never too big for the sense, but justly great in proportion to it: 'Tis the sentiment that swells and fills out the diction, which rises with it and forms itself about it. (Preface to *The Iliad*, *Twickenham Edition*)

Pope is trying to identify that use of language which D.W. Harding describes in his essay on Rosenberg, and which issues from the poet's bringing together 'idea' and 'expression' at any unusually early stage of the psycho-physiological process, so that they modify each other before coming to full consciousness. Professor Harding contrasts this with the more usual state of affairs, where the 'idea' is distorted slightly in order to fit the nearest convenient verbal formula or stock phrase (*Scrutiny*, iii, 365). As Pope puts it, in 'living words' the diction forms itself about the sentiments, rather than the sentiment being fitted to the diction.

To quote Pope, however, though it may be suggestive, leaves essential questions unanswered, and it is important to examine the features of eighteenth-century criticism which have disturbed modern critics.

A well-known case is Macbeth's:

> I have liv'd long enough: my Way of life
> Is fall'n into the sear, the yellow leaf.

Upon this Johnson comments, in his notes to his edition of Shakespeare:[1]

> As there is no relation between the 'way of life', and 'fallen into the sear', I am inclined to think that the 'W' is only an 'M' inverted, and that it was originally written,
>
> my *May* of life.
>
> 'I am now passed from the spring to the autumn of my days, but I am without those comforts that should succeed the spriteliness of bloom, and support me in this melancholy season.' (*Yale*, viii, 791-2)

Johnson does not, in fact, insert the emendation into the text, but it is clear which reading he prefers.

An oddly similar and even more outrageous instance, which Johnson *does* insert into his text, is Warburton's emendation of the Gentleman's description of Cordelia, after she hears what her sisters have done to her father:

> You have seen
> Sunshine and rain at once; her smiles and tears
> Were like a better way.

Warburton, on similar grounds to those given by Johnson in the previous instance, emends 'better way' to 'wetter May' (Johnson's *The Plays of William Shakespeare*, London, 1765, vi, 117). To fill out the picture, it may be remarked that Benjamin Heath, a noted Shakespearean of the time, while conceding that Warburton's suggestion is 'not absolutely without propriety', suggests 'April day' as an even greater improvement (*Revisal of Shakespeare's Text*, London, 1765, 343).

The tendency is clear and no further examples need be given. A modern

---

[1] Throughout this and the following chapter I shall refer to *Johnson on Shakespeare*, ed. A. Sherbo, which takes up volumes vii and viii of *The Yale Edition of the Works of Samuel Johnson*. The two volumes in question were published by the Yale University Press in 1968 and seem destined to become the standard reference work. I describe Johnson's footnote to Macbeth's lines here as '*Yale*, viii, 791-2', and this formula will be followed in all cases. As in the Yale edition, act, scene and line references (e.g. I.ii.24) follow W. Aldis Wright's Cambridge edition (revised 1891-3), but the text follows Johnson's first edition.

commentator would note that this tendency, if given free rein, would turn Shakespeare's speeches, alive as they are with the actual pressures of thought, feeling and language, into exhibitions of studied sentiment, of the kind that may be conveniently studied in Johnson's own play *Irene*.

But critics ought not to be judged by their worst attempts. Are these examples merely the visible part of a cold iceberg of incomprehending disapproval of Shakespeare's poetry, or relatively unimportant manifestations of a bias ? It will be argued that the latter is the fairer answer; and it may usefully be added that modern commentators on Johnson sometimes rigidly proceed with reference to pre-conceived ideas, rather than with reference to what is before them. One such example arises from Johnson's comment when Eleanor, in *King John*, urges a speedy reconciliation with the French, while they are in the mood for a parley,

> Lest zeal now melted by the windy breath
> Of soft petitions, pity and remorse,
> Cool and congeal again to what it was.

Johnson comments:

> We have here a very unusual, and, I think, not very just image of 'zeal', which in its highest degree is represented by others as a flame, but by Shakespeare as a frost. To 'repress zeal', in the language of others, is to 'cool', in Shakespeare's to 'melt' it; when it exerts its utmost power it is commonly said to 'flame', but by Shakespeare to be 'congealed'. (*Yale*, vii, 415)

Professor Sherbo, who is commonly anxious to defend Johnson, remarks that he is here 'disturbed by Shakespeare's deviation from poetic tradition', and adds:

> One must concede that zeal has rarely been equated with coldness, and no writer, even Shakespeare, Johnson is saying, should allow a desire for novelty to lead him into absurdity. Johnson was evidently disturbed by the terms of the metaphors, neglecting their total effect in his concentration on their constituent parts. (*Samuel Johnson, Editor of Shakespeare*, 77)

Sherbo seems to be bullied by the view that Johnson liked his tenors and vehicles separate. Johnson does not talk about the 'absurdity' of the effect, nor does he appeal merely to 'poetic tradition', nor does he attribute any desire for novelty to Shakespeare. In terms of Richards' thinking, Johnson notes a failure to triumph over the resistances of words, and appeals to the criterion elaborated in Richards' comment on Eliot's use of the word 'beauty' with reference to food. Behind the metaphor of 'flame' for 'zeal' is a whole interconnected system of words, such as 'fiery', 'hot-headed', 'hot-tempered', 'warm-hearted', and so on, and Shakespeare encounters the resistance of this system. It is noticeable that Johnson, with the accuracy that one expects, makes this a point about *usage*, not about the nature of 'zeal'; he does not claim that 'zeal' *is* 'hot'. Professor Sherbo does not say what the 'total effect' is, which Johnson is alleged to have neglected, and his point seems to be no more than an inert recall of the kind of allegation made by Tate. It is, in fact, hard to evade the conclusion that these lines of Eleanor's are some of the thousand that Ben Johnson wished Shakespeare had blotted.

That a 'defender' of Johnson can proceed in this fashion, indicates, perhaps more strongly than could anything else, the need for an examination of the doctrine of propriety.

2. Interinanimation and propriety

The doctrine of propriety concerns itself with inter-relations between words. Propriety is inter-relation, impropriety its absence. Propriety, that is, concerns itself with what Richards called 'interinanimation'. To pursue the resemblance, the basis of the doctrine is the criterion of realisation. The aim of 'proper' writing is to make the reader feel that he is grasping not merely words but things and experiences. The concern for 'propriety' of diction issues from a preoccupation with 'the force of poetry, that force which calls new powers into being, which embodies sentiment, and animates matter' (*Rambler*, 168). This common ground between Richards and eighteenth-century criticism is crucial.

Several objections may immediately arise. It may be said that, though the doctrine of propriety resembles Richards' theory of interinanimation in some respects, it is radically vitiated by rigid notions of what kinds of interinanimation are permissible; by irrelevant social criteria for judging poetic language; by rigid theories about the need for different types of diction in different genres; and by narrow views about 'correctness' of signification. It may also be said that the eighteenth-century critics, victims of Locke's description of the mind, were unable to formulate a *creative* account of poetic language.

The problem is one of degree; to what extent *were* the above factors disabling? The discussion has two broad aspects. First, the basis of the doctrine of propriety will be outlined; second, the doctrine will be examined in practice. Throughout, the flexibility of the doctrine will be emphasised.

To centre attention upon Johnson's Shakespearean criticism has several advantages. It has been considered a *locus classicus* of the alleged disabilities that we have to examine. Further, it excludes that aspect of propriety of diction which relates to the neo-classical interest in genre, thus indicating the secondary nature of that aspect. That Johnson does exclude that aspect of propriety may readily be illustrated from his preface to Shakespeare.

In the Preface, Johnson prefers Shakespeare to Addison, chiefly on the grounds that 'Addison speaks the language of poets, and Shakespeare, of men'. He says of Addison's *Cato*:

> [it] affords a splendid exhibition of artificial and fictitious manners, and delivers just and noble sentiments, in diction easy, elevated and harmonious, but its hopes and fears communicate no vibration

to the heart; the composition refers us only to the writer; we
pronounce the name of *Cato*, but we think on Addison. (*Yale*,
vii, 84)

On the other hand, he says of Shakespeare's plays:

> [they] are not in the rigorous and critical sense either tragedies or
> comedies, but compositions of a distinct kind, exhibiting the real
> state of sublunary nature. (*Yale*, vii, 66)

This dismissal of considerations of literary genre in so far as they affect
diction is not presented by Johnson as an apology, or as an incidental
point; it is closely related to his essential admiration for Shakespeare.
From the fact that Shakespeare uses the language of men, which communicates a 'vibration to the heart', follows this conclusion:

> This therefore is the praise of Shakespeare, that his drama is the
> mirrour of life; that he who has mazed his imagination, in following
> the phantoms which other writers raise up before him, may here be
> cured of his delirious extasies, by reading human sentiments in
> human language; by scenes from which a hermit may estimate the
> transactions of the world, and a confessor predict the progress of the
> passions. (*Yale*, vii, 65)

A point which may usefully be extracted from this, is the necessity for
rejecting compromises of the kind to be found in Professor Wimsatt's
account of Johnson's Shakespeare criticism. Professor Wimsatt argues as
follows:

> how he [Johnson] got to the heart of Shakespeare – perceived the
> progress and tenor of the drama – except through the aesthetic sur-
> face, the particulars of actions and words, may be difficult to under-
> stand. Doubtless we confront here some incompleteness of con-
> version, an unresolved tension between the neo-classic conscience
> and the liberating impulse. Johnson the lexicographer would of
> course be most painfully sensitive to the jaggedness of the verbal
> idiom – the maverick particularities. (*Johnson on Shakespeare*)

Since Johnson so firmly grounds his claim for Shakespeare's greatness
upon Shakespeare's *language*, it is hard to see how Professor Wimsatt's
position is tenable.

3. Particularity and propriety

It is convenient to preface an account of the working basis of the
doctrine of propriety with some orthodox remarks by Kames and with an
introductory example of the application of the doctrine. Kames notes
that language is a medium in which *connection* is a central feature, and
adds:

> We are so framed by nature, as to require a certain suitableness or
> correspondence among things connected by any relation. This
> suitableness or correspondence is termed *congruity* or *propriety*; and
> the want of it, *incongruity* or *impropriety*. (*Elements of Criticism*, ii,
> 5–6)

Propriety has two branches; one deals with the 'right choice of words or materials', the other with the 'due arrangement of these words or materials'. These two branches are not really separate; whether or not the 'right' word has been chosen will depend not only on its 'proper' meaning, but also on its relations with the other words in the context.

If we ask why the eighteenth-century critics demanded a 'proper' use of language, we quickly arrive at the point made by Richards in his attack on Kames; there is a very strong demand for concreteness, particularly of a visual kind. Lengthy illustration of this fact would be redundant, but some examples may be given to recall the point fully. Thomas Warton, for instance, discussing Pope's poetry, makes the central claim clearly:

> The use, the force, and the excellence of language certainly consists in raising clear, complete, and circumstantial images and in turning readers into spectators.

Addison, too, conducts his discussion on the 'imagination' in highly pictorial terms, and, elsewhere, refers to 'those beautiful descriptions and images which are the spirit and life of poetry'. Kames dwells at some length on the importance of 'ideal presence', which results from the calling up of ideas into the mind by an unusually deliberate and intense exertion of memory, and adds that 'the power of language to raise emotions depends on raising such lively and distinct images as are here described'. Erasmus Darwin sees this as the essential distinction between poetry and prose. Blair notes that the importance of metaphors springs from the following fact:

> they make an abstract conception, in some degree, an object of sense; they surround it with such circumstances as enable the mind to lay hold of it steadily, and to contemplate it fully.

Spence, discussing Pope, makes the same point: 'a metaphor is not to be used unless it gives a greater light and makes the thing more sensible to us'. So does Addison; a metaphor 'serves to convey the Thoughts of the Mind under Resemblances and Images which affect the Senses'. Absence of imagery is one of the chief grounds of Johnson's critique of the metaphysical poets: 'In forming descriptions, they looked out not for images, but for conceits.' His Dictionary defines a 'conceit' as 'a sentiment without an image'. It also defines the 'Fancy' as the 'power of forming ideal pictures'.

We shall waive, for the moment, Richards' objections to such naively 'imagist' views, and concentrate on the fact that they correspond with the emphasis, in critics like Leavis, on 'concreteness' or 'realisation'. It will be seen that they demand a high degree of sensory content, and that they involve criteria similar to those in Richards' own analysis of the words 'frail steel tissue of the sun', which, as was pointed out, consists of an enumeration of the properties or qualities of the objects described, which are brought out by the interactions of the words.

The common ground between Richards' theory of interinanimation and the doctrine of propriety is that both see concreteness or realisation as being achieved by a full exploitation of the implications of the words used.

This is clear, for example, in a comment by Spence on what Leavis would call some 'unrealised' lines from Pope's *Iliad*:

> From his eyes *poured down the tender dew*

and,

> But Anticlus unable to controul,
> Spoke *loud* the *languish* of his yearning soul.

Spence says: 'In these the action is described in words that import a violence, while the act to be expressed is plainly something still and gentle.' The implications of tender weeping are stillness and gentleness, and these implications should interweave with similar implications in the surrounding words. Evidently, the words 'poured down' and 'spoke loud' do not have such implications.

It may seem peculiar that there should be a need to show that eighteenth-century critics were, in fact, in possession of this, the most elementary principle of good writing. That there is such a need may be indicated by a more interesting example from Johnson's notes on Shakespeare.

Lepidus, in *Antony and Cleopatra*, attempting to gloss over Antony's weaknesses, says:

> His faults in him seem as the spots of heav'n,
> More fiery by night's blackness.

Johnson comments:

> If by spots are meant stars, as night has no other fiery spots, the comparison is forced and harsh, stars having been always supposed to beautify the night; nor do I comprehend what there is in the counterpart of this simile, which answers to night's blackness. (*Yale*, viii, 843)

The New Arden edition comments:

> His faults are made more conspicuous by his goodness, as the stars by night's blackness. The simile aims only at force of contrast, disregarding correspondence of quality in the things compared.

Johnson's principles are clear. That there is no 'correspondence of quality', as the Arden edition puts it, means that there is no realisation, because there is insufficient interconnection between the parts of the meaning. To recall for a moment Richards' key example, in the lines from *Venus and Adonis* the powers of the word 'star' are fully exploited; in the speech of Lepidus they are not. It is further evident that Johnson feels such a conspicuous lack of interconnection between 'blackness' and Antony's virtues, that the comparison seems entirely to elude him.

In the comment in the Arden edition there is mere abnegation of principle. The word 'aims' is totally unjustified, implying, as it does, some

mysterious insight into what was going on in Shakespeare's mind as he
wrote. The oblique suggestion that the disregard of 'correspondence of
quality' somehow adds to the 'force of contrast' will not bear scrutiny. In
the tenor the contrast is between faults and virtues, in the vehicle it is
between stars and blackness; the disparity between faults and stars, which
worries Johnson, is in no way effective.

The example illustrates the atmosphere in which confusion about
eighteenth-century critical principles flourishes, and as anyone who has
examined modern editions of Shakespeare will readily recognise, it is not
untypical. The desire to vindicate Shakespeare at every point and at any
cost is a familiar feature of modern Shakespeare criticism.

It would be easy to amass negative examples of Johnson's principle that
failure of interconnection between the implications of words is failure of
realisation, since it is the basic principle of his analytic technique; instead,
consider some more positive examples, in which Johnson records
approval of Shakespeare.

The observation about Captain Whitmore, in *Henry VI*, Part 2, has
already been noted:

> The gaudy, blabbing, and remorseful day
> Is crept into the bosom of the sea.

Johnson comments:

> The epithet 'blabbing' applied to the day by a man about to commit
> murder, is exquisitely beautiful. Guilt is afraid of light, considers
> darkness as a natural shelter, and makes night the confidante of those
> actions which cannot be trusted to the 'tell-tale day'. (*Yale*, viii,
> 591)

Here Johnson is sketching the network of implications through which the
metaphor of the day as an informer is realised. As Richards would put it,
the more the image is followed up the more relevant links are found. It is
by noting a network of a slightly different kind that Johnson defends the
word 'breed', in a speech by Angelo in *Measure for Measure*, against
Warburton's version. Angelo, roused by Isabella's virginal innocence,
says in an aside:

> She speaks, and 'tis such sense,
> That my sense breeds with it.

Johnson comments:

> Thus all the folios. Some later editor has changed 'breeds' to
> 'bleeds', and Dr Warburton blames poor Mr Theobald for recalling
> the old word, which yet is certainly right. 'My sense *breeds* with her
> sense', that is, new thoughts are stirring in my mind, new conceptions
> are 'hatched' in my imagination. So we say to 'brood' over thought.
> (*Yale*, vii, 185)

There is present a network of interconnection with a cluster of related
words, of the kind which Johnson found absent in the idea that zeal is

cold. The fertility with which he explores the meaning may usefully remind us of the metaphoric concreteness of his own poetry, which Leavis has so well described; a concreteness that issues from Johnson's sensitivity to the full powers of language. Here, the complex of associations that comes in with 'stirring', 'hatching' and 'brooding' are the source of the vivid strength of the lines.

In the same play, Johnson is moved to praise some lines in the Duke's attempt to prepare Claudio for death by making him despise life:

> Thou hast nor youth, nor age;
> But as it were an after-dinner's sleep,
> Dreaming on both.

Johnson comments:

> This is exquisitely imagined. When we are young we busy ourselves in forming schemes for succeeding time, and miss the gratifications that are before us; when we are old we amuse the languour of age with the recollection of youthful pleasures or performances; so that our life, of which no part is filled with the business of the present time, resembles our dreams after dinner, when the events of the morning are mingled with the designs of the evening. (*Yale*, vii, 193)

It may be thought that Johnson is merely indulging his taste for moralising, but his description of the tenor, in fact, fully brings out the power of the vehicle. That this is 'exquisitely imagined' is, for Johnson, a matter of the multiplicity of interconnection between the tenor and the vehicle.

The attentive habit of reading which goes with this principle appears not only at points where Johnson is praising or blaming Shakespeare, but where he is simply giving an explanatory gloss. When, for instance, Othello calls Desdemona as 'false as water', Johnson remarks: 'As water that will support no weight, nor keep any impression'.

4. Some eighteenth-century critical terms

Such is the essence of the doctrine of propriety. Its resemblance to Richards' theory of realisation through multiplicity of interconnection is obvious and central. These ideas also relate to such key terms in eighteenth-century criticism as *simplicity* and *ease*; terms which express a demand for concreteness. The linguistic medium should become, as it were, transparent, so that the reader feels himself in the presence not of words, but of things and experiences.

A quotation from Steele serves to clear away an initial possibility of confusion over the word 'ease': 'simplicity is of all things the hardest to be copied, and ease to be acquired with the greatest labour'. 'Ease' in eighteenth-century stylistic description, has a high sense and a low sense. The difficulty of attaining 'ease' in the high sense is stressed in Felton's *Dissertation on Reading the Classics*, where we find praised:

> that ornamental Plainness of Speech, which every common Genius thinketh so plain, that any Body may reach it, and findeth so very

elegant, that all his Sweat and Pains, and Study, fail him in the Attempt.

The relations between 'simplicity', 'plainness' or 'ease', the doctrine of propriety and the doctrine of realisation, may be illustrated from some basic observations by Dennis:

> Simplicity of Thought, is Thought which naturally arises from the Subject, Ideas which bear a just Proportion to the Things they represent, and which the Subject seems of itself as it were to offer to us, instead of our obtruding them upon that.

For Dennis 'Simplicity of Expression' is 'an Expression proportion'd to the Ideas, as they are to the Things'. The ground is covered by Johnson in the third number of *The Rambler*, in the remark that criticism may discover, in examining a given work, 'some secret inequality . . . between the words and sentiments, or some dissimilitude of the ideas and the original objects'. The ideal is the elimination of distraction from the subject that is being written about: the medium should attract no attention to itself. With this in mind, Johnson expresses dissatisfaction with the eighteenth-century tendency to indulge in 'poetical' language. The two senses of 'ease' are conveniently distinguished in a number of *The Idler*. Of the high sense Johnson says:

> Easy poetry is that in which natural thoughts are expressed without violence to the language . . . Language suffers violence by harsh or by daring figures, by transposition, by unusual acceptations of words, and by any licence which would be avoided by a writer of prose. Where any artifice appears in the construction of the verse, that verse is no longer easy. Any epithet which can be ejected without diminution of the sense, any curious iteration of the same word, and all unusual, tho' not ungrammatical, structure of speech, destroy the grace of easy poetry. (*Idler*, 77)

The rigour of the criterion is further stressed: 'To require from any author many pieces of easy poetry, would be indeed to oppress him with too hard a task.' Of particular interest is the example of 'un-easy' poetry which Johnson gives:

> The first lines of Pope's *Iliad* afford examples of many licences which an easy writer must decline.
>
> Achilles' *wrath*, to Greece the *direful spring*
> Of woes unnumber'd, *heav'nly* Goddess sing,
> The wrath which *hurl'd* to Pluto's *gloomy reign*
> The souls of *mighty* chiefs untimely slain.
>
> In the first couplet the language is distorted by inversions, clogged with superfluities, and clouded by a harsh metaphor; and in the second there are two words used in an uncommon sense, and two epithets inserted only to lengthen the line; all these practices may in a long work easily be pardoned, but they always produce some degree of obscurity and ruggedness. (*Ibid.*)

The low sense of 'ease' is defined in Johnson's comment on Pope's little society poem, 'On the Countess of Burlington Cutting Paper':

> Affectation, however opposite to ease, is sometimes mistaken for it, and those who aspire to gentle elegance, collect female phrases and fashionable barbarisms, and imagine that style to be easy which custom has made familiar. (*Ibid.*)

Two points may be made. First, when an eighteenth-century critic demands that poetry be 'easy', in the high sense, it is important not to see in it confirmation of the opinion put forward by Leavis:

> most eighteenth-century verse, and all verse of the Augustan tradition, has a social movement – a movement that suggests company deportment, social gesture and a code of manners: it is polite. (*The Common Pursuit*, 103)

The second point concerns Johnson's use of terms like *harsh* and *obscure*. They involve higher criteria than conventionality or ready intelligibility. They describe absence of 'ease', or failures of realisation, as Johnson's comments on the opening of *The Iliad* readily illustrate. The metaphor of a 'spring', which Johnson calls 'harsh', so far from being 'far-fetched' is something of a cliché, a vaguely appropriate figure which might readily come to mind as a substitute for 'origin'. In the light of the analytic procedure which we have seen Johnson using on Shakespeare's poetry, 'harsh' here must mean 'failing to fully exploit the powers of the words'. The implications of 'spring' (fertility, pleasantness, naturalness, and so on) are not only irrelevant but inappropriate. Nor does Pope use the one implication which might be relevant: the flowing of water as the flowing of tears. The relation between 'harshness' and 'obscurity' is indicated by Johnson's word 'clouded'; redundancy and deviation from common meanings call attention to the words and distract attention from the subject. His point is not that the lines (which are, in an obvious sense, conventional) are difficult to understand, or that their devices trespass beyond conventional bounds, but that they lack realising power.

It is worth showing what 'harshness' means for Johnson, because, as Dr Brown says (in *The Critical Opinions of Samuel Johnson*), perhaps 'no critical term used by Johnson has done more injury to his reputation as a critic'. Dr Brown himself makes the important point that Johnson, in using the term 'harsh', refers to the meaning rather than to sound of words, and to this it should be added that he is referring to it in the way described above.

The general background of terms like 'simplicity' and 'ease', though well known, should be recalled, because it has often been seen as revealing a spirit inimical to poetry. One of the main factors usually referred to in accounts of this aspect of eighteenth-century criticism is the influence of French neo-classicism, clearly a correct assessment.

Addison, for instance, holding up for our admiration the style recommended by Bouhours and Boileau, thus identifies it:

> that beautiful Simplicity, which we so much admire in the Com-

positions of the Ancients; and which no Body deviates from, but those who want this Strength of Genius to make a Thought shine in its own natural Beauties. (*The Spectator*, 62)

An influence readily lending itself to the pressure indicated here, was that of the Royal Society, in its attitude to language. For Sprat, as is notorious, the ideal was that language should say 'so many *things*, almost in an equal number of words'. For Hobbes 'the light of human minds is perspicuous words, but by exact definitions first snuffed, and purged from ambiguity ... and on the contrary, metaphors and senseless and ambiguous words are like *ignes fatui*'.

Such thinking *can* be inimical to poetry, but it has a more congenial side. An illustration of this occurs in *Ecclesiastes* – a book advising clergymen how to preach effectively – by John Wilkins, a member of the Royal Society, who introduced Sprat to the Society. Wilkins tells the following anecdote:

> [a scholar] meeting . . . a countryman as he was in a journey, and falling into discourse with him about divers points of Religion . . . observed the plain fellow to talk so experimentally, with so much heartinesse, and affection, as made him first begin to think, that sure there was something more in those truths, than his notionall humane learning had yet discovered.

Wilkins is praising that vigorous folk-speech, soaked in actual experience, which Leavis attributes to the common people of the seventeenth century. In preferring 'experimental' language to 'notionall' language, he is preferring concreteness to abstraction.

So far as literary criticism is concerned, the importance of sensory detail in the eighteenth-century view of realisation has already been seen. Let Shakespearean criticism provide a last illustration. When Timon of Athens has squandered his fortune, the Poet expresses astonishment at the readiness with which Timon's erstwhile followers have deserted him:

> *Poet*   I am rapt and cannot cover
> The monstrous bulk of this ingratitude
> With any size of words.
> *Timon* Let it go naked: men may see't the better.

Warburton comments (in Johnson's *The Plays of William Shakespeare*, London, 1765, vi, 264):

> The humour of this reply is incomparable. It insinuates not only the highest contempt of the flatterer in particular, but this useful lesson in general, that the images of things are clearest seen through a simplicity of phrase; of which, in the words of the precept, and in those which occasion'd it, he has given us examples.

In fact, the 'simplicity' is highly metaphorical, as is apparent in such words as 'cover', 'bulk', 'size', 'naked'. None the less, it is easy to see what Warburton means; there is a sense in which the words *are* simple, and the lines exhibit that astonishing directness which characterises Shakespeare's poetry. 'Simplicity', given this sort of application, is not at all inimical to poetry in the way in which Hobbes' remark, quoted above, is. Warburton's approach is one which finds the concrete vigour of Shakespeare's English a highly congenial mode.

5. Particularity and an emotive theory

The question remains whether the above ideas, even though basically sound, were too rigidly applied by eighteenth-century critics. Are they as wooden as Richards, in his account of Kames, suggests?

That last example from Warburton's notes to Shakespeare perhaps indicates the contrary. Warburton there talks of the 'images of things', but it seems clear that he does not mean it literally; it is hard to see what he might have been having an image *of*. It seems likely that Warburton is merely indicating (as people often do when they speak of 'images') a high level of vividness or power. As in the case of Richards' later development, there is no harm in so talking provided certain dangers are avoided. Coleridge himself can speak in a way which seems as 'imagist' as that of Hulme. The third and most important characteristic of the poetic imagination, for example, is said by Coleridge to be 'the power of so carrying on the eye of the reader as to make him almost lose the consciousness of words – to make him *see* everything'. And he can talk so despite the fact that he can elsewhere stress the importance of 'activity' just as heavily as Richards, as when he notes that in reading poetry there is:

> An endless activity of thought, in all the possible associations of thought with thought, thought with feelings, or with words, or of feelings with feelings, and words with words.

Abuse of the 'imagist' view can certainly be found in eighteenth-century criticism. Addison, for instance, in his method for exposing bad metaphors, adopts the stance for which Richards castigates Kames: 'It will most effectually discover the Absurdity of these monstrous Unions, if we will suppose these Metaphors or Images actually painted.' (*Spectator*, 595)

Professor Sherbo implies that Johnson uses this method with reference to the words in which, in *King John*, the dying Melun (telling the English who have fought on the French side that Lewis, in fact, intends to betray them once they have helped him to victory) urges them to,

> Unthread the rude eye of rebellion,
> And welcome home again discarded faith,
> Seek out King John and fall before his feet.

Johnson calls the metaphor, here, 'harsh', and Professor Sherbo suggests that Johnson 'was troubled by mental images of a tailor at his trade' (*Yale*, vii, 427 and *Samuel Johnson, Editor of Shakespeare*, 66).

Consider, therefore, some of the various modifications which are to be found, in eighteenth-century criticism, of the crudely 'imagist' view. One of the most striking of these, recorded by Samuel Holt Monk (in *The*

Sublime), is the way in which images are modified by feelings.

The relation between images and feelings is central in eighteenth-century critical thought, and Professor Elledge has illustrated the pervasiveness of the kind of view recorded by Quintilian. For Quintilian, Professor Elledge tells us, the generation of emotion is the essence of poetry, and this confronts him with this question:

> how are we to generate these emotions in ourselves, since emotion is not in her own power? I will try to explain as best I may. There are certain experiences which the Greeks call φαντασίαι, and the Romans *visiones*, whereby things absent are presented to our imagination with such extreme vividness that they seem actually to be before our very eyes. (*Theories of Generality and Particularity*, 158)

This is the view we have already seen adopted by Kames, and it may incidentally be remarked that it much resembles Eliot's idea of 'objective correlatives'. A similar emphasis is apparent in the Longinian stream in eighteenth-century criticism. For Longinus,

> an image has one purpose with the orators and another with the poets and . . . the design of the poetical image is enthralment, of the rhetorical-vivid description. Both, however, seek to stir the passions and emotions. (Roberts, *Longinus on the Sublime*)

In the development recorded by Monk, the emphasis is not only upon the way in which an image excites an emotion, but also on how it is *modified* by the emotion. Monk is tracing the emergence of the view that imagination shapes reality, the emergence of a 'romantic' critical theory.

A representative passage in his illustration of this emergence is the following from Robert Lowth, quoted in Monk (*Sublime*),

> The mind, with whatever passion it be agitated, remains fixed upon the object that excited it; and while it is earnest to display it, is not satisfied with a plain and exact description; but adopts one agreeable to its own sensations, splendid or gloomy, jocund or unpleasant.

In the thinking of Burke one finds some of the most sharp attacks on the idea that poetry must excite clear and exact images. Burke discusses the nature of poetic language:

> The truth is, all verbal description, merely as naked description, though never so exact, conveys so poor and insufficient an idea of the thing described, that it could scarcely have the smallest effect, if the speaker did not call in to his aid those modes of speech that mark a strong and lively feeling in himself. (*A Philosophical Enquiry*, 175)

And he uses this assertion to attack the following 'common notion':

> [that] the power of poetry and eloquence . . . is; that they affect the mind by raising in it ideas of those things for which custom has appointed them to stand. (*Ibid.*, 163)

Although Burke's development of his case is startling, in the extreme emphasis which it places on the auditory effects of poetry, it remains of great interest, which, for present purposes, may be summarised as follows: it calls attention to the fact that in metaphor there are inevitably relations not only between tenor and vehicle, but also between metaphor and speaker.

Johnson admired Burke's essay, calling it 'an example of true criticism', but Johnson of course finds no place in Monk's account of 'pre-romantic' criticism. At the level of general taste, Johnson's place might fairly be indicated by recalling his attitude to the enthusiasm for Ossian: 'Sir, a man might write such stuff for ever if he would *abandon* his mind to it.' It is evident that Johnson is not a 'pre-romantic' critic.

It also seems evident, from even a cursory examination of Johnson's criticism, that he did possess the ideas in which Monk is interested. Without wishing to question the validity of Monk's account of those critics with whom he deals, there are dangers in dwelling too much upon the development of critical theory, and ignoring actual critical performances; particularly in the case of critics who rise above the common run; critics, that is, whose work is more shaped by their response to poetry than by current aesthetic theories.

For example, Johnson, in a number of *The Rambler* (152) devoted to the discussion of epistolary literature, notes that such literature should usually employ the 'familiar style', and adds:

> But it is natural to depart from familiarity of language upon occasions not familiar. Whatever elevates the sentiments will consequently raise the expression; whatever fills us with hope or terror will produce some perturbation of images, and some figurative distortions of phrase.

Metaphor does not give clear pictures, but, in also conveying feelings, modifies the image presented. Johnson uses similar language in a discussion of the ambiguous significance of the word 'poverty'. He descants on the abuse of language in general, and adds that many people profess to find the most conspicuous examples of this abuse in the 'compositions of poets, whose stile is professedly figurative, and whose art is imagined to consist in distorting words from their original meaning' (*Rambler*, 202).

As his remarks on departures from the familiar style show, Johnson knows very well the value of such 'distortion'. It seems, consequently, necessary to disagree with a current view of Johnson's ideas about language. R. Downes, for example, says that, for Johnson, 'the mind perceives reality, retains mental pictures of it, and communicates these pictures by allotting them signs which are called words' (*Johnson's Theory of Language*). It will be noticed that Downes' view dovetails very readily with the kind of general stricture proposed by Allen Tate, that the trouble with eighteenth-century literary men was their assumption of a static relation between perceived and perceiver. It is possible to make out a case, as Downes does, by amassing quotations which show Locke's influence on Johnson, but Johnson was a critic, not a philosopher, and, as the quotations from *The Rambler* show, his insight into how poetic language works was penetrating and clear. Coleridge may well have despised

Johnson's way of putting it, but Johnson is describing the same phenomena that preoccupied Coleridge.

The point may readily be supported by well-known passages from
Johnson's literary criticism. For example, when Macbeth describes the
night-scene in a soliloquy before the murder of Duncan, Johnson quotes,
as a contrasting passage, a description of night by Dryden, and says:

> Night is described by two great poets, but one describes a night of
> quiet, the other of perturbation. In the night of Dryden, all the dis-
> turbers of the world are laid asleep; in that of Shakespeare, nothing
> but sorcery, lust and murder, is awake. He that reads Dryden, finds
> himself lull'd with serenity and disposed to solitude and contempla-
> tion. He that peruses Shakespeare, looks round alarmed, and starts
> to find himself alone. One is the night of a lover, the other, of a
> murderer. (*Yale*, vii, 769-70)

To use Lowth's phrase, quoted by Monk, the lover and the murderer
adopt descriptions 'agreeable to their sensations'.

In a similar vein is Johnson's comment on *L'Allegro* and *Il Penseroso*.
The two poems, he remarks, show 'how, among the successive variety of
appearances, every disposition of mind takes hold on those by which it
may be gratified' (*Lives of the Poets*, i, 166). Such comments issue not out
of any literary theory, but out of attention to the poetry and out of common
observation. It would certainly seem rather strained to cite them as
examples of the Longinian or 'pre-romantic' tendencies in eighteenth-
century criticism. The same might be said of Johnson's remark about
James Thomson:

> [he] had as much of the poet about him as most writers. Everything
> appeared to him through the medium of his favourite pursuit. He
> could not have viewed those two candles burning but with a poetical
> eye. (Boswell, *Life of Johnson*, i, 453)

An example, which has more of a feeling of being in contact with
eighteenth-century theories of the 'sublime', is Johnson's comment on
Edgar's description of the precipice, in *King Lear*. Johnson disagrees with
Addison's high estimate of it and adds:

> He that looks from a precipice finds himself assailed by one great and
> dreadful image of irresistible destruction. But this overwhelming
> idea is dissipated and enfeebled from the instant that the mind can
> restore itself to the observation of particulars, and diffuse its attention
> to distinct objects. The enumeration of the choughs and crows, the
> samphireman and the fishers, counteracts the great effect of the
> prospect, as it peoples the desert of intermediate vacuity, and stops
> the mind in the rapidity of its descent through emptiness and
> horror. (*Yale*, viii, 695)

A 'great and dreadful image of irresistible destruction' was the kind of
thing, no doubt, upon which enthusiasm for the 'sublime' loved to dwell,
but in this description of the way in which a passion modifies a perception,
Johnson is pursuing a line of thought which, as we have seen, was always

congenial to him. If we are to argue, in the end, that there *are* Longinian elements in Johnson's criticism, they are not to be seen as an excrescence, or a modifying tendency, on his central views, but as an integral part of them.

Johnson, in his account of the way in which images are 'perturbed' by figurative language, is noting, as was Richards in his remark that poetic language is non-referential, one of those things which are so obvious that they elude attention. In our examination of what consequences the idea has upon his critical practice, we shall begin with an extremely obvious example. The Fool says of Lear, when he has given up his throne, 'That's a sheal'd peascod' (*King Lear*, I, iv, 198). Johnson comments: 'i.e. Now a mere husk, which contains nothing. The outside of a king remains, but all the intrinsic parts of royalty are gone: he has nothing to give' (*Yale*, viii, 670). It may seem absurd to take such an example, but from it several points may be drawn for application to more interesting cases.

It would be foolish to suppose that Johnson might have felt tempted to condemn the metaphor for not conveying a picture. The Fool indicates Lear's emptiness not, to use Burke's words, by 'naked description', but by calling 'in to his aid those modes of speech that mark a strong and lively feeling in himself'. To put it in a different way, the junction of tenor and vehicle is effected largely by the speaker's feelings. The background in this particular case, could only be described by a wider reference to the play; there is an element of bitterness, even of contempt, and the metaphor suits well with the general character of a professional fool. This, in short, is the *dramatic* use of metaphor. If this background of feeling were removed, the metaphor would appear outrageously far-fetched; to compare a monarch who has abdicated with an empty pea-pod might then provoke a violent reaction from a neo-classical critic interested in 'decorum'.

It is here, it can be argued, that Johnson's failure with Donne may most fruitfully be discussed. He condemns Donne's metaphors as 'far-fetched' because he has not grasped the *feelings* which effect the essential junction between tenors and vehicles. It is not usually noticed that this is where the burden of Johnson's critique lies. He says of the metaphysical poets:

> they wrote rather as beholders than partakers of human nature; as beings looking upon good and evil, impassive and at leisure; as Epicurean deities making remarks on the actions of men and the vicissitudes of life, without interest and without emotion. Their courtship was void of fondness and their lamentation of sorrow (*Lives of the Poets*, i, 20)

The remainder of his critical commentary is an attempt to explain the literary basis of this lack of feeling. Had Donne been able to see Johnson's comments he might have remarked that Johnson didn't know very much about love. There, it may be, is where Johnson's incapacity lies, not in the rigidities of neo-classical literary theory.

With Shakespeare Johnson has no such problem; for him, Shakespeare's excellence lies precisely in his power of conveying feeling, in his power over language which communicates a 'vibration to the heart'.

Consider him, for instance, responding to a subtly dramatic use of a conceit, when Iachimo, in the process of making Posthumus believe that he has seduced Imogen, says that one of the paintings in Imogen's bedroom shows:

> Proud Cleopatra, when she met her Roman,
> And Cydnus swell'd above the banks, or for
> The press of boats, or pride.

Warburton had argued that the image here indicates that Iachimo 'is secretly mocking the credulity of his hearer, while he is endeavouring to persuade him of his wife's falsehood'. Johnson replies:

> If the language of Iachimo be such as shews him to be mocking the credibility [sic] of his hearer, his language is very improper, when his business was to deceive. But the truth is, that his language is such as a skilful villain would naturally use, a mixture of airy triumph and serious deposition. His gayety shows his seriousness to be without anxiety, and his seriousness proves his gayety to be without art.
> (*Yale*, viii, 886–7)

This is Johnson's criticism at its best. He unerringly reaches through to the state of feeling which dictates, and is expressed by, the poetry. The figure is of the same type as, though much more delicate than, the Fool's, quoted above. The 'far-fetched' conceit of the river swelling itself up like a vain man elicits no condemnation from Johnson, because the junction between tenor and vehicle is successfully made by Iachimo's feelings. Nor, consequently, is the figure said to be 'harsh'. Although there is only a single, and very arbitrary, point of resemblance between the river and the proud man (they both swell), the *disparity* is itself functional, and functional disparity is a species of interinanimation or propriety. The function of the disparity between tenor and vehicle here is to express, as Johnson says, Iachimo's 'airy triumph'.

It is not entirely an accident that Johnson's phrasing is reminiscent of Eliot's definition of 'wit' as an 'alliance of levity and seriousness'. The use of conceits (of which the most obvious feature is disparity between tenor and vehicle) is crucial to the poetry of 'wit'. As Eliot notes, the 'difference between imagination and fancy, in view of this poetry of wit, is a very narrow one'. If Eliot had had access to Richards' thinking at this point he might have expanded this into a remark that the distinction is narrow because in 'witty' poetry, the process of interinanimation involves the function of disparity. For Richards, the question, in a given case, would be the degree to which the disparity is connected with the speaker's feelings; and this also is the case with Johnson; he has no complaint here because the conceit is dramatically functional.

How the view which attributes to Johnson a desire for neatly separated tenors and vehicles would explain examples of this kind, is difficult to see.

It is, likewise, difficult to avoid the conclusion that Johnson's comment on Iachimo's lines issues from a response to Shakespeare's 'concrete specificity in the rendering of human experience', a response of which Leavis holds him to be incapable.

It would be easy to accumulate examples illustrating Johnson's response to the dramatic as opposed to pictorial functioning of metaphor. A useful example, used by Professor Sherbo, occurs when the Archbishop of Canterbury praises the transformation of the disreputable Prince Hal into a learned and eloquent monarch:

> When he speaks,
> The air, a charter'd libertine, is still.

Professor Sherbo says:

> One might expect this figure to be castigated as 'forced and un-natural', 'harsh', and 'far-fetched'. But Johnson proclaims it exquisitely beautiful. (76, cf. *Yale*, viii, 529)

Professor Sherbo feels compelled to see such things as surprising exceptions to the rigidity of Johnson's 'neo-classical principles'. The surprise, in fact, should not be at Johnson's failure to castigate the figure, but at the fact that he should be *expected* to castigate it. This case is similar to our previous ones. It is a conceit, in which the junction between tenor and vehicle is effected by reference to the speaker's feelings, of which the metaphor is, in turn, an expression. The speech in which the lines occur runs in a vein of exaltedly beautiful panegyric, and by the time these lines are reached the feeling has been firmly established, so that the effect feels perfectly 'natural', just as does the Fool's comparison of King Lear with an empty pea-pod.

A vivid illustration of one of the powers by which Coleridge characterised the imagination: 'the power by which one image or feeling is made to modify many others and by a sort of *fusion to force many into one*', occurs when Vernon, reporting to Hotspur before the battle of Shrewsbury, describes Hal and his companions as they wait for the battle:

> All furnisht, all in arms;
> All plum'd like estridges that wing the wind,
> Baited like eagles, having lately bath'd:
> Glittering in golden coats, like images,
> As full of spirit as the month of May,
> And gorgeous as the sun at Midsummer;
> Wanton as youthful goats, wild as young bulls.
> I saw young Harry, with his beaver on,
> His cuisses on his thighs, gallantly arm'd,
> Rise from the ground like feather'd Mercury;
> And vaulted with such ease into his seat,
> As if an angel dropt down from the clouds,
> To turn and wind a fiery Pegasus,
> And witch the world with noble horsemanship.

Johnson comments:

> This gives a strong image. They were not only plum'd like estridges, but their plumes fluttered like those of an estridge beating the wind with his wings. A more lively representation of young men ardent for enterprize perhaps no writer has ever given. (*Yale*, vii, 482)

To attempt to make pictures of the similes would result in absurdity. The extraordinary sequence of figures looks, on the face of it, a candidate for Pope's phrase a 'glaring chaos and wild heap of wit'. Those who like to dwell on Johnson's neo-classical rigidity should be surprised at his admiration. What unifies the images is the current of feeling, which comes across so strongly that Hotspur is provoked into a fit of irritation by Vernon's delighted admiration. It is worth noting that Johnson uses the words we have seen in Burke's account of images: 'strong' and 'lively'; the speaker is using 'those modes that mark a strong a lively feeling in himself'. Johnson uses them because there is no exact pictorial effect. It is tempting to quote here a beautiful description by Johnson of the effect that such imagery has. Speaking of a Greek hymn celebrating good health, he says that 'no one, who has ever languished under the discomforts and infirmities of a lingering disease, can read it without feeling the images dance in his heart' (*Rambler*, 48). It is hard to imagine a more vivid description of the way in which metaphor can blend visual, kinaesthetic and emotional elements. Further, Vernon's lines also exemplify, to a high degree, that 'tumbling' imagery which is characteristic of Shakespeare; a flow in which one figure gives birth to another, and which Johnson has no difficulty in admiring.

It is, of course, true that Johnson *can* use, and mis-use, the crudely 'imagist' doctrine. He applies it to the metaphical poets, where it is inapplicable, and argues that they cannot arouse emotion because they present no images. But his dealings with Shakespeare's dramatic poetry make it clear that his critique of the metaphysical poets does not spring from a mechanical application of theory.

6. On the moral function of poetry

The insistence, in eighteenth-century criticism, that an essential function of imagery is to arouse emotion is crucial, because it connects with the stress on the ideas of 'sympathy' and 'generality'. These should be outlined, because the idea of 'generality' is another modification of the crudely 'imagist' view, and, more importantly, because 'sympathy' and 'generality' cover the same ground as Richards' notion of 'self-realisation'.

In Richards' formulation verbal complexity, or interinanimation, is creativity, and, in re-creating the experience which a poem presents, the reader is realising himself. In eighteenth-century terms, propriety of diction realises images which arouse emotion; to feel emotion in this way is an act of sympathy; sympathy is possible because human nature is, fundamentally, always the same; consequently, what we are realising is, in the end, ourselves.

That eighteenth-century critics saw emotion as the end of imagery is a reflection of their generally emotive theory of poetry. This is apparent in Johnson's criticism, lying, for instance, at the heart of his discussions, in his preface to Shakespeare, of the mingling of tragic and comic scenes and of the 'unities'. With regard to the mingling of tragic and comic scenes, Johnson says that, by those who disapprove of it:

> It is objected, that by this change of scenes the passions are interrupted in their progression, and that the principal event, being not advanced by a due gradation of preparatory incidents, wants at last the power to move, which constitutes the perfection of dramatic poetry. (*Yale*, vii, 67)

Johnson disagrees with the objectors, but agrees that the 'power to move' is 'the perfection of dramatic poetry'.

With regard to the 'unities', it had been argued that to break the unity of time and place, breaks the dramatic illusion. Johnson says:

> It will be asked, how the drama moves if it is not credited. It is credited with all the credit due to a drama. It is credited, whenever it moves, as a just picture of a real original. (*Ibid.*, 78)

The insistence on the primacy of emotional effect is not restricted to Johnson's discussions of dramatic poetry. It is, as we have said, the basis of his critique of the metaphysical poets, and here the relevance of the idea of 'generality' is clear. The metaphysical poets, Johnson says:

> were not successful in representing or moving the affections. As they were wholly employed on something unexpected and surprising they had no regard to that uniformity of sentiment, which enables us to conceive and to excite the pains and the pleasure of other minds. (*Lives of the Poets*, i, 20)

The final ground of Johnson's principle, as is indicated by that phrase 'uniformity of sentiment', is the idea upon which he loved to dwell; 'that human nature is always the same'. Much illustration would be superfluous, but we may recall Imlac's claim, in *Rasselas*, that 'the province of poetry is to describe Nature and Passion, which are always the same', or Johnson's remark in *The Rambler*, that 'reason and nature are uniform and inflexible'. (*Rambler*, 125)

It is through an act of sympathy that we perceive this generality. Here lies Johnson's preference, for instance, for 'domestic' over 'imperial' tragedy:

> It is not easy for the most artful writer to give us an interest in happiness or misery, which we think ourselves never likely to feel, and with which we have never yet been acquainted. Histories of the downfall of kingdoms, and revolutions of empires, are read with great tranquillity. (*Rambler*, 60)

The point is repeated in his summary of *Timon of Athens*: 'the play of *Timon* is a domestic tragedy, and therefore strongly fastens on the attention of the reader'. His affection for biography is justified in similar terms:

Those parallel circumstances, and kindred images, to which we
readily conform our minds, are, above all other writings, to be found
in narratives of the lives of particular persons; and therefore no
species of writing seems more worthy of cultivation than biography,
since none can be more delightful or more useful, none can more
certainly enchain the heart by irresistible interest, or more widely
diffuse instruction to every diversity of condition. (*Rambler*, 60)

The tendency is towards the view that what we contemplate, when moved
by poetry, is, essentially, ourselves, and a general statement to this effect
appears in the same *Rambler*:

All joy or sorrow for the happiness or calamities of others is produced
by an act of the imagination, that realises the event however fictitious,
or approximates it however remote, by placing us, for a time, in the
condition of him whose fortune we contemplate; so that we feel,
while the deception lasts, whatever motions would be excited by the
same good or evil happening to ourselves.

The same line of thought runs through Johnson's preface to Shakespeare;
the drama represents 'to the auditor what he would himself feel, if he were
to do or suffer what is there feigned to be suffered or to be done'; or,
'Shakespeare has no heroes; his scenes are occupied only by men, who act
and speak as the reader thinks that he should himself have spoken or acted
on the same occasion' (*Yale*, vii, 78 and 64).

It is no accident that Johnson, in the words 'an act of imagination that
realises the event', anticipates one of Leavis' favourite phrases: 'the
realising imagination'. The phrase 'men, who act and speak as the reader
thinks that he should himself have spoken or acted', also indicates the
central importance for Johnson, of Shakespeare's *poetry*. The moving
power of the language is that from which all else follows.

This nexus of ideas is not, of course, peculiar to Johnson. Burke notes
the following effect of sympathy:

we enter into the concerns of others; . . . we are moved as they are
moved, and are never suffered to be indifferent spectators of almost
anything which men can do or suffer. For sympathy must be considered as a sort of substitution, by which we are put into the place
of another man, and affected in many respects as he is affected.(*The
Sublime*, 44)

The ideas are neatly summed up by John Upton in his *Critical Observations of Shakespeare* (1746), an important document in Shakespeare
criticism of the mid-eighteenth century:

how beautiful is it to see the struggles of the mind, and the passions
at variance . . . But what is tragic poetry without passion ? In a word,
'tis ourselves, and our own passions, that we love to see pictured; and
in these representations we seek for delight and instruction.

Upton's final words here indicate clearly that the essence of the eighteenth-
century view of the moral function of poetry, is the insistence that poetry
gives self-knowledge. It is, therefore, no surprise to find that Coleridge,

in a typical essay on the self-realising powers of poetry, adduces a passage from Warburton's preface to Shakespeare, as a satisfactory expression of his own views:

> Of all literary exercitations, whether designed for the use or entertainment of the world, there are none of so much importance, or so immediately our concern, as those which let us into the knowledge of our own nature. Others may exercise understanding or amuse the imagination; but these only can improve the heart and form the human mind to wisdom. (*The Friend*, i, 115)

To put this in a modern perspective, what Warburton is describing is what Leavis calls moral *enactment*, as opposed to moral *statement*.

It is difficult to avoid the conclusion that Leavis, in accusing Johnson of moralising crudity in his approach to Shakespeare, is being less than just. It is certainly true that Johnson very seriously accused Shakespeare of not making his 'moral' clear:

> he makes no just distribution of good or evil, nor is always careful to shew in the virtuous a disapprobation of the wicked; he carries his persons indifferently through right and wrong, and at the close dismisses them without further care, and leaves their examples to operate by chance. (*Yale*, vii, 71)

But, in view of the ideas which we have been examining, this must be seen as a point of secondary importance. Johnson is here concerned with the public responsibility of the poet, and he demands clear moral statement, *in addition* to moral enactment, in order that the 'examples' should not merely 'operate by chance'. His major point, which Leavis unfairly dismisses, is that 'he that thinks reasonably must think morally', and he is here referring to the complex of ideas that we have outlined. In evoking our response to fundamental human nature Shakespeare is teaching us about ourselves, and the reader of Shakespeare is 'cured of his delirious extasies, by reading human sentiments in human language'. It is in the purifying of the imagination that Johnson sees the essential value of Shakespeare.

Such are the most important aspects of the ideas of 'generality' and 'sympathy'. That they need to be stressed may be suggested by Professor Elledge's remark, in a discussion of a minor aspect of 'generality' (its relation with the Longinian stream in eighteenth-century criticism), that 'we suspect that the words "general" and "particular" were almost as useless and actually just as meaningless for the eighteenth-century critic as they are for the modern student of that period'. It is never a safe procedure to accuse Johnson of bandying meaningless words about.

The further point about the idea of 'generality' is that it modifies the crudely 'imagist' approach, since it demands that the images of poetry should be 'general' as well as 'particular'.

Johnson can quite happily employ both criteria. In the character of Imlac he can say:

> The business of a poet . . . is to examine, not the individual, but the

species; to remark general properties and large appearances: he does not number the streaks of the tulip, or describe the different shades in the verdure of the forest. He is to exhibit in his portraits of nature such prominent and striking features, as recall the original to every mind.

But he can also say of Rowe:

> I know not that there can be found in his plays any deep search into nature, any accurate discriminations of kindred qualities, or nice display of passion in its progress; all is general and undefined. (*Lives of the Poets*, ii, 76)

or, of Milton:

> his images and descriptions of the scenes or operations of Nature do not seem to be always copied from original form, nor to have the freshness, raciness, and energy of immediate observation. (*Ibid.*, i, 178)

The simultaneous demand for 'particularity' and 'generality' is only an apparent contradiction. That the imagination reconciles 'the individual, with the representative' was to be, for Coleridge, one of its central features.

CHAPTER FOUR

COMPLEXITY AND THE DOCTRINE
OF PROPRIETY IN JOHNSON'S
SHAKESPEARE CRITICISM

1. Johnson's approach to Shakespeare

The central principles of eighteenth-century criticism resemble those developed by Richards, and eighteenth-century critics applied them in a less rigid way than modern commentators are wont to suggest. This chapter examines that flexibility in detail, as it is exemplified in Johnson's Shakespeare criticism. As preface, some general features of Johnson's response to Shakespeare's poetry may be recalled. This raises interesting questions about some aspects of modern Shakespeare criticism.

According to Leavis, 'what Johnson acclaims in Shakespeare, it might be said, is a great novelist who writes in dramatic form', and this 'radical insufficiency [is] correlated with his abstraction of the "drama" from the "poetry" – with his failure to see the dramatic genius as a poetic and linguistic genius'. Johnson is seen, in short, as a precursor of Bradley, engaged in irrelevant discussion of Shakespeare's 'characters' (*Scrutiny*, xii, 198).

If one works with any sort of scheme resembling Richards', and talks in terms of complexity of language (a complexity which must involve aspects of tone and feeling) then a 'character' approach to Shakespeare is inevitable. One must find oneself talking in the way that Johnson talks in, say, his description of the tone and feeling of Iachimo's lines, since there is no other way in which the complexity of the poetry can be fully discussed. And to talk in that way of *all* Iachimo's lines is to discuss his 'character'.

If, on the other hand, a play is seen as a pattern of concretely realised images, one may be pursuing a legitimate and interesting line of enquiry, but will be examining less than the full complexity of the poetry. One will, in fact, be largely employing a crudely 'imagist' approach, and demanding nothing further than concrete particularity.

There is a need to enforce the point, especially since Johnson's admirers tend to fall back on the view, necessary if one accepts Leavis' arguments, that Johnson, in some mysterious fashion, pushed his way irritably past Shakespeare's poetry, to seize the human truths beneath.

Johnson's account of Polonius is a convenient example. Johnson is provoked to write at length on Polonius because he disagrees with Warburton, who sees the character as that of a 'weak, pedant, minister of state' (*Yale*, viii, 973). Johnson insists, against this, on the complexity of the character:

Polonius is a man bred in courts, exercised in business, stored with observation, confident of his knowledge, proud of his eloquence, and declining into dotage. His mode of oratory is truly represented as designed to ridicule the practice of those times, of prefaces that made no introduction, and of method that embarrassed rather than explained. This part of his character is accidental, the rest is natural. Such a man is positive and confident, because he knows that his mind was once strong, and knows not that it has become weak. Such a man excels in general principles, but fails in the particular application. He is knowing in retrospect, and ignorant in foresight. While he depends upon his memory, and can draw from his repositories of knowledge, he utters weighty sentences, and gives useful counsel; but as the mind in its enfeebled state cannot be kept long busy and intent, the old man is subject to sudden dereliction of his faculties, he loses the order of his ideas, and entangles himself in his own thoughts, till he recovers the leading principle, and falls again into his former train. This idea of dotage encroaching upon wisdom, will solve all the phaenomena of the character of Polonius. (*Yale*, viii, 974)

On the surface this account may seem to support the view that Johnson's strength is in getting the general drift of a character and in isolating the 'type' to which it belongs. But that procedure is, in fact, exemplified by Warburton's summary, not by Johnson's, of which the most impressive feature is the delicate response to the shifting qualities of the poetry in which Polonius, in the full sense of the phrase, *expresses himself*. An examination of Polonius' speeches (e.g. II.ii.120–40) reveals that, at *every* point, they respond to Johnson's account, and, as such analysis proceeds, it finds itself talking about subtly varying tones, feelings and movements; it is, in short, analysis of the *poetry*.

2. Propriety and the dramatic use of metaphor

In examining, with reference to Johnson's notes on Shakespeare, the flexibility of the doctrine of propriety, we shall look first at the question of permitted relations between tenors and vehicles in metaphors. This is important, because upon it hinge many of the uses of such terms (connected with the doctrine of propriety) as 'far-fetched', 'strained', 'harsh', and 'obscure'. A key idea, for the eighteenth-century critic, in this area is that of 'surprise' or 'novelty'.

The idea of surprise rests on the observation, in *The Rambler* (78), that 'nothing can strongly strike or affect us, but what is rare or sudden'. This is the element in the second half of Johnson's definition of 'wit' as that 'which is at once natural *and* new'; a definition which occurs in his critique of the metaphysical poets, who, he says, cultivated surprise at the expense of naturalness (*Lives of the Poets*, i, 20).

In its practical application the idea is important to Johnson's view of metre. In his review of Wharton's essay on Pope, he writes:

Unvaried rhymes, says this writer [Wharton], highly disgust readers

of good ear. It is surely not the ear but the mind that is offended. The
fault arising from the use of common rhymes is, that by reading the
past line the second may be guessed, and half the composition loses
the grace of novelty. (*The Works of Samuel Johnson*, v, 666)

The criterion behind this is, to use Richards' word, 'activity'; common
rhymes result in an easy and mechanical mode of interconnection between
the words, whereas rhymes which have 'novelty' issue in a greater
intensity of 'activity'. Johnson cannot be referring to mere and literal
'novelty', for, in that case, he would be reducing *all* rhymes to the level of
common rhymes after the first reading.

The same basic principle appears in his noting 'the frequent intersections of the sense, which are the necessary effects of rhyme' (*Lives*, iii,
299), in a passage where he is contrasting rhymed and blank verse. His
preference for the former is largely to be seen in terms of increased 'interinanimation' ('frequent intersections of the sense').

It follows that, for Johnson, metre is a movement of meaning. This
appears in his disagreement with Pope about representative metre (*Ibid.*,
230), and in his satirical exposure of Dick Minim's analysis of 'tied
imagery' (*Idler*, 60). The following summary of his views is more conveniently quotable:

> poetical measures have not in any language been so far refined as to
> provide for the subdivisions of passion. They can only be adapted to
> general purposes; but the particular and minuter propriety must be
> sought only in the sentiment and language. (*Works*, v, 664)

What concerns us more is the idea of surprise with regard to metaphor.
It appears clearly in the remark that a 'simile may be compared to lines
converging at a point and is more excellent as the lines approach from a
greater distance' (*Lives*, ii, 130). This principle is applied critically to one
of Dryden's similes, in which 'there is so much likeness in the initial
comparison that there is no illustration'; it is like saying 'of a brook, that
it waters a garden as a river waters a country' (*Ibid.*, i, 441).

It is therefore incorrect of Richards to see Johnson as exactly opposed
to André Breton. For Breton, according to Richards, the sole criterion of
success in metaphor is the greatness of the distance between tenor and
vehicle, 'whereas Johnson objected to comparisons being, like Cowley's,
"far-fetched"' (*Philosophy of Rhetoric*, 124).

Johnson's position, in fact, is like Richards' own, as can be seen in his
comment on Pope's comparison of the progress of study with a journey
through the Alps: 'the most exact resemblance is traced between things in
appearance utterly unrelated to each other' (*Works*, v, 666). Here 'exact
resemblance' corresponds with that multiplicity of inter-connection
which Richards describes in the comparison of the departing Adonis with
a falling star; and that the tenor and vehicle are 'utterly unrelated to each
other' corresponds with that disparity between tenor and vehicle which
Richards describes as 'the strength of the bow', or the source of the metaphor's energy (PR, 125).

When Johnson uses terms like 'far-fetched' or 'harsh' he is talking not about any absolute idea of distance between tenor and vehicle but simply about failure of junction, failure to utilise the full powers of the words involved.

Johnson's stress on the importance of surprise in metaphor relates to the importance he attached to the poet's memory. 'Wit', for instance, is defined on one occasion as:

> the unexpected copulation of ideas, the discovery of some occult relation between images in appearance remote from each other; an effusion of wit therefore presupposes an accumulation of knowledge; a memory stored with notions, which the imagination may cull out to compose new assemblages. (*Rambler*, 194)

This flexibility of memory pre-supposes a high power of receptiveness in the poet, a power which Johnson attributes, for example, to Savage, of whom he wrote:

> he could frequently recollect incidents, with all their combination of circumstances, which few would have regarded at the present time, but which the quickness of his apprehension impressed upon him. (*Lives*, ii, 429)

In terms of Richards' little illustration of the same theme, Savage would have noticed the colour of the water and the wheeling of the pigeons, as well as the drift of the speech, in the scene in Trafalgar Square.

The coincidence of views is not surprising. Richards and Johnson are simply noting that the poet is highly receptive to impressions and highly retentive of them. To revert to a theme touched on before, it is the kind of point that histories of criticism tend to neglect, because it is so commonplace; but its commonplace-ness is an index of its importance.

In examining particular examples of Johnson's views on these issues, it would be absurd to claim that one is measuring exactly, but suggestive instances may serve as a basis for some tentative conclusions.

Further examples of the dramatic junction between tenor and vehicle, where Johnson has no difficulty with metaphors which, summarily considered, might appear outrageously 'far-fetched', are to the point. By comparison, Kames, occupied in setting out the 'rules' for good metaphors, condemns a too 'slight resemblance' between tenor and vehicle, and continues:

> The expression, for example, *drink down a secret*, for listening to a secret with attention, is harsh and uncouth, because there is scarce any resemblance betwixt *listening* and *drinking*. (*Elements of Criticism*, iii, 155)

This is the sort of approach which Richards condemns as characteristic of eighteenth-century critics. There is, however, a difference between the wooden rigidities of a theorist and the practice of a perceptive critic. Ariel, in *The Tempest*, sent upon an errand by Prospero, says:

> I drink the air before me, and return
> Or e'er your pulse twice beat.

One might think that there is even less resemblance between drinking and travelling fast, than between drinking and listening. Johnson's comment is:

> 'To drink the air' is an expression of swiftness of the same kind as to 'devour the way' in *Henry IV*. (*Yale*, vii, 133)

This junction is effected by the idea of the eager avidity of a thirsty man. Further, in both 'drink the air' and 'devour the way' there is a clear function of disparity between tenor and vehicle; the *impossibility* of drinking air or eating a road dictates the tone and feeling of the metaphors. In Ariel's case this tone and feeling relate to his 'character' as a whole, since his *forte* is precisely to perform the impossible. Where there is a successful dramatic function of metaphor, the criteria to be found in Kames are, for Johnson, irrelevant.

The degree of flexibility which Johnson will exercise in this respect is nowhere more clear than in his comment on Macbeth's description of Duncan's corpse:

> Here, lay Duncan;
> His silver skin laced with his golden blood.

Johnson comments:

> It is not improbable, that Shakespeare put these forced and un-natural metaphors into the mouth of Macbeth as a mark of artifice and dissimulation, to show the difference between the studied language of hypocrisy, and the natural outcries of sudden passion. This whole speech, so considered, is a remarkable instance of judgement, as it consists entirely of antithesis and metaphor. (*Yale*, viii, 774)

This subtlety of response to the dramatic function of the poetry, even when it involves violating the neo-classic 'rules', is evident in Johnson's summary of *Antony and Cleopatra*:

> Upton, who did not easily miss what he desired to find, has discovered that the language of Antony is, with great skill and learning, made pompous and superb, according to his real practice. But I think his diction not distinguishable from that of others: the most tumid speech in the play is that which Caesar makes to Octavia. (*Yale*, viii, 873)

The speech (iii.vi.42–55) referred to is that in which Caesar, under pretence of indignation at Antony's casual treatment of Octavia, seeks further excuse for a break with Antony. The 'tumidity', that is, expresses Caesar's hypocrisy. That Johnson can single out this speech, in this way, is important testimony of his grasp of the essentially poetic nature of Shakespeare's drama.

In the light of this, consider his comment on Isabella's disgust at her brother's acquiescence in Angelo's offer to let her brother live if Isabella will sacrifice her virginity:

> Is't not a kind of incest, to take life
> From thine own sister's shame?

Johnson observes:

> In Isabella's declamation there is something harsh, and something forced and far-fetched. But her indignation cannot be thought violent when we consider her not only as a virgin but as a nun. (*Yale*, vii, 197)

Professor Sherbo says: 'the idea (Johnson would call it a conceit) that Claudio's taking life from his sister's prostitution can be likened to incest is so "far-fetched" that it displeases instantly' (*Samuel Johnson, Editor of Shakespeare*, 67). But Johnson, surely, is making a point not about Shakespeare's poetic infelicities, but about Isabella's character; she is indulging in 'declamation', just as Caesar is indulging in 'tumidity', or Macbeth in the 'studied language of hypocrisy'.

One may also set here Johnson's justification of the 'obscurity' of the language of Caliban in *The Tempest*:

> His diction is indeed somewhat clouded by the gloominess of his temper and the malignity of his purposes; but let any other being entertain the same thoughts and he will find them easily issue in the same expressions. (*Yale*, vii, 123)

The final part of this comment refers implicitly to the central cluster of ideas outlined earlier; the language of Shakespeare provokes in the reader the feelings which it expresses, and this is the ground on which is based Johnson's view of the moral function of poetry.

'Harshness', 'tumidity', 'forced-ness', and 'obscurity', then, are words which Johnson can use not merely in a condemnatory fashion but as indicators of one of the ways in which poetry functions dramatically.

3. Propriety and the non-dramatic use of metaphor

We shall now look at some instances where there is a rather delicate relation between tenor and vehicle but where there is no obvious dramatic function.

Richard II, uttering sinister threats about the consequences if Bolingbroke pursues his rebellious courses, says:

> ere the crown, he looks for, live in peace,
> Ten thousand bloody crowns of mothers' sons
> Shall ill become the flow'r of England's face.

Theobald was disturbed by the oddity of the metaphor, and wished to emend 'flower' to 'floor'. Warburton indulges in a typically rude remark about Theobald, explains that 'the flower of England' means 'the choicest youths of England, who shall be slaughter'd in this quarrel, or have "bloody crowns"', and goes on to remark that it is a 'fine and noble expression'. Johnson reproduces the note and says that the passage is thus 'very happily explained' (*Yale*, vii, 442). It is easy to see why Theobald was disturbed, and the generosity of Warburton and Johnson here perhaps goes too far. Warburton's reading entails firmly cutting out the literal sense of 'flower' and restricting attention to the metaphorical sense.

This means that the propriety of the diction here is very limited, since the powers of the words are not being fully used. The metaphor is a less extreme instance of the kind we have seen Johnson adversely criticising in Lepidus' comparison of Antony's faults with stars.

A more extreme case occurs when Timon of Athens, bankrupt and bitter, calls down a curse on the unprincipled opportunist, who

> his particular to foresee
> Smells from the gen'ral weal.

In reply to Warburton's emendation of 'foresee' to 'forefend', Johnson comments:

> The metaphor is apparently incongruous, but the sense is good. To 'foresee his particular', is 'to provide for his private advantage', for which 'he leaves the right scent of publick good'. In hunting, when hares have cross'd one another, it is common for some of the hounds 'to smell from the general weal, and foresee their own particular'.
> (*Yale*, viii, 733)

Here the main senses of 'foresee' and 'smell' have to be cut out, because, if stressed, they clash with each other in an absurd fashion. Johnson is quite willing to understress the chief senses, and let the relevant secondary implications come in. This is not to say that he is enthusiastic about the metaphor, but the breach of propriety evidently does not distress him.

He is, however, enthusiastic about the following complex, and typically Shakespearean, metaphorical play, in which the interactions of meaning are fleeting and delicate. Claudio, in *Measure for Measure*, tells the Provost that the condemned prisoner Barnadine is,

> As fast lock'd up in sleep, as guiltless labour
> When it lyes starkly in the traveller's bones.

Johnson glosses 'starkly' as 'stifly', and adds: 'these two lines afford a very pleasing image' (*Yale*, vii, 203). The lines contain a metaphor within a simile, and the metaphor contains a personification. The effect defies any neat account, and the reader is not allowed to press too far the triple comparison between sleep, a prison and bones. Johnson's gloss brings out the essential connecting link; 'starkly' carries, on the one hand, implications of being closely restricted, as in prison, and, on the other hand, of the stiffness or soreness of the bones of a weary man. If one presses the metaphor too hard, the idea of personified 'labour' being imprisoned inside a man's bones quickly becomes absurd. What carries off the effect is the power, or the 'propriety', of the relevant implications of 'starkly'.

That example offers a useful comparison with one on which Professor Sherbo comments, and which we have already glanced at:

> Unthread the rude eye of rebellion,
> And welcome home again discarded faith,
> Seek out King John and fall before his feet.

Sherbo says that for Johnson the 'fact that Rebellion is personified here contributes to the harshness of the metaphor, for how can Rebellion be a person and a needle at one and the same time ?' (*Samuel Johnson, Editor*, 66). Sherbo seems to be referring to the common eighteenth-century dictum that metaphors should not be crowded upon each other, and it is important to stress the inadequacy of this sort of plausible conjecture, which assumes an easy identity between the rules propounded by critical theorists and the actual practice of critics.

If we apply this 'rule' to Claudio's lines we must say, 'How can personified labour be locked up inside someone's bones ?' Nor is it the case that Johnson's admiration of the image is a surprising exception to his usual adherence to the 'rules'. It is the propriety of 'starkly' that carries the effect, and such propriety is conspicuously absent from the metaphor of the needle and thread; there is no network of relevant implications to be carried over from the vehicle to the tenor.

The point may be illustrated further by King John's angry dismissal of the impertinent French envoy, who has presented him with a box of tennis-balls:

> So, hence! be thou the trumpet of our wrath,
> And sullen presage of your own decay.

Johnson comments:

> By the epithet 'sullen', which cannot be applied to a trumpet, it is plain, that our author's imagination had now suggested a new idea. It is as if he had said, be a 'trumpet' to alarm with our invasion, be a 'bird' of 'ill-omen' to croak out the prognostick of your own ruin. (*Yale*, vii, 406)

Johnson does not ask, 'How can the man be at the same time a trumpet and a bird ?', but describes instead Shakespeare's habit of moving rapidly from one metaphor to another.

This last example represents a species of 'allusion'. If one were thoroughly to enquire into the sensitivity of eighteenth-century critics to the concrete vigour of Shakespeare's poetry, a large number of one's examples would come under this head. It is here that eighteenth-century critics place that oblique, half-explicit, metaphorical activity which is one of the leading characteristics of Shakespeare's poetry.

How the term 'allusion' is used is best recalled by example rather than by definition. Of Antony's lament,

> I am so lated in the world, that I
> Have lost my way for ever

Johnson simply says, 'Alluding to a benighted traveller' (*Yale*, viii, 857).

A similar example is Flaminius' question in *Timon of Athens*:

> Has friendship such a faint and milky heart
> It turns in less than two nights ?

Johnson comments: 'Alluding to the "turning" or acescence of milk' (*Ibid.*, 721). It would be easy to gather together examples of Johnson's sensitivity to this sort of effect, but it would be superfluous.[1] As we have seen in his comment on 'sullen presage' he has no objections to fleeting allusions even when they come in to complicate another metaphor.

The conclusion which offers itself from those examples is that where vehicles are bringing in relevant implications, Johnson is indifferent to questions of neatness, explicitness or logic, and it seems, therefore, necessary to reject views like the following:

> Clearly, what Johnson did was to analyse . . . [a] passage in the very process of reading it: he habitually interposed the demand that he understood how a figure works, and the qualification that its foundation be neither far-fetched nor difficult to discover, before allowing it to become poetically effective. (Abrams, 'Unconscious Expectation in the Reading of Poetry', 237–8)

4. Propriety and 'licentious' diction

'Allusion' involves, like all metaphorical modes, a shift of meaning within a word; as Johnson's *Dictionary* says, the basic feature of metaphor is the use of a word in other than its normal signification. The result is a double range of reference; as the mind of the reader selects from the normal range and from the new range, it grasps what is being presented in an unusually full way. In Johnson's words metaphor 'conveys the meaning more luminously', because it 'gives you two ideas for one' (Boswell, *Life of Johnson*, iii, 174).

We shall now look at some eighteenth-century opinions about those shifts of meaning which have none of the formal features of metaphor, and which are a notable characteristic of Shakespeare's poetry. In such cases a word is extended to a meaning it does not normally have, without any metaphorical basis for the extension, and in this area lies a good deal of what is usually called Elizabethan boldness and freedom with the English language. Our topic, in fact, is the eighteenth-century attitude to Shakespeare's linguistic 'licentiousness'; and our argument is that the doctrine of propriety is applicable in this field in the same way as in the field of metaphor proper, and that the eighteenth-century critic is happy with non-metaphorical extension of meaning when the normal range is relevant to the new range; when, that is, there is 'interinanimation' between the two ranges.

Take, first, two examples (of which Johnson disapproves), which illustrate the kind of shift of meaning that is at issue here. They occur

---

[1] Cf. *Timon of Athens*, I.ii.40; III.vi.4; and v.iv.8. (*Yale*, viii, 713; 727 and 744): *King Lear*, I.ii.97 (*Yale*, viii, 667): *Measure for Measure*, v.i.240 (*Yale*, vii, 211): *Much Ado*, III.i.112 (*Yale*, vii, 367): *Othello*, IV.i.118 (*Yale*, viii, 1041): *Troilus and Cressida*, I.iii.319 and v.i.55 (*Yale*, viii, 916 and 934): *Henry V*, I.i.33 and III.i.16 (*Yale*, viii, 528 and 545). This is a very incomplete list.

together in *Richard II.* Aumerle, challenged to a duel by Bagot, but
reluctant to fight a man who is his social inferior, exclaims:

> Shall I so much dishonour my fair stars,
> On equal terms to give him chastiment?

Warburton had wanted to amend 'stars' to 'stem', on the grounds that the
latter is nearer to the necessary idea of 'rank' or 'high birth'. Johnson
comments:

> I think the present reading to be unexceptionable. The 'birth' is
> supposed to be influenced by 'stars', therefore our author with his
> usual licence takes 'stars' for 'birth'. (*Yale*, vii, 444–5)

Seeing Aumerle's reluctance, Fitzwater, Bagot's ally, joins in:

> If that thy valour stand on sympathies,
> There is my gage, Aumerle, in gage to thine.

Johnson comments:

> Here is a translated sense much harsher than that of 'stars' explained
> in the foregoing note . . . 'Sympathy' is an 'affection' incident at once
> to two subjects. This 'community of affection' implies a 'likeness or
> equality of nature', and thence our poet transferred the term to
> 'equality of blood'. (*Yale*, vii, 445)

The idea of 'likeness or equality of nature' is in the range of meaning of
'sympathy', so Shakespeare isolates it, re-applies it, and cuts out the rest
of the normal range. It is evidently the last point which makes Johnson
call this a 'harsher' shift than that of 'stars'. 'Harshness' means conspicuous failure to exploit the powers of words. In the case of 'stars' the
usual implications are not relevant, and there is no particular *point* in the
extension of meaning. In the case of 'sympathies', the usual implications
are more than irrelevant, they are evidently *contrary* to the implications
required by this particular context. The speech is hostile, and the word
'sympathies' is therefore improper, since its usual meaning has to be cut
out, but struggles to get in. To use Richards' phrase again, Shakespeare
has failed here to 'triumph over the resistances of words' (PC, 212).

Here, the background of the problem should be outlined. Warburton
discusses it in his preface, arguing against those who had said that Shakespeare's freedom with language is the sign of a confused mind:

> The truth is, no-one thought clearer, or argued more closely than
> this immortal bard. But his superiority of genius less needing the
> intervention of words in the act of thinking, when he came to draw
> out his contemplations into discourse, he took up (as he was hurried
> along by the torrent of his matter) with the first words that lay in his
> way; and if, amongst these, there were two *Mixed-modes* that had
> but a principal idea in common, it was enough for him; he regarded
> them as synonymous and would use the one for the other without
> fear or scruple. (Johnson, *The Plays of William Shakespeare*, i,
> 135)

Warburton regards the habit as illustrating Shakespeare's boldness as well as his 'licentiousness', and he connects it with a 'genius less needing the intervention of words'. Warburton is being a moderate. For an enthusiast such as John Upton, one of the 'rules' which Shakespeare, being above the ordinary 'rules', invented for himself and which the reader must observe, is:

> He sometimes omits the primary and proper sense, and uses words in their secondary and improper signification. (*Critical Observations*, 304)

Among Warburton's notes to Shakespeare, the following is an illustration of what he has discussed in general in his preface. Of the lines in *A Midsummer Night's Dream*,

> Brief as the lightning in the collied night,
> That in a spleen unfolds both heav'n and earth

he says:

> Shakespear always hurried on by the grandeur and multitude of his ideas, assumes every now and then, an uncommon license in the use of words. Particularly in complex moral modes it is usual with him to employ one, only to express a very few *ideas* of that number of which it is composed. Thus wanting here to express the ideas 'of a sudden', or 'in a trice', he uses the word *spleen*; which, partially considered, signifying a hasty sudden fit, is enough for him, and he never troubles himself about the further and fuller signification . . . And it must be owned this sort of conversion adds a force to the diction. (*Johnson's Edition of Shakespeare*, i, 95)

'Force' occupies a high place in eighteenth-century stylistic description, and Warburton's acuteness here goes very far. So far from being uncomprehendingly repelled by Shakespeare's licentious diction, he sees clearly how it works and, despite a touch of nervousness about it, is happy to allow its strength.

How shrewdly the eighteenth-century critics discussed the problem is evidenced by Joshua Reynolds, in an Appendix to the 1765 edition of Johnson's Shakespeare. With reference to Brabantio's reply when the Duke tries to console him for his loss of Desdemona to the Moor:

> But words are words; I never yet did hear,
> That the bruis'd heart was pierced through the ear,

Warburton had suggested 'pieced' (i.e. mended) for 'pierced', but Reynolds remarks:

> Shakespeare was continually changing his first expression for another, either stronger or more uncommon, so that very often the reader, who has not the same continuity or succession of ideas, is at a loss for its meaning. Many of Shakespeare's uncouth strained epithets may be explained, by going back to the obvious and simple expression which is most likely to occur to the mind in that state. I

can imagine the first mode of expression that occurred to Shake-speare was this:

The *troubled* heart was never cured by words;

to give it poetical force, he altered the phrase:

The *wounded* heart was never reached through the ear;

'wounded heart' he changed to 'broken', and that to 'bruised', as a more uncommon expression. 'Reach', he altered to 'touched', and the transition is then easy to 'pierced', i.e. thoroughly touched. When the sentiment is brought to this state, the commentator, without this unraveling clue, expounds 'piercing the heart', in its common accep-tation, 'wounding the heart', which making in this place nonsense, is corrected to 'pieced the heart', which is very stiff, and as Polonius says, is a 'vile phrase'.

It says a great deal for literary criticism in Johnson's time that critical speculation at this level of persistence and detail could be offered by a non-specialist such as Reynolds. As a speculation about Shakespeare's method of composition, it is opposite to that offered by Warburton, and similar to that offered by Empson (*Seven Types*, 82–3). Of course, it may well be wrong, but it shows the level of acuteness at which the problem of Shakespeare's 'licentiousness' was discussed, and the way in which it is related to his 'poetical force'. The question for the eighteenth-century critic is, 'At what point does force over-reach itself and become im-propriety?' Reynolds believes that so much of the range of 'pierced' acts in a way contrary to that demanded by the context to which one part of its range has been transferred, that the consequence is 'nonsense'. It is a more extreme case of the kind we have seen in 'sympathies'. 'Impropriety' means absence of interinanimation.

This discussion brings out particularly clearly the fact that multiplicity of interconnection *was* the working principle of eighteenth-century critics. This is apparent in Warburton's remark that Shakespeare some-times uses only 'a few ideas of that number of which [the word] is com-posed'; the implication being that the better use is that which exploits as many of the ideas as possible. It is helpful to recall Locke's account of 'mixed modes'. Locke, in *An Essay Concerning Human Understanding*, ii, 44 and 52, stresses the *liberty* possessed by the mind in forming ideas of 'mixed modes':

in its complex ideas of mixed modes, the mind takes a liberty not to follow the existence of things exactly . . . Nor does the mind . . . examine them by the real existence of things; or verify them by patterns, containing such peculiar compositions in nature.

An example given by Locke illustrates the point:

Thus the name of procession: what a great mixture of independent ideas of persons, habits, tapers, orders, motions, sounds, does it contain in that complex one, which the mind of man has arbitrarily put together, to express by that one name.

Locke is talking of what Richards wished to stress in his use of a context theory of meaning:

> The multiplicity and interdependence of the meaning of words, so much insisted upon here, becomes obvious and necessary as soon as we conceive of interpretation in terms of sign-situations. (*Interpretation in Teaching*, 48, footnote)

For Richards a word is built up from a multiplicity of 'contexts'; for Locke it contains a large number of 'ideas'.

In practice, however, the eighteenth-century doctrine of propriety tends to treat *all* words as 'mixed modes'. For instance, Johnson's objection to the comparison of 'faults' with 'stars', rests on an appeal to the implications of 'stars', or the complex of 'ideas' which are usually attached to it.

Johnson had considered the problem of 'mixed modes' as attentively as had Warburton or Reynolds. This is clear, for instance, in his note on Lear's lines:

> Those wicked creatures yet do look well-favour'd,
> When others are more wicked.

Warburton had wished to emend 'wicked', in both its occurrences, to 'wrinkled', on the grounds that this makes a better 'connection' with 'well-favour'd'. Johnson rejects this and makes the following comment on Warburton's emendation:

> [he should have] remembered what he says . . . concerning 'mixed modes'. Shakespeare, whose mind was more intent upon notions than words, had in his thoughts the pulchritude of virtue, and the deformity of wickedness; and though he had mentioned 'wickedness' made the correlative answer to 'deformity'. (*Yale*, viii, 680-1)

In practice, the doctrine of propriety applies to the 'licentious' use of language in exactly the same way that it applies to metaphor. This point may be confirmed by looking briefly at further examples of Johnson's response to 'that perpetual slight alteration of language', to use Eliot's phrase, which characterises Shakespearean poetry.

Helena, in *All's Well that Ends Well*, referring to Bertram's unwitting seduction of her, talks of those occasions,

> When saucy trusting of the cozen'd thoughts
> Defiles the pitchy night.

Warburton had wished to emend 'saucy' to 'fancy', and insert a comma after it. Johnson comments:

> This conjecture is truly ingenious, but, I believe, the author of it will himself think it unnecessary, when he recollects that 'saucy' may very properly signify 'luxurious', and by consequence 'lascivious'. (*Yale*, vii, 398)

For Johnson the sense has to be deduced in the same way as with 'sympathy' in our earlier example, but there is no objection, because the usual implications of 'saucy' readily accommodate themselves to the new context.

A similar case occurs in *Two Gentlemen of Verona* when Julia says:

> The air hath starv'd the roses in her cheeks,
> And pinch'd the lilly-tincture of her face,
> That now she is become as black as I.

Warburton thought the reference was to being sun-burned and emended 'pinch'd' to 'pitch'd'. Johnson comments:

> This is no emendation – none ever heard of a face being 'pitched' by the weather. The colour of a part 'pinched', is livid, as it is commonly termed, 'black and blue'. The weather may therefore be justly said to 'pinch' when it produces the same visible effect. (*Yale*, vii, 172)

Here the new head sense of 'pinch'd' is only a small part of the normal range of implications, but it is acceptable because much of that normal range (such as a general feeling of discomfort and unpleasantness) is still relevant.

Such examples may seem, singly considered, trivial, but it is such *slight* distortion of meaning which, as Eliot notes, is the life-blood of Shakespeare's poetry.

It is, evidently, true that eighteenth-century critics did have a bias; a modern critic, for instance, would not be provoked into saying that the use of 'sympathy', examined above, is 'harsh'. But it is unjust of Leavis to say of the eighteenth-century literary man: 'He has no impulse to indulge in licentious linguistic creation, nor does it occur to him that such indulgence may ever with any propriety be countenanced' (*Scrutiny*, xii, 194). The border-line between the free use of language we have just looked at and metaphor proper is often very faint; where the new application of a word strongly invites in its old range of implications, the concreteness achieved is that which one associates with metaphor. And concreteness, as we have seen, so far from being something to which, as Leavis suggests, the eighteenth-century critic was insensitive, is central to the doctrine of propriety.

5. Summary

The main purpose of discussing the doctrine of propriety in eighteenth-century criticism has been to show its similarities with Richards' theories. I have wished to do so for two reasons: first, to illustrate the essential critical continuity, and, second, to support my contention that the better use of these theories is that exemplified in the criticism of Johnson, and not that exemplified in Richards' own attempts to distinguish between different modes of language, or different phases of literary history.

Used in the Johnsonian way, such an analytic method can have no pretence to rigorous exactness; its virtue lies in concentrating attention

upon the fact that poetry is 'the *best* words in the best order', and in providing a means for pointing suggestively to how, in a given case, the words
are working, or failing to work. The value of this kind of attentiveness lies
primarily in its gradual establishment of a perceptive habit of reading,
and in its promotion of fruitful discussion, rather than in the fixing of a
rigorous critical theory.

It is also hoped that our examination, though far from complete, may
have been sufficient to suggest that the doctrine of propriety does not
deserve the opprobrium that is now generally bestowed upon it. On this
note we may finally glance at a point in Johnson's preface to Shakespeare:

> In tragedy his performance seems constantly to be worse, as his
> labour is more. The effusions of passion which exigence forces out
> are for the most part striking and energetic; but whenever he solicits
> his invention, or strains his faculties, the offspring of his throes is
> tumour, meanness, tediousness, and obscurity. (*Yale*, vii, 72–3)

This may be related to Johnson's comment on Hamlet's, 'To be or not to
be . . .':

> Of this celebrated soliloquy, which bursting from a man distracted
> with contrariety of desires, and overwhelmed with the magnitude of
> his own purposes, is connected rather in the speaker's mind, than
> on his tongue, I shall endeavour to discover the train, and to show
> how one sentiment produces another. (*Yale*, viii, 981)

This, then, is one of the 'effusions which exigence forces out'; it suggests
that Johnson's preference is for the *mature* Shakespearean style, rather
than for the 'laboured' (i.e. manifesting an obvious carefulness of
execution) style of the earlier tragedies.

When Johnson adversely criticises Shakespeare's poetry, he is not
taking his own *Irene* as the rigid standard, and manifesting incompre-
hension of what Shakespeare was doing; he is, rather, making the sort of
point that Eliot was later to make when he referred to 'the strained and the
mixed figures of speech in which Shakespeare indulged himself' (*Selected
Essays*, 38). In the context of his own age Johnson was, in fact, consciously
resisting bardolatry, and it is in this respect that his Shakespeare criticism
is now particularly timely.

PART THREE

T.S. ELIOT and F.R. LEAVIS

CHAPTER FIVE

THE IDEA OF COMPLEXITY IN THE CRITICISM OF T.S.ELIOT

1. Complexity and realisation: Eliot and Richards

I aim to discuss ideas which Eliot, in his criticism, has in common with Richards and eighteenth-century critics, to outline his distinctive features, and to suggest in what ways these are closely connected with weaknesses.

The central point of similarity between Eliot, Richards and the eighteenth-century critics lies in Eliot's account of complexity of meaning and of 'realisation', and of the connection between the two. The key statement is his comment on 'Shakespearean' poetry:

> These lines of Tourneur and of Middleton exhibit that perpetual slight alteration of language, words perpetually juxtaposed in new and sudden combinations, meanings perpetually *eingeschachtelt* into meanings, which evidences a very high development of the senses, a development of the English language which we have perhaps never equalled. (*Selected Essays*, 209)

There is an emphasis, there, on alteration or distortion of language. For the moment we shall note that the idea of 'encapsulation' (in 'eingeschachtelt') is similar to 'interinanimation' and that the 'very high development of the senses' corresponds to the eighteenth-century stress on 'circumstantial particularity' or to Richards' enumeration of the *sensory* qualities of the objects in his analysis of 'frail steel tissue of the sun'. These similarities are central, not incidental. Though they use different terms, which have different implications, Eliot, Richards and the eighteenth-century critics are discussing the same poetic phenomena. The poet, by a complex use of language, makes the reader grasp with unusual power what is being presented by the poetry.

The same idea is central in Eliot's comment on the following lines by Lord Herbert of Cherbury:

> So when from hence we shall be gone,
>   And be no more, nor you, nor I,
>   As one another's mystery,
> Each shall be both, yet both but one.
>
> This said, in her up-lifted face,
>   Her eyes, which did that beauty crown,
>   Were like two starrs, that having faln down,
> Look up again to find their place:

> While such a moveless silent peace
> Did seize on their becalmed sense,
> One would have thought some influence
> Their ravished spirits did possess.

Eliot remarks on the power of the lines and says, 'a good deal resides in the richness of association which is at the same time borrowed from and given to the word "becalmed"' (*Selected Essays*, 284). This is Richards' theory in a nutshell, though it exists only at the level of an acute insight, and is nowhere in Eliot's criticism elaborated into an explicit theory.

The emphasis on sensory particularity is conspicuously developed in Eliot's notion of the 'objective correlative'. His basic statement occurs in the essay on *Hamlet*:

> The only way of expressing emotion in the form of art is by finding an 'objective correlative'; in other words a set of objects, a situation, a chain of events which shall be the formula of that *particular* emotion; such that when the external facts, which must terminate in sensory experience, are given, the emotion is immediately evoked. If you examine any of Shakespeare's more successful tragedies, you will find this exact equivalence; you will find that the state of mind of Lady Macbeth walking in her sleep has been communicated to you by a skilful accumulation of imagined sensory impressions. (*Selected Essays*, 145)

Eliot's notion of an 'objective correlative' has, of course, further implications, developed in his application of it in *Hamlet*; for our purpose, it is the simple core of the notion that matters, and this appears most clearly in the remark about Lady Macbeth. This core closely resembles the eighteenth-century insistence on imagery as the crucial means for the evocation of feelings. There is nothing odd about the resemblance; the fact is one with which any reader of poetry is familiar.

2. Realisation and moral function

For Richards and the eighteenth-century critics there is a direct connection between the 'realisation' produced by a complex use of language, and the moral function of poetry; what one is 'realising' is, in the end, oneself. In Eliot's case, though this moral function may be shrewdly touched upon, it is in no way related to his thinking about poetic language.

In 'The Three Voices of Poetry', for instance, he says, mulling over his own experience of creating fictional characters, 'I can't see, myself, any way to make a character live except to have a profound sympathy with that character'. He elaborates the point as follows:

> Some bit of himself that the author gives to a character may be the germ from which the life of that character starts. On the other hand, a character which succeeds in interesting its author may elicit from the author latent potentialities of his own being. (*On Poetry and Poets*, 93)

Eliot makes the connection between this and the moral function of poetry by way of a point about structure, when he suggests that Ford's plays lack the 'significance' that one finds in Shakespeare and adds:

> a dramatic poet cannot create characters of the greatest intensity of life unless his personages, in their reciprocal actions and behaviour in their story, are somehow dramatizing, but in no obvious form, an action or struggle for harmony in the soul of the poet. (*Selected Essays*, 196)

Eliot makes the point more simply, and in a fashion reminiscent of Johnson's preference for 'domestic' over 'imperial' tragedy, in this remark:

> Iago frightens me more than Richard III: I am not sure that Parolles, in *All's Well That Ends Well*, does not disturb me more than Iago. (And I am quite sure that Rosamund Vincy, in *Middlemarch*, frightens me far more than Goneril or Regan.) (*On Poetry and Poets*, 93)

The more nearly a character comes home to us, the greater the effect, and for most of us the villainy of Richard, Goneril or Regan is a remote, though real, possibility, whereas the vanity of Parolles or the impenetrable egotism of Rosamund Vincy is only too familiar.

These elements, interesting and suggestive as they may be, are not, however, related to Eliot's thinking about poetic language. Indeed, at the points in his criticism where he talks most penetratingly about poetic language there is a positive anxiety to avoid any attribution of a moral function to poetry. This is clear, for instance, in his insistence (*Selected Essays*, 327) that Swinburne's 'morbidity is not of human feeling but of language' or his noting how completely in the evaluation of great poetry, 'any semi-ethical criterion of "sublimity" misses the mark'. This is followed by the assertion that the intensity with which a variety of elements are fused is the better criterion (*Ibid.*, 19).

It would be hard to overemphasise the importance of Eliot's central ideas on the relations between linguistic complexity and realisation. These ideas are basic to the work of Leavis, and are the means by which Leavis contrived to put into practice his urgent insistence that literary studies should be a *literary* discipline, and not be allowed to become a sub-division of philosophy or history. Whatever exaggerations it may have been subjected to, the notion of complexity, associated with the criterion of realisation, had the great merit of re-introducing a Johnsonian discipline: a discipline which, for Johnson, centred on the idea of 'propriety'; and it did permit a concern with wider judgements. Eliot's central ideas, being pondered and applied, generated a great deal of critical relevance.

Eliot's account of the complexity of poetic language has, however, several distinctive features, which are connected with the emphasis on 'disparity' evident in his phrase 'perpetual slight alteration of language' in the passage quoted above. The root of this stress is to be found in his definition of 'impersonality', and in his idea of the 'objective correlative'. The poet, he says,

> has, not a personality to express, but a particular medium, which is only a medium and not a personality, in which impressions and experiences combine in peculiar and unexpected ways. (*Selected Essays*, 19)

This closely relates to a well-known illustration in his essay on the meta-physical poets. The ordinary man, Eliot says,

> falls in love, or reads Spinoza, and these two experiences have nothing to do with each other, or with the noise of the typewriter or the smell of cooking; in the mind of the poet these experiences are always forming new wholes. (*Ibid.*, 287)

In his denial of the importance of 'personality' Eliot uses the phrase 'art-emotion'. The poet's actual emotions may be crude, ordinary and un-interesting, but his 'art-emotions' are complex, because they combine 'a number of floating feelings, having an affinity to this emotion by no means superficially evident' (*Ibid.*, 20). To transfer this back to the illustration, and to re-introduce the idea of the 'objective correlative', the formula by which the emotion of love is conveyed is composed of feelings associated with reading Spinoza, the noise of a typewriter, the smell of cooking, and so forth.

Eliot in his own way, is covering ground that Richards covers in his account of the poet's memory, the poet's ability to connect disparate areas of experience. The difference is that Eliot puts more emphasis on the *surprise* caused by the disparity between the experiences associated. This is apparent, to quote another well-known remark, in his comment on Johnson's critique of the metaphysical poets. Johnson had said that in metaphysical poetry the 'most heterogeneous ideas are yoked by violence together'; Eliot replies that 'a degree of heterogeneity of material com-pelled into unity by the operation of the poet's mind is omnipresent in poetry' (*Selected Essays*, 283).

This emphasis has several consequences for Eliot's thinking. It relates, first to his preoccupation with the poet's alteration of language; second, to his interest in the poetry of 'wit'; and, third, to his fondness for a high degree of 'suggestiveness' in poetic language. These are the distinctive features of Eliot's notion of complexity, and we shall examine them in turn.

3. Dislocation of language

Eliot's emphasis on the poet's alteration of language (which might lead, for instance, to poetry such as some of Dylan Thomas') is counter-acted by strong opposite tendencies in his thinking. These may be focussed by recalling his fondness, in describing the diction of some poetry which he admires, for such terms as 'correct', 'pure' or 'simple'. There are, however, some points at which the emphasis on alteration or distortion is noticeable, and these are of particular interest, since they relate very closely to the tendency, which we have already seen in some remarks by Leavis, to insist that creativity in poetic language *necessarily* involves 'licentiousness'.

Eliot, for example, contrasting Shakespeare with Milton, quotes some lines from *Macbeth*:

> Light thickens, and the crow
> Makes wing to the rocky wood.

Eliot comments:

> With Shakespeare, far more than with any other poet in English, the combinations of words offer perpetual novelty; they enlarge the meaning of the individual words joined: thus . . . 'rooky wood'. In comparison, Milton's images do not give this sense of particularity, nor are the separate words developed in significance. His language is, if one may use the term without disparagement, *artificial* and *conventional*. (*On Poetry and Poets*, 140)

This is powerful and suggestive criticism. It will be clear that, although Eliot is stressing the way in which Shakespeare alters language ('the combinations of words offer perpetual novelty'), he is basically using the principle which Richards called interinanimation. The key contrasting example he gives from Milton comes from *Comus*:

> paths of this drear wood
> The nodding horror of whose shady brows
> Threats the forlorn and wandering passenger.

Eliot does not comment on this beyond saying that it is 'artificial and conventional'. As it turned out, subsequent critics found it hard to believe that such terms *can* be used undisparagingly.

Eliot's comparison of Shakespeare with Milton is similar to Richards' comparison of Gray with Blake, or Donne with Dryden, and the resemblance is not coincidental. One would not quarrel with Eliot's comment on Shakespeare, but he has neglected to notice the complexity of Milton's language. Milton sees the trees as demon-bandits. To show how the metaphor 'enlarges the meaning of the individual words joined', one has only to note that 'shady' refers to the bandits' hats, pulled over the eyes, as well as to the hanging branches of the trees, and consequently how much, for example, would be lost by changing 'brows' to 'boughs'.

Novelty is prominent in Shakespeare's words, but any difference between them and Milton's words cannot be accounted for in terms of interinanimation or complexity. It is also arguable that the most striking effect that Eliot quotes from Shakespeare is 'Light thickens', and here the interinanimation is, as in Milton's lines, the consequence of an implied metaphor. The enlarging of the meaning is produced by a metaphorical action of the same kind as is exhibited by Milton's lines.

Eliot is appealing not only to a criterion of interinanimation but also to one of particularity. The lines from *Macbeth*, he says, 'convey the feeling of being in a particular place at a particular time' (*On Poetry and Poets*, 140). The same criterion is applied to some lines from *L'Allegro*:

> While the ploughman near at hand,
> Whistles o'er the furrowed land,
> And the milkmaid singeth blithe,
> And the mower whets his scythe,
> And every shepherd tells his tale,
> Under the hawthorn in the dale.

Eliot comments:

> It is not a particular ploughman, milkmaid, and shepherd that Milton sees (as Wordsworth might see them); the sensuous effect of these verses is entirely on the ear, and is joined to the concepts of ploughman, milkmaid, and shepherd. (*Ibid.*, 140)

Eliot is using the cluster of ideas contained in our initial quotation; complexity of language corresponds with sensory particularity. It is probable, in fact, that Eliot's reaction to these lines of Milton was, 'There is no particularity, therefore there is no complexity of language.' Be that as it may, Eliot is again ignoring the interactions of Milton's words. The effect depends not only upon the sounds of the words but upon the sounds that the words describe, and it is a typically Miltonic effect. The passage fuses together the ideas of work and happiness through the connections of 'whets' with 'whistles' and 'scythe' and 'blithe'. To some extent this is a connection of sound: the effect, as Eliot notes, is on the ear. But the effect on the ear is in the closest possible co-operation with the *meaning* of the lines. The whetting of the scythe gathers, by the connections, the feeling of gaiety in 'whistles' and 'blithe', and it gives back to them a feeling of business and briskness. By this process of interinanimation the feeling of 'happy work' is created. As Richards would say, the movement of the metre ('scythe/blithe') is a movement among meanings. Richards derived that way of talking from Coleridge, and it is closely connected with Coleridge's definition of the imagination as that 'power by which one image or feeling is made to modify many others and by a sort of *fusion to force many into one*' (*Shakespearean Criticism*, ii, 188). In Milton's lines, work and gaiety are fused together and the linguistic complexity is the symptom of this fusion.

That Eliot, besides ignoring interinanimation unless it is prominent enough to appear as novelty of meaning, is here using a crude criterion of particularity, is worth dwelling on. Johnson's account of Milton's imagination provides a convenient framework:

> Whatever be his subject he [Milton] never fails to fill the imagination. But his images and descriptions of the scenes or operations of Nature do not seem to be always copied from original form, nor to have the freshness, raciness, and energy of immediate observation. (*Lives*, i, 178)

This includes Eliot's point but goes beyond it. For Johnson, as we have seen, there were other criteria than concrete particularity.

The effect in those lines from *L'Allegro* was claimed to be typical of Milton. The point may be supported by a brief examination of some fairly representative lines from *Paradise Lost*, Book IV, which confirm the way in which the imaginative modification of images is accompanied by complexity of language:

> now glowed the firmament
> With living Saphirs: Hesperus that led
> The starry Host, rode brightest, till the moon
> Rising in clouded Majestie, at length
> Apparent Queen unvaild her peerless light,
> And o're the dark her silver mantle threw.

This is a representative example of Milton's 'magnificence', which hinges upon the comparison of the night-sky with a state occasion; the stars are the ceremonial soldiery. Hesperus is the chief of the general staff; the moon is the queen. The culmination of the effect is the fine imperious gesture of the queen, casting away her cloak; here the commonplace metaphor is made bold and surprising almost to the point of being a conceit. What prevents it from obtruding itself as a conceit is the success with which it is carried off. For instance, the imperiousness of the gesture has a retro-active effect upon 'apparent', giving it the implication: 'It is obvious from her behaviour that she really *is* queenly'. 'Apparent' is also firmly given the sense 'becoming visible'. The moon's imperiousness relates back to her 'clouded Majestie' giving it, especially in connection with the fact that Hesperus 'rode brightest', the implication that the queen–moon is a little cross at being outshone. That is a crude way of putting it. It is difficult to find a word which describes that type of haughtiness which is a sort of 'cloudedness'. The complexity of Milton's language here, as in the lines above from *L'Allegro*, consists of a full and subtle exploitation of the powers of the individual words.

These lines exemplify Johnson's remark; they fill the imagination, rather than give a particular observation of nature. 'Glowed' and 'living Saphirs' are examples of a recurrent Miltonic effect. 'Glowed' scarcely seems to be the 'proper' word here, if one were looking for accurate observation; and, it might be asked, how can there be a high degree of interinanimation in a phrase like 'living Saphirs', when the chief implications of 'living' are warmth, vitality and movement, while the chief implications of 'Saphirs' are hardness, lifelessness, and so on? But Milton, of course, uses this type of oxymoron frequently, and to call it oxymoron is to indicate that there is a conspicuous disparity effect. Some other examples from *Paradise Lost* are useful, because they serve to make a further point about Eliot's use of the criterion of concrete particularity and, with it, a criterion of alteration of language.

The 'pavement' of heaven 'like a sea of jasper shone' (Book III, 363). The relation between 'sea' and 'jasper', or 'sea' and 'pavement' is exactly

like that between 'living' and 'Saphirs'. Satan wings his way 'through the
pure marble air'. Raphael's wings are described as 'downy gold' or
'feathered mail'. The fruit in Eden is 'burnished with golden rind'. In the
midst of Eden stands,

> the Tree of Life,
> High eminent, blooming ambrosial fruit
> Of vegetable gold.

It is no accident that Leavis seizes on this last example, claiming that the
words exhibit no 'fusion' (*Revaluation, Tradition, and Development in
English Poetry*, 50). It is, indeed, typical, but Leavis' remark is, I think,
misleading.

What the examples make clear is that Milton, in using this type of
effect, is describing not an actual but an imagined world, of which an
important feature is that it is not like the real world. To quote Johnson
again, 'Milton's delight was to sport in the regions of possibility: reality
was a scene too narrow for his mind'. The important point, for us, is that
where a disparity action is so used, it is functional. The clash between the
implications of the words is precisely what makes these implications
relevant, and there is, in such cases, a high degree of interinanimation. As
with Ariel's claim that he will 'drink the air', which we looked at earlier,
these Miltonic effects are an assertion of the existence of the impossible.
The idea of a 'sea of jasper' is plainly intended to astonish the reader and
the astonishment is generated by the disparity between the implications
of the two words; the sea is ceaselessly moving, of vast extent and soft so
that one sinks in it; jasper is unmoving, small and hard. It is clearly not
possible to demonstrate conclusively that there is any difference between
any one of these Miltonic effects and disparities of a merely absurd or
unsatisfactory nature. All one can do, after making detailed comments of
the kind made above, is to point out that this is the local action of the
fundamental Miltonic power to create visionary worlds, worlds imaginatively transformed by feelings of awe; and that this local action involves,
through the deliberate disparity effects, complexity of language.

A further point to be made about Eliot's criticism is that elsewhere, he
can waive the criterion of concrete particularity, but when he does so, he
talks in terms of 'simplicity' of diction, and is therefore consistent in
assuming that where there is no particularity there is no complexity of
poetic language.

4. Suggestiveness

It is convenient to begin describing Eliot's fondness for a high degree
of suggestiveness by quoting his remark that, in the poetry of Shakespeare, Donne, Webster and Tourneur, the 'words have often a network
of tentacular roots reaching down to the deepest terrors and desires'
(*Selected Essays*, 155). Eliot, so far as I am aware, never goes into this
satisfactorily, but the same metaphor of depth occurs in another of his

descriptions of Shakespeare's poetry:

> The re-creation of word and image which happens fitfully in the poetry of such a poet as Coleridge happens almost incessantly with Shakespeare. Again and again, in his use of a word, he will give a new meaning or extract a latent one; again and again the right imagery saturated while it lay in the depths of Shakespeare's memory, will rise like Anadyomene from the sea. (*The Use of Poetry and the Use of Criticism*, 146)

It is easy to associate this with Eliot's well-known account, in the same book, of the 'auditory imagination':

> What I call the 'auditory imagination' is the feeling for syllable and rhythm, penetrating far below the conscious levels of thought and feeling, invigorating every word; sinking to the most primitive and forgotten, returning to the origin and bringing something back, seeking the beginning and the end. It works through meanings, certainly, or not without meanings in the ordinary sense, and fuses the old and obliterated and the trite, the current, and the new and surprising, the most ancient and the most civilised mentality. (*Use of Poetry*, 118)

In this passage Eliot is talking not about 'images' but about the tied imagery or the direct effects of words, as is shown by his stress on 'syllable and rhythm'. In a much later essay, Eliot quotes Valéry:

> 'I prize the theories of Poe, so profound and so insidiously learned; I believe in the omnipotence of rhythm, and especially in the suggestive phrase.' (*To Criticise the Critic*, 37)

Eliot is far from identifying himself with this 'credo of a very young man', as he calls it, but none the less goes on to remark that 'within this tradition from Poe to Valéry are some of those modern poems which I most admire and enjoy'. One is here reminded of his remark about Baudelaire:

> It may be that I am indebted to Baudelaire chiefly for half a dozen lines out of the whole of *Fleurs du Mal*; and that his significance for me is summed up in the lines:
>
> Fourmillante Cité, cité pleine de rêves,
> Ou le spectre en plein jour raccroche le passant . . . (*Ibid.*, 126)

One is also reminded of the way in which haunting lines from other poets stick in Eliot's mind, of which he himself has given some examples; or, most obviously, one may note Eliot's own extraordinary power in creating haunting lines himself.

That Eliot tends, in his use of metaphors of depth, to associate imagery with the direct effects on the grounds that both are mysterious in their operation, may be confirmed by the way in which he develops the theme with reference to images in his own poetry:

> Why, for all of us, out of all that we have heard, seen, felt, in a lifetime, do certain images recur, charged with emotion, rather than others? The song of one bird, the leap of one fish, at a particular place and

time, the scent of one flower, an old woman on a German mountain path, six ruffians seen through an open window playing cards at night at a small French railway junction where there was a water-mill: such memories may have symbolic value, but of what we cannot tell, for they come to represent the depths of feeling into which we cannot peer. We might just as well ask why, when we try to recall visually some period in the past, we find in our memory just the few meagre arbitrarily chosen set of snapshots that we do find there, the faded poor souvenirs of passionate moments. (*Use of Poetry*, 148)

This is from the same area as the remark about Shakespeare's imagery rising like Anadyomene from the sea, but Eliot is clearly talking about himself rather than about Shakespeare. The relevant lines, from *Journey of the Magi*, run:

> Then at dawn we came down to a temperate valley,
> Wet, below the snow line, smelling of vegetation;
> With a running stream and a water-mill beating the darkness,
> And three trees on the low sky,
> And an old white horse galloped away in the meadow.
> Then we came to a tavern with vine-leaves over the lintel,
> Six hands at an open door asking for pieces of silver,
> And feet kicking the empty wine-skins.

Professor Gardner notes that these lines effect a 'transformation of this personal memory to give it general symbolic significance' (*The Art of T. S. Eliot*, 125), that the gamblers foreshadow the dicers at the foot of the cross, and that the three trees imply the three crosses on Calvary. She offers no comment on the water-mill, the old white horse or the smell of vegetation, and this may seem to support Eliot's remark that 'such memories may have symbolic value, but of what we cannot tell'.

It is that element of mysteriousness which makes Eliot talk in the same way about images as he talks about the direct effects; but in doing so he exaggerates beyond all need the element of mystery in imagery. This exaggeration is connected with the mysteriousness which pervades Eliot's account of the way in which the poet's mind works. A poem is, he says,

> a concentration, and a new thing resulting from the concentration, of a very great number of experiences which to the practical and active person would not seem to be experiences at all; it is a concentration which does not happen consciously or of deliberation. (*Selected Essays*, 21)

The stress here on the unconsciousness of the process reminds us that this is in turn connected with that aspect of the idea of 'objective correlatives' to which Yvor Winters so strongly objected. Eliot says, in his definition of 'objective correlatives', that they are the only way in which the poet can express emotion, and he seems also to suggest that they are the nearest the poet can come to *understanding* his emotions; to use the words quoted above, 'they come to represent the depths of feeling into which we cannot peer'. The vividly remembered image is an 'objective correlative' for feelings which the poet does not understand.

In objecting to this notion, Winters points out that Eliot himself later rejects it, without seeming to be aware that he is doing so (Winters 1947, 468). Contrasting Lancelot Andrewes with Donne, and preferring Lancelot Andrewes, Eliot says:

> [Donne] is constantly finding an object which shall be adequate to his feelings; Andrewes is wholly absorbed in the object and therefore responds with the adequate emotion. (*Selected Essays*, 351)

Andrewes, that is, knows what the actual motive for his emotion is. As Winters notes, Eliot makes the comparison between Andrewes and Donne in 1926, but is still talking in terms of 'objective correlatives' in the essay on Tourneur in 1931. He is still talking in those terms in *The Use of Poetry and the Use of Criticism*.

Eliot's preoccupation with images which stand for a depth of emotion which cannot be expressed in any other way, and cannot be understood, is clearly of great interest for any general study of Eliot. For our purposes, its significance is that it makes Eliot, in his criticism, attach exaggerated importance to the 'haunting' line; and the atmosphere of such lines is one of the key elements in Eliot's notion of 'complexity' in poetic language.

What does 'exaggerated importance' mean here? In *The Use of Poetry and the Use of Criticism*, talking further of the kind of image which, in Shakespeare's poetry, 'rises like Anadyomene from the sea', Eliot adds that it will, in its poetic context, 'have its rational use and justification'. This is what criticism is primarily concerned with. To refer to Eliot's own examples, why the image of the water-mill meant so much to him may be of interest to the biographer or the psychoanalyst, but the critic's concern is with the effect, not its origin. The critic may find it difficult to describe this effect in abstract terms, but if it remains, for the critic, as shrouded in mystery as the origin, then the image can only be regarded as a failure. The reference to the water-mill presents no more difficulty than such a detail would present in a narrative section in a novel; it establishes the scene and creates a suitable atmosphere. A description of this atmosphere would involve subtle reference to other parts of the poem, but would not require speculation about the depths of Eliot's unconscious associative processes.

To describe the second, more important, consequence of Eliot's exaggeration of the importance of the haunting, suggestive line, we return to our earlier point about Ben Jonson. In the essay on Jonson, which we quoted at the beginning of our account of suggestiveness, Eliot says: the words of 'Shakespeare, and also Donne and Webster and Tourneur (and sometimes Middleton) . . . have often a network of tentacular roots reaching down to the deepest terrors and desires. Jonson's most certainly have not.'

Eliot is describing the way in which Jonson's poetry is 'of the surface' though not 'superficial', and the most prominent positive word in his description is 'simple'. He quotes from a speech by Sylla's ghost in *Catiline*:

> Dost thou not feel me, Rome? not yet! is night
> So heavy on thee, and my weight so light?
> Can Sylla's ghost arise within thy walls,
> Less threatening than an earthquake, the quick falls
> Of thee and thine? Shake not the frighted heads
> Of thy steep towers, or shrink to their first beds?
> Or as their ruin the large Tyber fills,
> Make that swell up, and drown thy seven proud hills? (1.i.7–8)

Of this Eliot says: 'it is the careful, precise filling in of a strong and simple outline', and adds that the 'words themselves are mostly simple words, the syntax is natural, the language austere rather than adorned' (*Selected Essays*, 151).

Though the poetry is not suggestive, its language *is* certainly complex. Consider, for instance, the bold condensation of a phrase like 'quick falls', or the grotesque metaphor of the towers shaking with fright or pulling the bed-clothes over their heads, or the relations between 'swell up' and 'proud' in the last line, or the way in which violent upward and downward movements relate and contrast with each other throughout the passage, giving a sickening nightmare atmosphere ('heavy', 'light', 'arise', 'quick falls', 'shrink', 'ruin', 'fills', 'swell up', 'drown'). The lines, in short, exhibit a high degree of interinanimation.

And yet it is perfectly clear what Eliot is driving at, and his essay on Ben Jonson is criticism of the highest quality, so that to insist that the language of these lines is complex rather than simple may seem to be merely a quibble. That it is more than a quibble will be clear when we discuss Eliot's exaggeration of the importance of 'suggestiveness' and his corresponding misconception of 'simplicity' of language, in the context of the notion of a 'dissociation of sensibility'. For the moment we shall rest with the point that Eliot's ideas of 'complexity' and 'simplicity' are misleading, in the way we have seen.

5. Wit

The third distinctive element in Eliot's thinking about poetic language is 'wit', as defined and discussed in the essay on Marvell. This element has two separable strands.

The first may be illustrated by the following observation about the nature of 'wit':

> it implies a constant inspection and criticism of experience. It involves, probably, a recognition, implicit in the expression of every experience, of other kinds of experience which are possible. (*Selected Essays*, 303)

This, together with the claim that it involves an 'internal equilibrium', an 'equipoise, a balance and proportion of tones', or an 'alliance of levity and seriousness' (*Selected Essays*, 304, 302, 296), indicates what it has in common with Richards' definition of 'irony', in *Principles of Literary Criticism*, as 'the bringing in of the opposite, the complementary impulses' (250). The difference is that the process, for Richards, involves the direct effects of language and is, consequently, beneath the level of observation, whereas for Eliot there is an observable complexity of *tone*.

One consequence of Eliot's stress upon 'wit' appears in a remark on Dryden and Milton. Dryden is a 'witty' poet:

> Sometimes the wit appears as a delicate flavour to the magnificence, as in *Alexander's Feast*:

> > Sooth'd with the sound the king grew vain;
> > Fought all his battles o'er again;
> > And thrice he routed all his foes, and thrice he slew the slain.

The great advantage of Dryden over Milton is that while the former is always in control of his ascent, and can rise or fall at will (and how masterfully, like his own Timotheus, he directs the transitions!), the latter has elected a perch from which he cannot afford to fall, and from which he is in danger of slipping:

> > food alike those pure
> > Intelligential substances require
> > As doth your Rational; and both contain
> > Within them every lower faculty
> > Of sense, whereby they hear, see, smell, touch, taste,
> > Tasting concoct, digest, assimilate,
> > And corporeal to incorporeal turn. (*Selected Essays*, 311)

This quotation is rather unfair, because Milton is not often in such acute danger as this. The point is more justly made by Johnson, in his remark that Milton's 'confusion of spirit and matter' in his presentation of the angels is particularly noticeable in the narration of the war in heaven, and that this narration is consequently 'the favourite of children, and gradually neglected as knowledge is increased'. Eliot's phrase, 'he is in danger of slipping', in fact, feels a little odd; had he put 'occasionally' it would have weakened his point, and had he put 'frequently' it would have clearly been an exaggeration.

It may be that the absence of 'wit' in Milton is one reason why Eliot assumed that Milton's language is without complexity; we have already noted, in our discussion of Richards, a tendency among some modern critics to assume that where there is no complexity of tone, there is no complexity at all. But the more important point is that there is an ambiguity in the term 'wit', which results in a criticism of Milton far more damaging than the mere assertion that he lacks 'wit' in the sense in which it is exhibited by Dryden.

Eliot makes the claim that Marvell blends thought with feeling, by adducing Coleridge's remark that the 'imagination' reconciles 'judgment' with 'enthusiasm', and 'emotion' with 'order', and by comparing Marvell with William Morris, whose poetry is characterised by feeling without thought (*Selected Essays*, 298).

This claim corresponds with Eliot's views on the metaphysical poets in general, as, for example, in the remark that 'Tennyson and Browning are poets, and they think; but they do not feel their thought as immediately as the odour of a rose.' (*Ibid.*, 287) This last capacity is pre-eminent in Donne and his followers, says Eliot, and is eroded by Milton and Dryden: 'Each of these men performed certain poetic functions so magnificently well that the magnitude of the effect concealed the absence of others.' (*Ibid.*, 288)

At this point, as Leavis has noted, there is a blur in Eliot's thinking about 'wit', but Eliot's case against Milton and Dryden is clear enough in outline; Dryden's poetry has insufficient feeling, Milton's insufficient thought. This case involves the idea of a 'dissociation of sensibility' and needs to be examined at length. The examination has to include points from our account of the various elements in Eliot's notion of complexity in poetic language, and to add some further description of his notion of 'simplicity'.

6. Eliot's idea of 'simplicity'

Eliot's most elaborate account of simplicity of poetic language occurs in a discussion of Dante. It is claimed that 'Dante's attempt is to make us see what he saw. He therefore employed very simple language.' (*Selected Essays*, 243) In so far as visual vividness is related to sensory particularity, this position contradicts that held by Eliot about the language of the Elizabethan and Jacobean poets, since, as we have seen, Eliot there associates particularity with complexity. The contradiction springs from the inadequacy of his notions of both complexity and simplicity. His notions are, in fact, impressionistic. Up to a point, this does not matter, especially when the impressions are as vivid and sensitive as those of a critic of Eliot's genius. But, in the end, his reliance upon insufficiently worked out impressions leads to confusion.

Having asserted the highly visual quality of Dante, Eliot compares Dante's Italian with the English language:

> [English] words have associations, and the groups of words *in* association have associations, which is a kind of local self-consciousness, because they are the growth of a *particular* civilisation. (*Selected Essays*, 240)

This gives English words 'opacity', whereas Dante's words have 'lucidity'. Mario Praz has taken issue with this, (Unger, *T. S. Eliot: A Selected Critique*) and, indeed, it seems that what Eliot attributes to English must be a fundamental feature of *any* language, and that Eliot's impression of Dante's 'lucidity' is the consequence of his knowing

Italian far less well than he knows English.

It would be presumptuous of me to pretend to any analysis of Dante, but a brief comment on a Dante-esque passage in Eliot's own poetry can, I think, serve as an adequate substitute. Eliot comments on this passage in 'What Dante Means to Me' (*To Criticise the Critic*, 129), refers to 'this very bare and austere style', to the 'simple words and simple phrases', and notes that the language is 'very direct'. It seems impertinent to question Eliot's judgement, but it is unlikely that words like 'simple' and 'direct' would naturally spring to the mind of a reader asked to comment on it. The first line contains a deliberate ambiguity; the second and third deliberate paradoxes; the fourth and fifth a metaphor of 'metaphysical' surprisingness; the sixth a simile of striking boldness; and so one could go on:

> In the uncertain hour before the morning
> Near the ending of interminable night
> At the recurrent end of the unending
> After the dark dove with the flickering tongue
> Had passed below the horizon of his homing
> While the dead leaves still rattled on like tin
> Over the asphalt where no other sound was
> Between three districts whence the smoke arose
> I met one walking, loitering and hurried . . .

the lines would, in fact, offer a good opportunity for a Richards to display the intense 'activity' of poetry; as, for instance, in the complex interaction between tenor (a departing bomber) and vehicle in,

> After the dark dove with the flickering tongue
> Had passed below the horizon of his homing.

The reader has to search among the possibilities, and his search, being successful, is the re-creation of what the lines are about.

In claiming that Dante is 'simple', Eliot also uses, for purposes of contrast, some lines from *Antony and Cleopatra*:

> she looks like sleep,
> As she would catch another Antony
> In her strong toil of grace.

This, I think, is a loaded example, because it is highly complex, even for Shakespeare, but it is, in any case, not difficult to pick lines from Eliot's own Dante-esque passage, which approach it:

> First, the cold friction of expiring sense

or,

> The bitter tastelessness of shadow fruit.

It is probable that one of the reasons why Eliot liked to use the word 'simple' of this sort of writing, is connected with that feature of his later poetry which caused Leavis to remark, 'Eliot's poetic technique is a technique for sincerity' (*English Literature in our Time and the University*, 120). There is no indulgence in spectacular effects or 'brilliant' ironies; or, to use the terms by which we have described Eliot's notion of complexity, there are no mysteriously haunting images, no daring distortions of language, and no 'witty' stances. However, though it lacks such things, it is not 'simple', but highly complex.

7. Dissociation of sensibility

It is in the idea of a 'dissociation of sensibility' that Eliot's unsatisfactory notions of simplicity and complexity are most damaging. The two key poets here are Dryden and Milton.

The idea of a 'dissociation of sensibility' is that the ability to fuse thought with feeling in poetry, conspicuous in 'the time of Donne or Lord Herbert of Cherbury' has disappeared from English poetry. In Eliot's view Dryden and Milton were instrumental in hastening the disappearance (*Selected Essays*, 287).

The way in which Dryden's role is discussed may most conveniently be recalled by quoting Eliot's comparison of him with Swinburne; Dryden, Eliot says,

> bears a curious antithetical resemblance to Swinburne. Swinburne was also a master of words, but Swinburne's words are all suggestions and no denotation; if they suggest nothing, it is because they suggest too much. Dryden's words, on the other hand, are precise, they state immensely, but their suggestiveness is often nothing.
> (*Selected Essays*, 314)

This relates very directly to Eliot's comparison of Marvell with William Morris; Morris, like Swinburne, is all suggestion, whereas Marvell is both precise and suggestive, and fuses thought with feeling (*Ibid.*, 299). After some very fine comments on Dryden, Eliot remarks:

> The question, which has certainly been waiting, may justly be asked: whether, without this which Dryden lacks [i.e. suggestiveness], verse can be poetry? (*Ibid.*, 315)

Eliot then notes the impossibility of giving a definition of 'poetry', quotes from Dryden's elegy on Oldham, and says:

> From the perfection of such an elegy we cannot detract; the lack of suggestiveness is compensated by the satisfying completeness of the statement. (*Ibid.*, 316)

In spite of all his insight, Eliot is, in the end, adopting the 'romantic' attitude to Dryden; the bent of his argument is towards the view that Dryden thinks powerfully, but feels insufficiently. But, in fact, the excellence of his account of Dryden is that it points to the triviality of the criterion of 'suggestiveness', exposes the falsity of equating 'suggestiveness' with 'feeling', and gives the essential hint about the complexity of Dryden's language.

For instance, Eliot quotes the famous lines on Shaftesbury (Achitophel):

> A fiery soul, which working out its way,
> Fretted the pigmy body to decay:
> And o'er informed the tenement of clay,

and comments: 'These lines are not merely a magnificent tribute. They create the object which they contemplate.' (*Ibid.*, 310). This is so, and in creating the object they go beyond anything that might be implied by the idea of 'statement'. The creativeness, further, involves complexity of language. This is most obvious in the multiple exploitation of 'fretted'. The *New Oxford English Dictionary* gives three strands of meaning, all of which are here relevant: (1) 'of slow and gradual destructive action . . . as of corrosives'; (2) 'to distress oneself with constant regret or discontent; to chafe, worry. Often with additional notion of querulous utterances'; (3) 'to move in agitation or turmoil'. These meanings interact with 'working out', which is also complex. First, 'leaving the body which has been destroyed by the corrosive fretting'; second, 'plotting its political course, which involves a lot of worry'. But 'working out' has also the kind of meaning which appears in such phrases as 'working out his apprenticeship'; Shaftesbury is completing an allotted task, so there is a suggestion that he is, in the end, merely working out his allotted destiny.

This analysis is useful because it indicates the way in which a large number of feelings enter into the creative effect; by 'feelings' is meant all the implications or connotations which the meanings involve. In a real sense the lines *suggest* immensely, though their suggestiveness is not of the kind that one associates with Swinburne.

That the quality of hauntingness, or suggestiveness (in Eliot's sense) upon which the idea of a 'dissociation of sensibility' so much depends, is a trivial criterion, is also apparent in Eliot's essay on Blake, another of his best performances as a critic. Eliot says memorably, of Blake:

> because he was not distracted, or frightened, or occupied in anything but exact statements, he understood. He was naked, and saw men naked, from the centre of his own crystal.

This feature of Blake is illustrated by:

> Love seeketh only self to please,
> To bind another to its delight,
> Joys in another's loss of ease,
> And builds a Hell in Heaven's despite.
> (*Selected Essays*, 319–20)

Eliot is here talking about Blake in the way that he talks about Dryden; they both excel at 'exact statements'. It is unlikely that Eliot wished to suggest that Blake and Dryden have much in common, of course, but he is, in any case, making an essential point. The point is that to which attention was drawn in our discussion of Richards' comparison of Blake with Gray. Whatever the difference is between Blake and the 'neo-classical' poets, it cannot be convincingly demonstrated as differing degrees of complexity in the use of language.

Eliot's impression of Blake here records itself in language similar to that in which he recorded his impression of Dryden. In one sense, he is mistaken in both cases; the language of Blake is as complex as that of Dryden, and the phrase 'exact statements' is consequently misleading. But it is hard to see anything intrinsically objectionable in this collocation of the two poets, in so far as poetic language is concerned. Had Richards, for instance, taken the above stanza by Blake for comparison with some representative lines by an Augustan poet, he would have found it impossible to even embark on an attempt to distinguish them in terms of different kinds of complexity. In Eliot's case what is here demonstrated, as was noted above, is the unimportance of 'suggestiveness'.

8. Verbal music

With reference to Milton, who is the other key poet in the disappearance of a unified sensibility, we have already seen that his poetry responds to analysis in the same way as does Dryden's, or Donne's, or Shakespeare's. It is creative, and reveals to a high degree the complexity which Coleridge attributes to 'imaginative' poetry. But some further remarks about Eliot on Milton are in place, since they illustrate some other features of Eliot's views on poetic language.

The essential case against Milton is implied in the term 'magniloquence'. In his critique, Eliot remarked that he found it necessary to read Milton twice: once for the sound and once for the sense. The swell of the Miltonic music distracted Eliot from the meaning of the words, and closer inspection revealed that it had already distracted Milton himself in the same way (*On Poetry and Poets*, 142). 'Magniloquence' involves insensitivity to subtlety of sense, hence Milton is the opposite of Dryden, whose poetry exhibits precision of statement. To illustrate the point, Eliot quotes a typically long sentence from *Paradise Lost* and says, 'the complication is dictated by a demand of verbal music, instead of by any demand of sense' (*Ibid.*, 141). Eliot's view is summarised in the remark that in Milton there is a 'hypertrophy of the auditory imagination at the expense of the visual and tactile' (*Ibid.*, 143).

The chief question here is what Eliot meant by 'verbal music'. An investigation of it throws light on Eliot's second Milton essay, which Leavis thinks was merely the result of a loss of nerve on Eliot's part. It seems more likely, in fact, that it represents a failure of critical rather than of general principles.

Eliot has two distinct ideas about 'music' in poetry, and we shall describe them in turn.

In 'The Music of Poetry' Eliot insists that 'the music of poetry is not something that exists apart from the meaning', and goes on to say:

My purpose here is to insist that a 'musical poem' is a poem which has a musical pattern of sound and a musical pattern of the secondary meanings of the words which compose it, and that these two patterns are indissoluble and one. (*On Poetry and Poets*, 33)

Alongside this one may set Richards' remark:

> The perceived relations between temporal parts of an utterance, which seem to the ear to constitute good metre, derive from relations between parts of its meaning. (CI, 120)

For Richards, that is, metre heightens the process of interinanimation. Another quotation from Eliot makes the resemblance more clear:

> The music of a word is, so to speak, at a point of intersection: it arises from its relation first to the words immediately preceding and following it, and indefinitely to the rest of its context; and from another relation, that of its immediate meaning in that context to all the other meanings which it has had in other contexts, to its greater or less wealth of association. (*On Poetry and Poets*, 32)

It may well be that Eliot is at this point specifically indebted to Richards, because there is some reason to believe that he is not really in command of the implications of this view. This is clear in the same essay, when he says, discussing successive poetic schools, 'when we reach a point at which the poetic idiom can be stabilized, then a period of musical elaboration can follow'. If one really accepts the theory of meaning assumed by Richards' account of music, then to talk of a 'poetic idiom' being 'stabilized' is impossible, since the powers exerted by a word in one context will be different from those it exerts in any other context. It may also be noted that, if one accepts Richards' definition of music in poetry, and Eliot's account of Milton's language, then Milton cannot be 'musical'. Music involves complexity of meaning, and Milton's language, according to Eliot, is not complex.

When Eliot talks of Milton's music he is, in fact, appealing to an idea different from that of Richards. This idea appears, for instance, when Eliot notes the importance of 'definiteness' as a condition for successful 'music' in the diction of Pound. Eliot observes:

> Words are perhaps the hardest of all material of art: for they must be used to express both visual beauty and beauty of sound, as well as communicating a grammatical statement. (*To Criticise the Critic*, 170)

This implies a separation of music and meaning, and the point is made explicitly in a comparison of Swinburne with Campion. Eliot quotes Campion's lines;

> Shall I come, if I swim? wide are the waves, you see;
> Shall I come, if I fly, my dear Love to thee?

and comments:

> It is an arrangement and choice of words which has a sound-value and at the same time a coherent comprehensible meaning, and the two things – the musical value and meaning – are two things, not one. (*Selected Essays*, 324)

Campion's special relation with music is not here regarded as making him an unusual case, and Eliot, on the same page, makes the same point about some lines by Shelley, which are said to be like Campion's in that they have 'a beauty of music and a beauty of content'.

This idea, evidently, is directly opposed to that expounded in 'The Music of Poetry', where the patterns of music and meaning are said to be 'indissoluble and one'. Further, it is not a very far step from the comment on Campion to the critique of Milton's 'magniloquence':

> To extract everything possible from *Paradise Lost*, it would seem necessary to read it in two different ways, first solely for the sound, and second for the sense. (*On Poetry and Poets*, 143)

Consequently, it is no surprise that Eliot, in his second Milton essay, and wishing to praise Milton, says that Milton can teach the modern poet that 'the music of verse is strongest in poetry which has a definite meaning expressed in the properest words' (*Ibid.*, 160). The word 'definite' here is pointing in the same direction as the remarks on Campion and Shelley and is also, it may be suggested, hinting at a rejection of Richards' sort of theory, which sees 'music' as necessarily connected with complexity of meaning, rather than with 'definiteness'.

There is, essentially, little difference between Eliot's critique of Milton and his 'recantation'. In the 'recantation' it is still noted that Milton lacks 'particularity' (*Ibid.*, 156), and, as we have said, there is little change in the account of Milton's 'music', except that what is now called 'music' was previously dismissed as 'magniloquence'.

The important point is that neither the critique nor the recantation gives any indication of the complexity of Milton's poetry, nor, consequently, any indication of what the Miltonic 'music' is *doing*. In fact, as has always been said, his music is 'sublime' and is in the closest relation with his imaginative power, so that the music and the meaning are perfectly consonant. In Eliot's second essay on Milton, the Miltonic 'music' seems to be felt merely as an abstract pattern of sound, beautiful for its own sake.

Eliot nowhere shows any interest in the 'sublime', and, evidently, it is harder to imagine a mode more alien from his own poetry. Here, probably, is the root of his lack of sympathy for Milton, in much the same way as Johnson's critique of Donne springs from his lack of sympathy with Donne's subject matter. Further, just as Johnson's antipathy was confirmed by his use of eighteenth-century literary principles, so is Eliot's by certain features in his notion of complexity. Milton is not 'witty', he does not cultivate the hauntingly suggestive line, and he does not dislocate language in the way that some Elizabethan poets do. It is not, consequently, surprising that Eliot fails to point out the ways in which Milton's language *is* complex.

9. Summary

The foregoing account of Eliot's views on poetic language has concentrated on the distinctive elements, and, more particularly, on the points at which those distinctive elements are of dubious value. This may seem rather like giving an account of Johnson by referring only to his views on 'metaphysical' poetry. The importance of that valuable core in Eliot's criticism, and especially in his early criticism, which was described at the beginning of the account, should therefore be stressed again. It was present in the form of suggestive hints rather than of consistent exposition. Its value, and the difficulties that lie in the way of extracting it, are recorded in Leavis' account of Eliot's criticism. Leavis, as he continued over the years to read and re-read Eliot, found much in the early criticism to ponder upon and learn from. He also found much to reject, and, in Eliot's later criticism, a distinct falling off.

That is an account from which it is difficult to dissent, but it may be suggested that the falling off was due not to a lapse of integrity on Eliot's part, but to the fact that his criticism had always been impressionistic. It is, certainly, not possible to trace in Eliot's work the coherent and consistent appeal to fully grasped critical principles that one finds in Leavis' own work.

As far as our own particular interests are concerned, Eliot's failure to extract principles from his impressions is reflected in the fact that there is very little analysis in his criticism. It is, in fact, somewhat puzzling that he should have acquired such a reputation for analysis. Eliot's unwillingness to test his notions by sustained and detailed analysis is the factor which allows free play to the distinctive features, or biases, in his idea of complexity.

It is apparent that these biases (in favour of wit, suggestiveness and distortion of language) correspond with important features in modern poetic taste, though an illustration of this is beyond the scope of my enquiry. Perhaps what most needs insisting upon is that in Eliot's criticism, as in the criticism of other innovators, such as Dryden and Wordsworth, the biases are less important than the core of true insight. It would be unfortunate were Eliot eventually to be treated in the same way as Johnson, and his biases presented as a full account of his criticism; but without a proper sense of the continuities of the critical tradition this might well happen.

CHAPTER SIX

THE IDEA OF COMPLEXITY IN THE CRITICISM OF F.R.LEAVIS

1. Leavis and Richards

The following account of F.R.Leavis will follow the same pattern as my study of Eliot: common ground first, then the distinctive features of Leavis' views on poetic language. He is, in my opinion, notwithstanding some of the following emphases, the best of the modern English critics, because he keeps to the central road of criticism, responding as a full human being to literature seen as full human utterance, and because his power to respond has shown itself over a very wide area of English literature.

For the common ground, Leavis' key critical terms are 'complexity', 'realisation', and 'self-realisation'. The poet, by a complex use of language, enables us to grasp fully, or realise, whatever it is that he is talking about, and the grasping involves awareness or self-realisation. The process is sometimes described by Leavis in Coleridgean terms, as a fusion of thought with feeling; the reader has the experience and knows what it is. These ideas result in a view like that of Richards' theory of 'pseudo-statement'. For Leavis the 'truth' of poetry is a question of degree of realisation.

It is not necessary to illustrate these ideas at great length, since they will be familiar to any reader of Leavis' work, but a few quotations may be adduced as reminders. With regard to complexity, Leavis wrote, in an article in *Scrutiny* (XIII, 119): 'What we are concerned with in analysis are always matters of complex verbal organisation.' The relation between this and realisation is exemplified in the following comment on Joyce:

> There is prose in *Ulysses*, the description, for instance, of Stephen Dedalus walking over the beach, of a Shakespearean concreteness; the rich complexity it offers to analysis derives from the intensely imagined experience realized in the words. (*Scrutiny*, ii, 194)

The relation, in turn, between that and self-realisation is exemplified in the following remark, in *New Bearings in English Poetry*, 13:

> [the poet's] capacity for experiencing and his power of communicating are indistinguishable; not merely because we should not know of the one without the other, but because his power of making words express what he feels is indistinguishable from his awareness of what he feels.

The essence of poetry for Leavis, as for Warburton or Coleridge, is self-

knowledge. The idea of self-realisation should be further illustrated with
reference to specific poets:

> The activity of the thinking mind, the energy of intelligence, in-
> volved in the Metaphysical habit means that, when the poet *has*
> urgent personal experience to deal with it is attended to and con-
> templated – which in turn means some kind of separation, or distin-
> tion, between experiencer and experience. 'Their attempts were
> always analytic' – to analyse your experience you must, while keeping
> it alive and immediately present as experience, treat it in some sense
> as an object. (*Scrutiny*, xiii, 61)

This may be put simply in terms of 'sincerity', as in Leavis' comment on
Ash Wednesday:

> it is impossible not to see in it a process of self-scrutiny, of self-
> exploration; or not to feel that the poetical problem at any point was
> a spiritual problem, a problem in the attainment of a difficult
> sincerity. (*New Bearings*, 117–8)

2. Realisation: the case of *St Mawr*

A more detailed probing of such basic ideas, as they appear in
Leavis' work, is afforded by his view of poetry as pseudo-statement. To
put it in that way is justifiable even though he does not use the word
'pseudo-statement' or present an explicit theory. His way of putting it is
to say that poetry is 'enactment' as opposed to 'statement'. We have
already seen examples of this line of thought, in our discussion of Johnson,
so we shall concentrate on a point at which the ideas appear in a rather
interesting and provocative way.

The case is Leavis' discussion of Lawrence's *St Mawr*, in *D.H.
Lawrence, Novelist*, with which Professor Buckley in *Poetry and Morality*
has registered disagreement. This disagreement offers an opportunity to
make some necessary points.

Leavis' exposition of *St Mawr* begins, if the metaphor is permissible,
from the 'surface', the words on the page:

> Lawrence writes out of the full living language with a flexibility and
> a creative freedom for which I can think of no parallel in modern
> times. (226)

The power of the language is, Leavis claims, a realising power which
presents its subject fully; it gives us the 'potent actuality of Mrs Witt';
ensures that the mountains (the setting of the close of the story) are
'marvellously evoked'; and gives us the horse, St Mawr, 'by a wealth of
poetic and dramatic means'. Leavis offers no detailed analysis of this,
restricting himself largely to general comments on the complexity of
tone. He quotes, for instance, a conversation between the heroine and her
mother and says:

> These exchanges, intimately *tête-à-tête*, between Lou and her
> mother are marvellous in their range and suppleness, their harmonic
> richness, and the sureness of their inflexion, which, since the surface,

belonging to the conversational everyday world, is always kept in
touch with the depths, can blend in one utterance the hard-boiled
sardonic with the poignant. (237)

The subtly conveyed tones of the dialogue set before us not stereotypes,
but people who seem to live. That Leavis offers no close analysis is an
interesting point, which will be commented upon later.

Implicit in this realisation are moral judgements, which are not stated
but enacted. The most interesting example is the enactment of the
positive values by which the various characters are dramatically 'placed'.
These values may be pointed to in some such phrase as 'integrity of
being', or 'sincerity' (in the sense in which it appears in Richards'
utilisation of Confucianism). Of these values the whole story itself is the
enactment. The heroine, for example, wants a man with such integrity,
and Leavis comments:

> The kind of intelligence, 'burning like a flame fed straight from
> underneath', that Lou postulates – the intelligence of a full thinking
> man who, more than merely intuitive, can sit the stallion as Lewis
> does – doesn't prove its possibility by being presented in any
> character: Lou, at the close, has little hope of meeting the man she
> would care to mate with. But it *is*, nevertheless, irresistibly present
> in *St Mawr* the dramatic poem; it is no mere abstract postulate. It is
> present as the marvellous creative intelligence of the author. (234)

A further quotation, along the same lines, is useful, because it serves fully
to clarify the issues involved:

> The power of the affirmation lies, not in any insistence or assertion
> or argument, but in the creative fact, his art; it is that which bears
> irrefutable witness. What his art *does* is beyond argument or doubt.
> It is not a question of metaphysics or theology – though no doubt
> there are questions presented for the metaphysician and the theo-
> logian. Great art, something created and *there*, is what Lawrence
> gives us. And there we undeniably *have* a world of wonder and
> reverence, where life wells up from mysterious springs. It is no
> merely imagined world; what the creative imagination of the artist
> makes us contemplate bears an unanswerable testimony. (235)

It will be seen that Leavis' path from the surface of the work to this final
position is very direct; poetic realisation is testimony of spiritual health.
The train of thought is, in important respects, like that pursued by
Richards in *Coleridge on Imagination*; the poet gives us the 'fact of mind',
which may be translated into doctrine, of various kinds, and these
doctrines are open to doubt, argument, questioning, disagreement, and
so on. The 'fact of mind', realised by the poet's complex use of language,
is *not* open to questioning of that kind, and the only relevant question is,
'Is it realised?'. That question is evidently important. For the moment
we may summarise Leavis' argument as follows: the central value of *St
Mawr* is realised with such power that it has the irresistible immediacy of
fact.

The assertion that realisation is rectitude, if one may so put it, seems a bold view (one with which Professor Buckley disagrees). However, if one accepts what may be called the Coleridgean definition of the 'imagination', the assertion, so far from being bold, is included in the definition. Coleridge, at the beginning of his description of the 'imagination' (*Biographia Literaria*, ii, 12) says:

> The poet, described in *ideal* perfection, brings the whole soul of man into activity, with the subordination of its faculties to each other, according to their relative worth and dignity.

Imaginative language, as defined by Coleridge, is witness to the presence of imagination; imagination is essentially defined in terms of spiritual health; hence realisation is rectitude. With regard to the moral element, Coleridge's definition is like Richards' definition of value in *Principles of Literary Criticism*, which says that the highest value is attained by an organisation of impulses in which the less important are arranged so as not to interfere with the more important. The objection likely to be registered here is not that these remarks are strange but that they are something in the nature of truisms.

How the Coleridgean definition of imagination relates to Leavis' discussion of *St Mawr* may be indicated by a remark from Richards' commentary on Coleridge:

> The extracted abstract doctrine (if we arrive at any such) is a skeleton of the living knowledge [given by the poem], deformed and schematized for the legitimate purposes of comparison (as well as for the irrelevant purposes of argument). In the poem [the ideas] . . . are autonomous, sanctioned by their acceptability to the whole being of the reader. Out of the poem, they are doctrine merely, and a temptation to dispute. (CI, 211)

Leavis' 'unanswerable testimony' corresponds with Richards' 'acceptability to the whole being of the reader', and his 'questions presented for the metaphysician and theologian' correspond with Richards' 'extracted abstract doctrine.'

The Coleridgean basis of Leavis' views on poetic *language* may be conveniently recalled by his remark on Coleridge's distinction between fancy and imagination:

> [it] is a way of calling attention to the organic complexities of verbal life, metaphorical and other, in which Imagination manifests itself locally. (*Scrutiny*, ix, 63)

The moral element in the definition of imagination implies that the language of poetry has an inescapably evaluative function. This point is made, and accepted, by Leavis, in his essay 'Literary Criticism and Philosophy', in the remark that words in poetry 'realize a complex experience . . . [and] a certain valuing is implicit in the realizing'. That words in poetry have an evaluative function follows from their possession of elements of tone and feeling, for whenever tone and feeling are present the question of their *appropriateness* must always arise.

As Richards emphasises, Coleridge's definition of the imagination contains the idea of 'impersonality', which Coleridge describes as the appeal of imaginative poetry to the '*all in each* of human nature'. The idea of 'impersonality' occupies a similar place in Leavis' thinking, and it is fully illustrated in Buckley's chapter, 'F.R.Leavis: Impersonality and Values' (*Poetry and Morality*, 184ff). The way in which Leavis uses the term may be recalled by his remark that in Lawrence's fictional presentation, in *The Rainbow*, of a child-parent relation similar to that between himself and his mother, 'the experience is wholly impersonalized (and, in being impersonalized, extended)' (*D.H.Lawrence*, 131).

The importance of the idea of 'impersonality', here, serves as a reminder that the high claims for the poet made by Coleridge and Leavis are not, of course, new-fangled. In Johnson's *Rasselas* (Chapter x), Imlac says of the poet:

> He must divest himself of the prejudices of his age or country; he must consider right and wrong in their abstracted and invariable state; he must disregard present laws and opinions, and rise to general and transcedent truths which will always be the same ... He must write as the interpreter of nature, and the legislator of mankind, and consider himself as presiding over the thoughts and manners of future generations; as a being superior to time and place.

Imlac is described here as feeling the 'enthusiastic fit' upon him, but the joke is against the enthusiasm and not against the ideal. It is in the light of the same ideal that Johnson himself gives Shakespeare a supreme place. This perennial claim for poetry arises from the acute sense of 'there-ness' felt by the reader, who seems to be in the presence of experiences undistorted by the poet's personality or time.

Consider, briefly, another of Leavis' quotations from *St Mawr*. Lou sees the stallion for the first time:

> The wild, brilliant, alert head of St Mawr seemed to look at her out of another world. It was as if she had had a vision, as if the walls of her own world had suddenly melted away, leaving her in a great darkness, in the midst of which the large, brilliant eyes of that horse looked at her with demonish question, while his naked ears stood up like daggers from the naked lines of his inhuman head, and his great body glowed red with power.
>
> What was it ? Almost like a god looking at her terribly out of the everlasting dark, she had felt the eyes of that horse; great, glowing, fearsome eyes, arched with a question, and containing a white blade of light like a thread. What was his non-human question, and his uncanny threat ? She didn't know.

Leavis says that this is not 'an indulgence of the imagination or fancy that cannot, by the mature, be credited with any real significance or taken seriously' (*D.H.Lawrence*, 229). The woman's vision of the horse is 'realised', and it is also, as the story and Leavis' further commentary make clear, Lawrence's own vision, with the addition that Lawrence *does* know what St Mawr's question is.

If we look even cursorily at the passage we see that there is a process of valuing involved in the presentation. It is not a picture which we *first* absorb and *then* judge. The opening predominantly carries a feeling of approval and admiration, as do phrases like 'the large, brilliant eyes'. But the resemblance of the ears to 'daggers', the 'inhuman head', and the eyes 'arched with a question' and containing a 'white blade of light', carry feelings of fear. In an account of *St Mawr* analysis would go into more detail, but those few points are sufficient to show the inevitably evaluative function of the language.

Consequently, any adverse moral judgement of a work must be translatable into a literary judgement. Indeed, to put it in that way is to falsify, because the moral judgement and the literary judgement are inseparable. By 'literary judgement', here, is meant the kind of judgement that is connected with the idea of 'realisation'. For example, of the above passage, the critic who finds Lawrence unsatisfactory will say: 'the tone and feeling here indicate that the horse and its significance for Lou, and for Lawrence, are intended to be of great importance. I myself cannot attach that degree of importance to these things, and I therefore judge the tone and feeling to be inappropriate.' In Coleridgean terms it would be said that the faculties of the soul are not here subordinated to each other according to their relative worth and dignity.

On these grounds, then, Professor Buckley's disagreement with Leavis is ill founded; but, since it expresses a not uncommon point of view, it should be briefly outlined. His central argument is that literature cannot be its own sanction; we should test literary works as follows:

> not only by referring them to our own personal 'sense of health', but by referring them, as well, to whatever institutions or bodies of belief from which that sense is partly derived, and by which, too, it is tested. (*Poetry and Morality*, 233)

This sounds just a little like reading a poem and then going to ask a priest what one ought to think about it. However, the chief point is that Buckley seems to have an odd idea of what Leavis means in claiming that *St Mawr* is its own sanction. In fact, Leavis' whole point is that *St Mawr* is 'unanswerable' precisely because of the response it elicits from our deepest self, and that deepest self includes our 'sense of health' and the beliefs involved in that 'sense'. Leavis is claiming that *St Mawr* exhibits that transcendence which Imlac attributes to great poetry.

Professor Buckley appears to be disagreeing with Leavis' *theory* but he is, in fact, merely disagreeing with Leavis' estimate of *St Mawr*, and he only appears to himself not to be doing so because he uses the word 'great' in a different sense from Leavis. Buckley's position is this: 'While finding Lawrence a great artist, I find much of his work hateful in some of its tendencies.' (*Ibid.*, 211). Exactly what this means is not explained, but, Buckley's argument being what it is, it can only mean that he finds

Lawrence 'great' and 'hateful' simultaneously. For Leavis, who is adopting a Coleridgean view of the function of imagination, this is merely a self-contradiction.

Granted the Coleridgean definition, there can be no theoretical objection to Leavis' discussion of *St Mawr*, but even if we grant it, there are obvious and important difficulties. In the first place, Coleridge is, like Imlac, describing the imagination in 'ideal perfection', and when we descend, as we must, to discussing poetry written by mere mortals we shall find less than perfect harmony of soul. In the second place, we are far from any state of perfection in our methods of analysing poetic language. Consequently, the question as to whether or not a given work *is* 'realised', or 'imaginative' (in Coleridge's sense) is one that can elicit no easy or certain answers.

In the case of *St Mawr* the second of those difficulties is particularly prominent, because it is a *prose* work, and so lacks the local concentration which makes the language of poetry more responsive to analysis. The point can be conveniently illustrated by referring to another description of a horse, highly admired by Coleridge, but not commented on in detail by him, because he thought it rather too 'strong' for a public lecture. Adonis' horse, in *Venus and Adonis*, sees a 'breeding jennet':

> Imperiously he leaps, he neighs, he bounds,
> And now his woven girths he breaks asunder;
> The bearing earth with his hard hoof he wounds,
> Whose hollow womb resounds like heaven's thunder;
>   The iron bit he crusheth 'tween his teeth,
>   Controlling what he was controlled with.

To recall this is to see that when Leavis says that Lawrence, 'invoking the essential resources of poetic expression, can hazard the most intense emotional and imaginative heightening' is pressing a little too hard. It is not merely that prose cannot encompass the rhythmic effects of poetry, so powerful in the lines above, but also that it cannot, I think, achieve quite the direct concentration here shown in words such as 'bearing', 'wound' and 'hollow womb'.

The first of the difficulties (that actual writers do not attain 'ideal perfection') is also prominent. Professor Buckley, considering Leavis' assertion that *St Mawr* 'bears an unanswerable testimony' says, 'Leavis can say this here with such conviction only because he so obviously assents to Lawrence's attitudes.' (*Poetry and Morality*, 35). This is an easy remark and Buckley does not say how it is obvious, any more than he says why he finds Lawrence 'hateful', but it is obviously true that there will always be room for error in such matters. A conviction that a work is of the highest imaginative power may turn out to be a delusion. In this case the difficulty is prominent because Lawrence is a recent and in some respects a controversial writer. To say, as Johnson used to say, that time plays an essential part in the settling of judgements of literary merit, is not

to assume some mysterious and automatic process, but to see the necessity for long testing, involving a whole succession of individual judgements. Dr Leavis has no illusions on this score, and has always insisted on
the collaborative nature of criticism. He takes as his description of the
critical enterprise Eliot's phrase 'the common pursuit of true judgement'.
Consequently he has no illusions about the power of analysis:

> A critical account of any poetry can only point, or draw a line round.
> It must always be left to each reader to grasp for himself what is
> concretely presented. (*Scrutiny*, xi, 267)

There is no question of 'proof'. Leavis also describes very well the use of
analysis in inculcating a habit of careful reading:

> What we call analysis is, of course, a constructive or creative
> process. It is a more deliberate following-through of that process of
> creation in response to the poet's words which reading is.

By this deliberateness 'we ensure a more than ordinary faithfulness and
completeness' (*Education and the University*, 70).

The advantage of the ideas used by Leavis in his discussion of *St
Mawr* is that they open the road for literary enquiry, whereas Buckley's
position, by separating literary judgements from moral judgements,
closes that road. Professor Buckley's procedure is to extract the doctrine
from a work and then conduct a discussion (moral, metaphysical, theological, and so on) of that. There are many difficulties in Leavis' path, but
it is a path that always leads towards literature, not away from it.

3. Distinctive features of 'complexity'

Having outlined Leavis' use of the ideas of complexity and realisation, and having noted their resemblance to the work of Richards, we
should now look at some of the distinctive features of his criticism.

One of the most important of these is the idea of 'exploration'. The idea
(by no means *unique* to Leavis) points simply to the poet's ability to bring
language to bear upon experience in an unusually intimate way; but
Leavis' applications of it indicate, I think, an important bias, which may
be summed up by saying that Leavis tends to assume that Eliot's *Four
Quartets* are the *standard* manifestation of the 'exploratory-creative' use
of language.[1] This bias is very much like that we saw when discussing
Richards' use of Coleridge's lines,

> To thee do all things live from pole to pole
> Their life the eddying of thy living soul.

There, Richards was misled by concentrating on an example which is
about a philosophical problem. The similarity between that and Leavis'
use of Eliot can be indicated by quoting his remark about *Burnt Norton*:

---

[1] See F. R. Leavis, *English Literature in our Time and the University*,
p.104, for a typical occurrence of the phrase 'exploratory-creative'. This
book is the published version of the Clark Lectures of 1967. I shall refer
to it henceforth as *English Literature in our Time* (ELT).

it seems to me to be the equivalent in poetry of a philosophical work – to do by strictly poetical means the business of an epistemo-logical and metaphysical enquiry. Of course, in this given case examination of the instruments is necessarily at the same time a use of them in the poet's characteristic kind of exploration. (*Education and the University*, 94)

Whether or not the word 'instruments' (one of Richards' favourite words) is a nod in Richards' direction, the ideas here are certainly like those of Richards. This may be more fully illustrated by Leavis' summary of his discussion of *Four Quartets*, in the Clark Lectures. He says that Eliot's poem,

compels a close attention to the subtleties of linguistic expression – to the ways in which the conceptual currency may affect the problem of how and what one believes and what believing is, and in which linguistic conventions and habits partly determine experience. That the creative battle to vindicate spiritual values should be associated, as it is in *Four Quartets*, with the subtlest kind of analytic interest in language seems to me a piece of good fortune that we, who are concerned for humane education at a time when linguistic science, or scientific linguistics, is making its victorious advances, have a duty to exploit. (ELT, 131–2)

Four Quartets demands, that is, the sort of attention to language which we saw in Richards' programme for the *further use* of the study of poetry, a programme demanding not only awareness of what the words are doing, but also of how they are doing it. Herein lies the peculiarity of *Four Quartets*, and one has no wish to quarrel with Leavis' account of it. It is the use of *Four Quartets* as a *standard* which is unjust, and it is interesting to see how this injustice comes about.

Dr Leavis' account of the language of *Four Quartets*, sketched above, dovetails very readily with a similar but more general sort of remark that he is wont to make. In *Education and the University*, for example, he says that Eliot, in *Burnt Norton*, is essentially faced with certain difficulties of belief, and adds : 'Those difficulties are such that they certainly cannot be met by any simple re-imposition of traditional frames'. What we find in Eliot, rather than such re-impositions, are the following :

explorations into the concrete actualities of experience below the conceptual currency ; into the life that must be the *raison d'être* of any frame – while there is life at all. (*Education and the University*, 103)

This is more general because it does not involve, necessarily, a linguistic interest of the peculiar type described above. It is, one would say, an account of what *any* poet ought to be doing, if he is to avoid mere cliche.

The phrase 'conceptual currency' is directly connected with Leavis' grand indictment of the eighteenth century :

The Augustan cannot conceive the need for . . . [the exploratory-creative] use of language. The ideas he wants to express are adequately provided for – and this is true of poetry as of prose – in the common currency of terms, put together according to the conventions of grammar and logic. (*Scrutiny*, xii, 194)

The charge is repeated in the Clark Lectures, in the context of a discussion of Eliot. The eighteenth century 'had no place for the distinctively poetic use of language, the exploratory-creative, exemplified supremely by Shakespeare'. Although Shakespeare is the *stated* standard here, I would suggest that, in view of the context, Eliot's *Four Quartets* are the actual standard. That point may be pressed by noting an important link between Leavis' account of *Four Quartets* and his discussion of exploratory-creative language in the essay 'Tragedy and the "Medium"', which also contains an adverse account of the eighteenth century.

In 'Tragedy and the "Medium"', Leavis says that Santayana, in some remarks on *Macbeth*, is 'proposing for the poet as his true business the lucid arrangement of ready-minted concepts'. Against this Leavis quotes Professor Harding's account of Isaac Rosenberg:

> Usually when we speak of finding words to express a thought we seem to mean that we have the thought rather close to formulation and use it to measure the adequacy of any possible phrasing that occurs to us, treating words as servants of the idea. 'Clothing a thought in language', whatever it means psychologically, seems a fair metaphorical description of most speaking and writing. Of Rosenberg's work it would be misleading. He – like many poets in some degree, one supposes – brought language to bear on the incipient thought at an earlier stage of its development. Instead of the emerging idea being racked slightly so as to fit a more familiar approximation of itself, and words found for *that*, Rosenberg let it manipulate words almost from the beginning, often without insisting on the controls of logic and intelligibility. (*Scrutiny*, iii, 363)

Dr Leavis also notes that Harding connects this use of language with Rosenberg's open-ness to experience, and quotes Harding's following comment on Rosenberg:

> [he had a] willingness . . . to let himself be new-born into the new situation, not subduing his experience to his established personality. (*Common Pursuit*, 133)

Leavis makes the same association of a breaking down of language, as it were, with a breaking down of the 'established personality', in his account of Shakespearean tragedy:

> The sense of heightened life that goes with the tragic experience is conditioned by a transcending of the ego – an escape from all attitudes of self-assertion. (*Ibid.*, 131)

This, for Leavis, is the essence of the tragic effect. When we respond to a Shakespearean tragedy it is in the following way:

> It is as if we were challenged at the profoundest level with the question, 'In what does the significance of life reside?', and found ourselves contemplating, for answer, a view of life, and of the things

giving it value, that makes the valued appear unquestionably more
important than the valuer, so that the significance lies, clearly and
inescapably, in the willing adhesion of the individual self to something other than itself. (*Ibid.*, 132)

In linking this with the exploratory-creative use of language Leavis
shows a certain tentativeness:

The attainment in literature of this level, and of organisation at this
level, would seem to involve the poetic use of language, or of processes that amount to that. (*Ibid.*, 130)

Dr Leavis does not explain what these other 'processes' might be. There
is a similar tentativeness in his account of the non-exploratory use of
language and its relation with an incapacity for expressing tragic experience:

It may not be altogether true to say that in such a use of language – in
the business of expressing 'previously definite' ideas – one is necessarily confined to one's 'established ego', one's 'readily-defined self'.
But it does seem as if the 'tragic' transcendence of ordinary experience that can be attained by a mind tried to such a use must
inevitably tend towards the rhetorical order represented by Mr
Santayana's account of Seneca's tragic philosophy. (*Ibid.*)

Despite the tentativeness, however, the point is clear, and it is a very
interesting one. The place allotted in this scheme to eighteenth-century
literature is indicated by the assertion that Johnson is even less perceptive
than Santayana: he is incapable of understanding language used for
'exploratory creation'.

It is in the idea of a defeating of the ego that this essay links very closely
with Leavis' account of Eliot's later poetry. In 'Tragedy and the
"Medium"' the idea is developed by reference to Lawrence. Leavis
quotes an attack, from one of Lawrence's letters, on some of the political
thinkers of the day:

They all want the same thing: a continuing in this state of disintegra-
tion wherein each separate little ego is an independent little princi-
pality by itself. What does Russell really want ? He wants to keep his
own established ego, his finite and ready-defined self intact, free
from contact and connection. He wants to be ultimately a free agent.

As opposed to this, the 'tragic experience' involves an 'adhesion of the
individual self to something other than itself'. Leavis is talking about
what is in a general sense a religious impulse, and here lies a central part
of his interest in Lawrence, of course. For instance, Leavis elsewhere says
that the remark sometimes made about George Eliot, that she is 'ethical'
rather than 'religious', could not have been made about Lawrence, and
gives, as a brief example, Lawrence's account of Tom Brangwen, in *The
Rainbow*:

But during the long February nights with the ewes in labour, looking
out from the shelter into the flashing stars, he knew he did not
belong to himself. He must admit that he was only fragmentary,

something incomplete and subject. There were stars in the dark heaven travelling, the whole host passing by on some eternal voyage. So he sat small and submissive to the great ordering. (*D.H. Lawrence*, 110)

The defeat of the ego is a large theme in Leavis' account of Eliot in the Clark Lectures. He says, for example, that the 'unwilled' quality of *East Coker*, 'is given in the opening lines of the poem':

> Because I do not hope to turn again
> Because I do not hope
> Because I do not hope to turn
> Desiring this man's gift and that man's scope
> I no longer strive to strive towards such things.

'if striving involves the will, and willing involves self-assertion and the desire to exalt the self, then there is to be no more striving' (ELT, 118–9).

In Leavis' account, the self-searching implied here involves the exploratory use of language.

For Leavis, the idea of the exploratory-creative use of language is thus linked with Eliot's later poetry. He needs that poetry, peculiar as it is (in the way indicated above), to buttress his critique of eighteenth-century literature, because, without it, his critique will not stand. It is true that eighteenth-century writers did not use language for exploration of the kind exhibited in *Four Quartets*, an exploration which involves a scrutiny of the linguistic instrument that can only be called philosophical. It is not true that their language is not exploratory-creative in the more general sense.

That last claim can, in fact, be amply supported by referring to Leavis' own account of Pope or Johnson. In his chapter on Pope in *Revaluation*, Leavis gives a forceful account of Pope's poetic creativity. He says, for instance, of a passage from *The Rape of the Lock*:

> The beauty here is, for our contemplation, created, just as the immediately following lines evoke the delighted eagerness of the chase. (*Revaluation*, 96)

He notes, elsewhere, of Johnson:

> [he gives] moral declamation the weight of lived experience and transforms his eighteenth-century generalities into an . . . extraordinary kind of concreteness. (*Common Pursuit*, 119)

In that word 'transform' there is indicated a different relation between experience and the 'common currency of terms' from that postulated in Leavis' adverse account of eighteenth-century literature. The point can be reinforced by his remark that, in *The Dunciad*, '"Order" for Pope is no mere word, but a rich concept imaginatively realized'. (*Ibid.*, 92) The exploratory-creative use of language does not necessarily require an abandonment of the 'common currency of terms'; such terms may simply be enriched by being re-soaked in experience.

Dr Leavis' phrase 'imaginatively realized' brings in, of course, that cluster of ideas which we have seen as central in his literary criticism. What is important here is not that Leavis is contradicting himself, but that his *positive* account of eighteenth-century poetry is the correct one, and that it should be pressed a little further. When Leavis remarks on the 'weight of lived experience' felt behind *The Vanity of Human Wishes*, he is on the way to noting that the poem deals with experience of a kind very urgent to Johnson. The view of life it expresses is very grim. Its grimness is brought out strongly in the one passage in the poem which may be said to strike a false note, the appeal to Democritus:

> Once more, Democritus, arise on earth,
> With cheerful wisdom and instructive mirth,
> See motley life in modern trappings dress'd,
> And feed with varied fools th'eternal jest.

It is no jest to Johnson, and to see this no recourse to biography is needed; the poem itself is sufficient testimony. The poem, however, conveys resolution as well as an acute sense of the grimness of life, and we might draw attention to this not only by reading out passages to get the feel of it, but by pointing to the recurrent metaphor of life as a battle, which runs through the whole poem. The feelings attendant upon that recurrent metaphor fuse with the characteristic tone of the poem.

It is convenient, at this point, to generalise by referring to some remarks by Professor Harding. In 'The Hinterland of Thought', he pursues the line of thought that we have seen in his account of Rosenberg. He uses Susanne Langer's account of 'presentational symbolism', and associates it with Jung's idea of 'archetypes'. 'Presentational symbolism' occurs when a word or image carries a number of meanings simultaneously, without putting these meanings into an explicit and logical relation with each other. The horse St Mawr is for us a convenient example of such a symbol.

Professor Harding makes, for our purposes, two important points about presentational symbols: first, that they may carry with them traces of pre-conscious activity, second, that the symbol itself need not arise from the pre-conscious. His registering of a disagreement with Jung most conveniently conveys the two points:

> The difficulty I find in accepting Jung's full idea of the archetype is the implication that the image itself which conveys the meaning arises from the depths or remotenesses of the body. For instance some sense of surging animal vitality and its huge potential power may arise in any of us and may emerge into conscious experience from below, in the way that the experience of hunger emerges out of bodily processes. As it comes towards 'symbolic transformation' the most appropriate image to hand may be, or may have been for many centuries past, the horse; and the horse may then serve as the symbol of a very complex mass of inarticulate potential experience, including a sense of the delight, the danger, the power, the vulnerability, the

wildness and the managableness of animal vitality. But although the meaning of the symbol may have come towards definition out of the remoteness of the whole psychosomatic person, the image – the horse – seems most likely to have entered by way of the sensory surfaces, especially the eye. (Harding, *Experience into Words*, 194–5)

Professor Harding then points out that:

> The choice of objects to carry the symbolic meaning may be largely an individual matter, or it may be culturally institutionalized.

If we transfer these ideas to *The Vanity of Human Wishes*, we can say that the image of life as a battle is a presentational symbol. The image in itself is commonplace and does not rise from the depths of Johnson's pre-conscious. However, it carries with it a complex of attitudes, present in the tone and feeling of the poem, which have been partly formed at the pre-conscious level; and the presence of this complex of attitudes is what makes the poem 'Johnsonian': the poet has articulated his deepest self by exploratory creative use of language.

Professor Harding remarks that:

> The less sensitive writer skids from the potentially new thought into the fluent old words, accepting a compromise which burkes what might have been an original creation.

That is, the 'fluent old words' are not faithful to the writer's deeper experience; they do not carry with them traces of pre-conscious activity. The following is a representative example from *The Vanity of Human Wishes* of the way in which the complex of attitudes referred to above carries itself into the language of the poem:

> Should Beauty blunt on fops her fatal dart,
> Nor claim the triumph of a letter'd heart;
> Should no disease thy torpid veins invade,
> Nor Melancholy's phantoms haunt thy shade;
> Yet hope not life from grief or danger free,
> Nor think the doom of man revers'd for thee:
> Deign on the passing world to turn thine eyes,
> And pause awhile from letters, to be wise;
> There mark what ills the scholar's life assail,
> Toil, envy, want, the patron, and the jail.

The recurrent image is plain throughout this: 'blunt', 'fatal dart', 'triumph', 'invade', 'danger', 'assail'. The lines carry a strong feeling of the hostility of life and, at the same time, a great energy of resolution; the more the hostility is stressed, the greater the resoluteness seems to be.

Further, it is important to take into account here the effects of sound and rhythm. It is there above all that one would expect to find the sort of faithfulness to the depths of experience that Professor Harding describes. As has often been said, analysis of sound and rhythm is always difficult, but it seems safe to remark upon the energy of Johnson's lines, and to suggest that this energy is largely a matter of a strategic deployment of

powerful verbs. 'Blunt', 'invade' and 'assail' are here particularly noticeable, and particularly relevant to our other comments on the passage. It is
also important to note the general effect of Johnson's 'medium'. Its
dignity, in both diction and movement, is a large element in what one
means by calling the poem 'Johnsonian'. This dignity, which is suggested,
not stated, ensures that, despite the overtly destructive tenour of the
poem – its setting up and knocking down of a variety of human aspirations – there is no sense of mere carping or belittlement. It is, it appears to
me, this dignity which qualifies the poem for the adjective 'tragic', a word
to which, in its general applicability to Johnson, Leavis draws attention.

It is difficult therefore to agree with Leavis' view of the Augustan 'use
of language':

> [it] must tend to turn forms and conventions from agents of life into
> debilitating conventionalities, such as forbid the development of the
> individual sensibility and set up an insulation against any vitalizing
> recourse to the concrete. (*Common Pursuit*, 111)

Why *must* the medium which is successful in Johnson's poem be doomed
to failure elsewhere ? It is worth pursuing the point a little further, again
with regard to Leavis' admiration for Eliot.

4. Exploration and public and private imagery

Leavis' view that the eighteenth century denied itself the exploratory-creative use of language is, I have argued, related to his taking *Four
Quartets*, which explores the linguistic instrument itself in an unusually
conscious manner, as a standard. Professor Harding's account offers an
opportunity for noting another way in which Leavis seems to take Eliot as
a standard.

Eliot's poetry is remarkable in its use of images which are individual
rather than 'culturally institutionalized', and he is in this respect, one
supposes, a typical modern poet. The figure of Coriolanus, the voices of
children in an apple-tree, a girl with hyacinths, a figure opening a door
along a corridor, a bird singing in the mist, come to random recollection.
Eliot's own metaphor of images 'rising like Anadyomene from the sea'
conveys very vividly the process which seems to be involved here. The
images appear to come from the depths of the poet's personal experience.

The exploration of images from specific personal experiences is a key
element in Leavis' account of Eliot. In *Lectures in America* he deals at
length with *La figlia che piange*, of which the following are the opening
lines:

> Stand on the highest pavement of the stair –
> Lean on a garden urn –
> Weave, weave the sunlight in your hair –
> Clasp your flowers to you with a pained surprise –
> Fling them to the ground and turn
> With a fugitive resentment in your eyes:
> But weave, weave the sunlight in your hair.

Leavis says:

> the memory obviously represents something very important for
> Eliot, some vital node of experience – something felt as perhaps a
> possibility of transcending disgust, rejection and protest. We know
> this not just from the power of the poem itself, but from the part
> played by closely related evocations in his later poetry. (43)

We are not here concerned with the validity of Leavis' point, but with the
importance he attaches to the image which is ingrained into 'some vital
node of experience'.

When Leavis discusses Eliot's later poetry, in the Clark Lectures, an
important feature is the contrast between Eliot and the eighteenth-
century poets. He says of *Four Quartets*:

> It required a capacity for intensely private or non-social (or non-
> .currency) experience – which amounts to saying, for bringing to
> expression in language what language doesn't readily lend itself to.
> (ELT, 115)

He says of eighteenth-century poetry:

> what . . . the poet 'has to say' must be suited to a mode that implies
> overtly social and 'civilized' presentation: experience that doesn't
> lend itself to such treatment is implicitly told that it doesn't exist, or
> is of no consequence. (*Ibid.*, 105)

The eighteenth century 'in essential intention, eliminated creativity', and
this elimination is, for Leavis, to be largely explained by referring to
Locke and Newton, the prophets of mechanism as opposed to creativity.

To discuss the implications of Locke and Newton is beyond the scope
of this essay. What is unsatisfactory in Leavis' thinking, is the suggestion
that where there is no overt exploration of specific private experience,
there is no creativity of poetic language: that the eighteenth century 'had
no place for the distinctively poetic use of language, the exploratory-
creative'. There are, evidently, great differences of some kind between
Eliot's poetry and Johnson's, but they are not to be explained in terms of
fundamental differences of language. This is the same point as we made
earlier when discussing Richards' comparison of Gray with Blake, or
Donne with Dryden.

A work such as *Gulliver's Travels*, which very fully exemplifies the
Augustan virtues of clear prose statement (virtues which Leavis finds
debilitating), is exploratory-creative in a high degree. The Yahoos, for
instance, are imaginatively realised presentational symbols which embody
'Swiftian' experience of an intimate nature. That they are presented in
language which has the form of clear prose statement, and that the words
have an air of simplicity, has no effect whatever upon the creative
process.

5. Wit

A further distinctive feature of Leavis' theory of poetic language is an
exaggeration of the importance of disparity-action. This is reinforced by

his interest in 'wit', which we shall consider first. Leavis says, of Pope's 'wit':

> [it creates] a readiness for surprise that amounts in the end to an implicit recognition, at any point, in accepting what is given, of other and complementary possibilities. (*Revaluation*, 72–3)

We recall Eliot's saying that wit 'involves, probably, a recognition, implicit in the expression of every experience, of other kinds of experience which are possible'.

The idea of wit, as used by Leavis, has something in common with Richards' idea of 'irony', or the reconciliation of opposed attitudes. This is seen in such remarks as that, in *The Waste Land*, there is a 'co-presence in the mind of a number of different orientations, fundamental attitudes, orders of experience'; or that in *Mauberly*, 'there is a subtlety of tone, a complexity of attitude, such as we associate with seventeenth-century wit' (*New Bearings*, 107 and 141).

This relation between Leavis and Richards is worth looking at in a little more detail. It is most clear in the essay 'Tragedy and the Medium'. Leavis uses, again, Professor Harding's account of Rosenberg, which contains the following remark about Rosenberg's poetry on death in battle:

> The value of what was destroyed seemed to him to have been brought into sight only by the destruction, and he had to respond to both facts without allowing either to neutralize the other. It is this which is most impressive in Rosenberg – the complexity of experience which he was strong enough to permit himself. (*Scrutiny*, iii, 363)

This is close to Richards' idea of a reconciliation of opposed attitudes. Leavis, who does not like that idea, says, having quoted Professor Harding, that he will merely 'note the stress laid by Harding on "complexity" and "technique"'. Leavis is toning down the idea so that it will dovetail with a more *general* notion of 'complexity of attitude'.

This cluster of notions, comprising 'wit', 'poise', 'complexity of attitude' and so on, in itself is unobjectionable, particularly since Leavis is quite happy to waive it when confronted with 'un-witty' poetry which he likes. Being a first-hand critic he is no wooden applier of principles. For example, he says of Hardy:

> Hardy is a naive poet of simple attitudes and outlook ... His greatness lies in the integrity with which he accepted the conclusion, enforced, he believed, by science, that nature is indifferent to human values ... (*Common Pursuit*, 50 and 52)

Hopkins, too, is 'in a certain obvious sense simple-minded', and is contrasted with the seventeenth-century poets in this respect. Leavis, of course, has a very high regard for both Hardy and Hopkins.

Further, the ideas of 'wit' and 'complexity of attitude' refer, for Leavis, to a deeper and simpler criterion: the presence of 'thought' in poetry. This is apparent in the Clark Lectures where he says that the importance of seventeenth-century 'wit', as an influence on Eliot's earlier poetry, is that it 'implies that the poet appeals to the full waking and thinking mind of the reader' (ELT, 102–3). The point appears earlier in his comment on Coleridge's account of *Venus and Adonis*. Coleridge noted the 'perpetual activity of attention' required on the part of the reader, and Leavis remarks that 'Coleridge has given an account of the element of "wit" that is in *Venus and Adonis*' (*Scrutiny*, ix, 68). Leavis, in the same vein, says elsewhere:

> an essential part of the strength of good Metaphysical poetry turns out to be of the same order as the strength of all the most satisfying poetry: the conceitedness, the Metaphysicality, is the obtrusive accompaniment of an essential presence of 'thought' such as we have in the best work of all great poets. (*Scrutiny*, xiii, 61)

Coleridge's phrase 'perpetual activity of attention', above, is a reminder of the connection between all this and Richards' idea of 'realisation'. Leavis' point about the metaphysical poets is that made by Johnson:

> To write on their plan it was at least necessary to read and think. No man could be born a metaphysical poet, nor assume the dignity of a writer by descriptions copied from descriptions, by imitations borrowed from imitations, by traditional imagery and hereditary similes, by readiness of rhyme and volubility of syllables. (*Lives of the Poets*, i, 21)

Leavis' interest in wit, then, is subject to a number of checks. It does, however, play an important part in his overstress upon disparity-action in poetic language. This is clear, for example, in his discussion of Pope's *Elegy to the Memory of an Unfortunate Lady*, which merits detailed examination.

His discussion is conducted in a context informed by the idea of wit:

> Seriousness for Pope, for the Metaphysicals, for Shakespeare, was not the sustained, simple solemnity it tended to be identified with in the nineteenth century: it might include among its varied and disparate tones the ludicrous, and demand, as essential to the total effect, an accompanying play of the critical intelligence. (*Revaluation*, 71)

In the light of this claim, Leavis comments on the lines:

> Most souls, 'tis true, but peep out once an age,
> Dull sullen pris'ners in the body's cage:
> Dim lights of life, that burn a length of years
> Useless, unseen, as lamps in sepulchres;
> Like Eastern Kings a lazy state they keep,
> And close confin'd to their own palace, sleep.

His analysis runs as follows:

> the associations of 'peep' are not dignified, and one's feelings towards the 'souls' vary, with the changing imagery, from pitying contempt for the timorous peepers, through a shared sense (still qualified with

critical contempt, for one is not oneself dull and sullen) of the
prisoners' hopeless plight, and a solemn contemplation in the
sepulchral couplet of life wasted among shrivelled husks, to that
contempt mixed with humour and a sense of opulence that is appropriate to the Kings lazing in their palaces. (*Ibid.*, 71–2)

This seems persuasive commentary, but the feeling is, surely, a good deal
less *varying* than Leavis suggests, and one should therefore draw attention to the 'propriety' of the language, rather than to its action through
disparity. The central point is that the prisoners *are* helpless, as Leavis
indicates in referring to their 'hopeless plight'. Our feeling that they are
helpless mitigates any feeling of contempt for them, and this mitigation
is connected with an important element in the whole poem: the fact that
the lady's soul is a rare one. She is not, as are the mass of souls, fated to
mediocrity. That she is *fated* is indicated by such lines as,

> Why bade ye else, ye Pow'rs! her soul aspire
> Above the vulgar flight of low desire?

This touches upon the poem's total 'statement', which is: 'There are a
few remarkable souls, which leaven the heavy lump of mankind, and it is
the function of the poet, whose own soul responds to their greatness, to
sing their praises.' The mediocre souls' helplessness springs from the
fact that they too are fated. The phrase 'burn a length of years', for instance, carries that feeling. The helplessness is the key point in the final
simile. The kings are 'close confin'd' (i.e. prisoners), and a 'sense of
opulence', which Leavis wants us to feel here, is surely irrelevant.
'Opulence' carries with it a broad and generous feeling which is inappropriate to the starved souls that Pope is describing. The passage is characterised, in fact, by a unity of feeling, which readily lends itself for comment in terms of propriety. The current of feeling is apparent in words
such as 'dull', 'dim' and 'lazy', and the three similes have a cumulative
effect of oppressive confinement. The propriety of the first and third
similes also consists in the fact that the prisoners, though feeling op-
pressed, are reconciled to their situation. Like some 'old lags', they have
largely lost the desire for freedom. It is difficult to see, in the sequence of
similes of imprisonment, death and sleep, that one's 'feelings towards the
"souls" vary, with the changing imagery'.

That Leavis' eye is rather fixed upon a pre-determined idea that 'wit'
must be present, is further evidenced by his next comment:

> The kings are at least dignified, and they make the transition to the
> complete dignity of the Lady, who enters again in the next couplet.
> (*Ibid.*, 72)

'Transition' is a word that Leavis is fond of, and he possibly owes it to
Eliot, who uses it in a similar way when comparing Dryden with Milton.
But if Pope had needed a transition from one tone to another, surely the
sepulchre is even more 'dignified' than the palace. The fact is that no
transition is needed. In a curious sort of way Leavis' view of Pope is a

post-romantic one, in its assumption that there is great difficulty involved in moving from a serious to a light tone.

This is also the case in his comment on the lines:

> Is it, in heav'n, a crime to love too well?
> To bear too tender, or too firm a heart,
> To act a Lover's, or a Roman's part?
> Is there no bright reversion in the sky,
> For those who greatly think, or bravely die?

For Leavis this is an example of the habit of 'critical "placing"' which goes along with the 'witty' mode. What is being 'placed' here is a 'rather histrionic exaltation'. Leavis offers no analysis, but, if there is such an effect, it must hinge largely on the legal metaphor of 'reversion'. Leavis, it seems, reads this as introducing, because its surprisingness verges upon conceitedness, that cool note which is characteristic of prominent disparity-action in metaphor. But, again, it is the propriety of the metaphor which most needs to be pointed out. The uncle who has driven the girl to suicide was her legal guardian, and the immediate implication of the legal metaphor here is that he has cheated her out of her inheritance, spiritual inheritance, primarily, though there may well be a veiled reference to the literal sense, also. The chief effect is to bring in the idea of the 'gods' as just guardians; they not only look after heroic souls but protect cheated orphans. The over-all feeling generated is noble and pathetic. Pope is coming on as strong as he can, and would, surely, not have liked to be told that he was 'critically placing' the feeling. Dr Johnson, who much admired the poem, saying that there is no other poem of Pope's in which 'the sense predominates more over the diction', at the same time castigated Pope for 'the illaudable singularity of treating suicide with respect', and added, more violently, that poetry 'has not often been worse employed than in dignifying the amorous fury of a raving girl' (*Lives of the Poets*, iii, 226 and 101). Johnson took the poem 'seriously', as it should be, and his reading is more accurate than Leavis'.

What was called the 'post-romantic' element in Leavis' reading also appears in his comment on the lines:

> As into air the purer spirits flow,
> And sep'rate from their kindred dregs below;
> So flew the soul to its congenial place,
> Nor left one virtue to redeem her Race.

He writes:

> The 'mean' element in the texture of the previous passage can be safely carried on in 'dregs'. The very violence of this directed as it is upon her contemptible family ('her Race'), draws the attention away from the value it gives, retrospectively, to 'spirits', though enough of this value is felt to salt a little, as it were, the sympathetically tender nobility that is opposed to 'dregs'. (*Revaluation*, 72)

This seems a subtle description of the ways in which the words interact, and, again, it involves the idea of a disparity-action in the metaphor. The contrast of the 'mean' element in the vehicle with the exalted element in the tenor is a species of wit ('salt'). The wit ensures that the lady's 'dignity is not a precarious one, to be sedulously guarded from all possible risible associations'. This last comment is noticeably reminiscent of Richards' account of 'irony' (PLC, 250). But there seem to be no real grounds for supposing that witty salt is being sprinkled here. What is there 'mean' about the metaphor of distillation? A romantic poet might find it startling, but not Pope. Pope chiefly needed a metaphor from a natural process, to re-inforce the idea that the conduct of the lady and of her family is, their natures being what they are, inevitable. To point the interaction of this with the poem as a whole one can quote the beautiful lines:

> Yet shall thy grave with rising flow'rs be drest,
> And the green turf lie lightly on thy breast:
> There shall the morn her earliest tears bestow,
> There the first roses of the year shall blow.

The suggestion that the girl's greatness of soul is part of the natural scheme of things is here extended into the claim that nature will look after her now that she is dead. In these lines no stretch of ingenuity could discover a 'critical placing' of the exalted sentiment.

Such is the way in which Leavis' preoccupation with wit, and his consequent overemphasis on the action of disparity in the interconnections of words, distorts his reading of Pope's *Elegy*.

6. Disparity

The above interest in disparity-effects, there supported by a desire to discover 'wit', also stands, of course, in its own right in Leavis' criticism. He discusses the point in a theoretical way in a comment on Donne's metaphor comparing farm-labourers with 'country-ants':

> It is from some such complexity as this, involving the telescoping or focal co-incidence in the mind of contrasting or discrepant impressions or effects that metaphor in general – live metaphor – seems to derive its life: life involves friction and tension – a sense of arrest in some degree.
>
> And this generalization suggests a wider one. Whenever in poetry we come on places of especially striking 'concreteness' – places where the verse has such life and body that we hardly seem to be reading arrangements of words – we may expect analysis to yield notable instances of the co-presence in complex effects of the disparate, the conflicting or the contrasting. (*Scrutiny*, xiii, 120)

Leavis is talking quite explicitly about disparity-action in metaphor, and may be indebted here to Richards. Likewise, the word 'telescoping' may be an echo of Eliot's comment that in metaphysical poetry there is often a 'sudden contrast of associations' or a 'telescoping of images' (*Selected Essays*, 283). But the stress is, in any case, highly characteristic of Leavis' approach to poetic language.

The bias here is exactly the opposite of that to be found in eighteenth-century analytic method. While recognising the value of 'surprise', particularly in the matter of distance between tenor and vehicle in metaphor, the eighteenth-century critic analysed predominantly in terms of propriety, of *consonance* between the 'impressions or effects', as Leavis calls them. While perfectly familiar with the general idea of propriety, Leavis tends to stress the importance of disparity. To criticise him is not to assert that contrast-effects are unimportant but that he too much neglects propriety.

This is clear even in the chief example with which Leavis immediately illustrates his generalisation: a fragment from the invocation to the corpse, in Tourneur's *The Revenger's Tragedy*, to which Eliot, while developing the view of poetic language which we have seen as central in his criticism, had drawn attention:

> Does the silkworm expend her yellow labours
> For thee? For thee does she undo herself?
> Are lordships sold to maintain ladyships
> For the poor benefit of a bewildering minute?

Leavis comments:

> The key-word in the first line is 'expend'. In touch with 'spin', it acts with its force of 'spend' on the 'yellow', turning it to gold, and so, while adding directly to the suggestion of wealth and luxury, bringing out by a contrasting co-presence in the one word the soft yellowness of silk. To refer to silk, emblem of luxurious leisure, as 'labours' is in itself a telescoping of conflicting associations. (*Scrutiny*, xiii, 120–1)

This seems rather far-fetched. 'Yellow labours' is, more obviously, a vehicle for the feeling of disgust at physical corruptibility which pervades the whole speech, and the chief implication is, 'The stuff which people prize so much comes from a worm's innards – and indeed this is fitting because the bodies which silk covers are themselves disgusting.' The Swiftian possibilities of 'yellow labours' need no elaboration. Leavis' suggestion that 'yellow' brings in the idea of 'gold' seems merely to distract from the main point. I agree that 'expend' is in touch with both 'spin' and 'spend' in the sense, I think, of 'destroy' or 'waste', as in phrases like 'his strength was spent'. This associates it not with an idea of gold but with 'undo' and the consequence of the 'bewildering minute' of the sexual act. The multiple propriety of 'undo' is obvious, and had Leavis been less intent on stressing the importance of contrast effects, he would presumably have noted it. 'Undo' means 'unwind', 'undress' and 'ruin'. The second and third of these meanings are not logically present, but are imposed by the pervasive feeling of disgust.

Leavis' commentary on that fragment from Tourneur is not, in itself, important. The misreading, as I think it, of Pope's *Elegy* is a more important consequence of his overemphasis on contrast-effects, not only because the poem is an important one, but also because Leavis, in placing it in the 'metaphysical tradition', as he does by stressing its 'wit', is implicitly attempting to remove from the Augustan tradition an essentially Augustan achievement. A still more important consequence is his analysis of Milton.

Of the speech in which Comus tempts the Lady, Leavis writes:

> It may look less mature, less developed, than the verse of *Paradise Lost*; it is, as a matter of fact, richer, subtler and more sensitive than anything in *Paradise Lost*, *Paradise Regained*, or *Samson Agonistes*. (*Revaluation*, 48)

Leavis comments specifically on the lines:

> And set to work millions of spinning Worms
> That in their green shops weave the smooth-hair'd silk . . .

> The Shakespearian life of this is to be explained largely by the swift diversity of associations that are run together. The impression of the swarming worms is telescoped with that of the ordered industry of the workshop, and a further vividness results from the contrasting 'green', with its suggestion of leafy tranquility. 'Smooth-hair'd' plays off against the energy of the verse the tactual luxury of stroking human hair or the living coat of an animal. (*Ibid.*)

This is a fine commentary but, again, in omitting any mention of the propriety of the language Leavis is giving a misleading emphasis. The propriety is dramatic, and in ignoring this and treating the lines almost as if they were a hymn to nature in a lyrical poem, Leavis is also showing a tendency of inappropriately applying the criterion of 'concreteness'. It is necessary to set the lines in their immediate context, in order to illustrate the point:

> Wherefore did Nature pour her bounties forth
> With such a full and unwithdrawing hand,
> Covering the earth with odours, fruits, and flocks,
> Thronging the seas with spawn innumerable,
> But all to please and sate the curious taste?
> And set to work millions of spinning worms,
> That in their green shops weave the smooth-haired silk,
> To deck her sons; and, that no corner might
> Be vacant of her plenty, in her own loins
> She hutched th'all-worshipped ore and precious gems
> To store her children with.

That Comus' exhortation to the Lady to indulge her appetites is supposed to be evil is clear not only from the wider context but from the speech itself. The excessiveness of the thing begins to be felt at 'Covering the earth with odours . . .', which has a smothering feeling, and is carried on in the next line. This excessiveness is commented on in the phrase 'sate the curious taste', and the unpleasant fact that the taste is being sated with 'spawn innumerable' needs no elaboration. Presumably the meaning is that the fish grow up to be eaten, but the unpleasant notion of sating oneself with spawn still intrudes itself. The feelings thus set in motion inevitably colour the next line, so that the 'millions of spinning worms' present by no means an entirely pleasing picture and the redundancy of 'haired' in 'smooth-haired silk' is a voluptuous excess. The unpleasantness reaches a climax in the grotesquerie of:

> in her own loins
> She hutched th'all-worshipped ore and precious gems
> To store her children with.

This quite explicitly presents the idea of the children ransacking the mother's womb. An analysis of the lines, in terms of unity and propriety, adopts the procedure that was used in our earlier examination of some lines from *Paradise Lost*. Contrast-effects do have a vivifying effect, but they are secondary to those interconnections of meaning which unify the feeling of the passage. The distinction between these lines and anything in *Paradise Lost* (and, evidently, they *are* different from anything in *Paradise Lost*, as Leavis says) has to be made in terms of rhythm and movement, not in terms of a fuller exploitation of meaning.

Similar comments might be made on the other passage from Milton which Leavis, in *Revaluation*, analyses in terms of contrast-effects:

> Not that fair field
> Of Enna, where Proserpin gath'ring flow'rs
> Herself a fairer Flow'r by gloomy Dis
> Was gather'd – which cost Ceres all that pain
> To seek her through the world – . . .
> . . . might with this Paradise
> Of Eden strive.

Leavis comments:

> It is in the repeated verb that the realizing imagination is irresistibly manifested; it is the final 'gathered' that gives concrete life to a conventional phrase and makes Proserpin herself a flower. And to make her a flower is to establish the difference between the two gatherings: the design – the gathered gatherer – is subtle in its simplicity. (*Revaluation*, 63)

Again the commentary is impressive, but again one needs to make the obvious point that the consonances of meaning are more important than the contrasts or disparities. Milton has brought back to full life one of the oldest of metaphors (the girl as flower) and the bringing back to life is very clearly a matter of releasing all the reverberations of feeling and implications that the metaphor can contain. Detailed analysis would be superfluous, and it would be foolish to suppose that Leavis himself could not have given it.

It is not possible to say with any precision what part this overemphasis on contrast effects, and the sometimes unsatisfactory style of analysis that goes with it, played in Leavis' over-all estimation of Milton. It seems likely, in fact, that his radical objection to *Paradise Lost* (which is where the critical focus has been) is moral rather than aesthetic. For example, we are told that Milton, in *Paradise Lost*, 'offers as ultimate for our worship mere brute assertive will, though he condemns it unwittingly by his argument and by glimpses of his own finer human standard' (*Ibid.*, 58). Since a sense of God's terrible and overwhelming power is precisely what lies at the heart of the 'sublime', one may fairly rephrase Leavis' comment, and say that the 'sublime' is a mode which he finds repellent. It seems likely, then, that Leavis' work on Milton is much like that of Johnson on the metaphysical poets; he has no sympathy with the attitudes and experiences which the poetry characteristically expresses, and his lack of sympathy is readily re-inforced by his habitual style of analysis. This point has already been made about Eliot's criticism of Milton, and it is, of course, evident that the religious poetry in which Leavis is most interested is Eliot's *Four Quartets*-poetry as far removed as may be from that of *Paradise Lost*.

7. Language and particularity

It has been argued that Leavis holds potentially misleading views about the exploratory use of language and about the importance of contrast-effects. We shall now look at his occasionally doubtful application of the criterion of 'concreteness', and see that he can, at strategic points, fall into a crudely 'imagist' approach, even though he is, at other points, well aware of its limitations.

One factor here is Leavis' view of the 'direct effects' of poetic language. His comments on Keats' apples in the opening lines of 'Ode to Autumn' are an apt starting point:

> It is a matter, among other things, of the way in which the analogical suggestions of the varied complex efforts and motions compelled on us as we pronounce and follow the words and hold them properly together (meaning, that is, has from first to last its inseparable and essential part of the effect of the 'sound') enforce and enact the paraphrasable meaning. The action of the packed consonants in 'moss'd cottage trees' is plain enough: there stand the trees gnarled and sturdy, their leafy entanglements thickly loaded. If is not fanciful, I think, to find that (the sense being what it is) the pronouncing of 'cottage-trees' suggests, too, the crisp bite and the flow of juice as the teeth close in on the ripe apple. (*Common Pursuit*, 16)

One willingly concedes that Leavis isn't being merely fanciful, much as an unsympathetic reader might disagree with him. However, it is useful to remember here Richards' view of the 'direct effects' of language, which he called 'tied imagery':

> Too much importance has always been attached to the sensory
> qualities of images. What gives an image efficacy is less its vividness
> as an image than its character as a mental event peculiarly connected
> with sensation. It is, in a way which no one yet knows how to explain,
> a relict of sensation and our intellectual and emotional response to it
> depends far more upon its being, through this fact, a representative
> of a sensation, than upon its sensory resemblance to one. An image
> may lose almost all its sensory nature to the point of becoming
> scarcely an image at all, a mere skeleton, and yet represent a sensation
> quite as adequately as if it were flaring with hallucinatory vividity.
> (PLC, 119-20)

In his analysis of Keats, Leavis takes the 'tied imagery' as being *imitative*
of sensation, and is quite justified in doing so. Richards' point, however,
seems to be generally valid, and Leavis, in fact, elsewhere implicitly
registers agreement with it, as can be shown in the following way.

In his analysis of Keats, Leavis is seizing upon an unusually *prominent*
example of the way in which the direct effects work. It is perhaps signifi-
cant that he twice uses the same lines from the 'Ode to Autumn', and that
he twice uses some lines by Donne for the same sort of purpose. One
might be tempted to conclude that convincing examples are not very
easy to come by.

A similar prominence is seized upon by Leavis in his discussion of
Hopkins' use of the direct effects of language. He refers, without quoting
it, to 'Tom's Garland', and to Hopkins' own comments on the poem:

> [Hopkins] indicates now and then in notes the kind of thing he is
> doing. 'Here comes a violent but effective hyperbaton or suspension,
> in which the action of the mind mimics that of the labourer – surveys
> his lot, low but free from care; then by a sudden strong act throws it
> over the shoulder or tosses it away as a light matter.' Effects of this
> order may be found on any page of his work. (*New Bearings*, 172)

The passage to which Hopkins refers is:

> Tom Heart-at-ease, Tom Navvy: he is all for his meal
> Sure, 's bed now. Low be it: lustily he his low lot (feel
> That ne'er need hunger, Tom; Tom seldom sick,
> Seldomer heartsore; that treads through, prickproof, thick
> Thousands of thorns, thoughts) swings though.

No one would question the success of this bold effect, but its unusualness
needs no stressing. Hopkins himself says that it is 'in point of execution
very highly wrought', and Leavis refers to 'the peculiarities of [Hopkins']
technique' (*New Bearings*, 167). However, he insists at the same time that
Hopkins is only accentuating the natural qualities of the language, and
tries to enforce the point by comparing Hopkins' lines with two passages
from Shakespeare. It seems obvious that neither of these two passages is
nearly so 'highly wrought' as Hopkins' lines; but there is no need to

examine them in detail, because the essential point is conceded elsewhere
by Leavis himself. After a characteristic analysis of Shakespeare's use of
the direct effects of language, he says:

> In the mature Shakespeare it is pervasive, but it can be fixed on for
> convincing comment only where the working is comparatively
> simple and obvious. (*Scrutiny*, v, 162–3)

For the most part, that is, the working of the direct effects is not simply
imitative and is beyond analysis. These are the points insisted on by
Richards.

Leavis, we have agreed, is justified in his comments on Keats and
Hopkins; it is with regard to Milton that his reliance on an imitative
theory of the direct effects is suspect. When he *praises* this aspect of
Milton's language, he appeals to an imitative criterion:

> Nor was his name unheard or unador'd
> In ancient Greece; and in Ausonian land
> Men called him Mulciber; and how he fell
> From Heav'n, they fabl'd, thrown by angry Jove
> Sheer o're the Chrystal Battlements: from Morn
> To Noon he fell, from Noon to dewy Eve,
> A Summer's day; and with the setting Sun
> Dropt from the Zenith like a falling Star,
> On Lemnos th'Aegean Ile: thus they relate,
> Erring. . . .

Leavis comments:

> What is most important to note is that the heavy stresses, the charac-
> teristic cadences, turns and returns of the verse, have a peculiar
> expressive felicity. (*Revaluation*, 45)

He makes the same point of the same passage in 'Mr Eliot and Milton',
and uses the same criterion when praising the speech of Comus, part of
which we have already examined. If the Lady's austere doctrine were
universally practised, says Comus, Nature,

> would be quite surcharged with her own weight,
> And strangl'd with her waste fertility;
> Th'earth cumber'd, and the wing'd air dark't with plumes,
> The herds would over-multitude their Lords,
> The sea o're fraught would swell, [and th'unsought diamonds
> Would so emblaze the forehead of the deep,
> And so bestud with stars, that they below
> Would grow inur'd to light, and come at last
> To gaze upon the sun with shameless brows.]

Leavis quotes only as far as 'swell' and says:

> To cut the passage short here is to lame it, for the effect of Nature's
> being strangled with her waste fertility is partly conveyed by the
> ejaculatory piling-up of clauses, as the reader, by turning back, can

verify. But one way in which the verse acts the meaning – not merely says but does – is fairly represented in the line,

> Th'earth cumber'd, and the wing'd air dark't with plumes,

> Where the crowding of stressed words, the consonantal clusters and the clogged movement have a function that needs no analysis. (*Revaluation*, 51–2)

Cutting the passage short, in fact, allows Leavis to evade the difficulty which was raised earlier with regard to the whole speech. The speech expresses a certain style of exaggeration and the direct effects of the language have reference to *that*, rather than to the objects which the verse is describing. It would be difficult for Leavis to comment on 'bestud with stars' in the way in which he comments on,

> Th'earth cumber'd, and the wing'd air dark't with plumes,

because the sound and rhythm are not simply imitative. Even in the line isolated, the reader's attention, surely, is on Comus rather than on the objects he is describing. Rhythm, as Richards said, is the organisation of the direct effects in the service of the movement of meaning. In this speech the meaning is primarily a matter of Comus' feelings, tone and intention.

It is when Leavis *adversely* criticises Milton's verse that one is most worried by the consequences of appealing to a simply imitative theory of the function of tied imagery. According to Leavis, Milton's 'characteristic cadences', which have in the Mulciber passage 'a peculiar expressive felicity', have, as a rule, a 'routine thump' (*Revaluation*, 46). Those cadences have, in fact, an intimate relation with Milton's 'sublimity'. To use Johnson's phrasing again, one recalls the remark that Milton's 'natural port is gigantick loftiness' (*Lives of the Poets*, i, 177). 'Port' is an apt word for referring to movement, and Johnson is implicitly noting the obvious relation between movement and feeling in *Paradise Lost*. To revert to Richards' language, the tied imagery of *Paradise Lost* functions with reference to Milton's characteristic feeling, tone and intention. As we have already noted, Leavis is far from being in sympathy with that feeling, and it is consequently no surprise that for him Milton's rhythm does not come to life. Further, the lack of sympathy is re-inforced and confirmed by an appeal to a critical principle which is always congenial to Leavis and, in some cases, valid. In this case the principle is that of 'concreteness', with particular reference to the function of the tied imagery.

8. Dangers of particularity

Leavis is also capable, at important points, of misusing the ideal of 'concreteness' not simply with reference to tied imagery but in a general way. One says 'at strategic points' because he is perfectly well aware in theory of the limitations of such an approach. One such strategic point is his critique of Milton, but the necessary comments on that have already been made with regard to Eliot's similar procedure. We shall look instead at some of his analysis of Shelley's poetry. He comments at length on 'When the lamp is shattered' and the final two stanzas receive the severest strictures:

> When hearts have once mingled
> Love first leaves the well-built nest;
>   The weak one is singled
> To endure what it once possessed.
>   O Love! who bewailest
> The frailty of all things here,
>   Why choose you the frailest
> For your cradle, your home, and your bier?
>
>   Its passions will rock thee
> As the storms rock the ravens on high;
>   Bright reason will mock thee,
> Like the sun from a wintry sky.
>   From thy nest every rafter
> Will rot, and thine eagle home
>   Leave thee naked to laughter,
> When leaves fall and cold winds come.

The first two stanzas, which lead into this, consist of a series of figurative illustrations of things dying when their container, so to speak, is broken: for instance, the first two lines of the poem:

> When the lamp is shattered
> The light in the dust lies dead.

The stanzas we have quoted elaborate this idea with regard to love; when the heart, which contains love, is broken, love dies.

Leavis professes puzzlement at the penultimate stanza:

> It would be unpoetically literal to suggest that, since the weak one is singled, the truant must be the mate, and, besides, it would raise unnecessary difficulties. Perhaps the mate, the strong one, is what the weak one, deserted by Love, whose alliance made possession once possible, now has to endure? (*Revaluation*, 219)

He dismisses this last alternative as unlikely, and concludes that we are not being invited to respond to any 'realization of the metaphors', but to react unthinkingly to the 'sentimental commonplaces'. Leavis then concludes, having decided that there is no 'realization' in the penultimate stanza, that 'thee' in the first line of the last stanza is the poet himself, and that Shelley is making 'self-pity a luxury'.

But the penultimate stanza *does*, in fact, have a plain enough meaning, though it does not 'realize' its objects in the way that Leavis demands. Two people fall in love. One of them is level-headed and can exercise emotional control ('the well-built nest'), and he, or she, stops loving before the other. The other is the 'weak one', who is left alone, and for him, or her, love is now an unwelcome inmate of the heart, merely to be endured. The question is then asked; why love chooses to stay in such weak hearts, which will be unable to sustain him?

In the last stanza love, as the syntax obviously demands, is *still* being addressed. The weak heart, subject to wild fluctuations of emotion, will rock love about. Alternating with these fits of passion will be cynical mockery of love. Eventually, the weak heart will rot itself by these various excesses, and reasonable people, having observed the whole sequence of events, will conclude that love is a very silly sort of business. Throughout the poem 'love' has the sense 'romantic passion'.

It is possible that 'bright reason' belongs to the people who will also laugh at love at the close of the poem. On the other hand, it is possible that the final laughter will come from the weak one, reacting against his sentimental excess with an ensuing cynical excess. The words, and the situation, can in fact, comfortably bear both of these interpretations simultaneously.

The function of the metaphors here is not to achieve 'realization', in the simple sense. Its function is that which is generally described in Richards' remark that 'the poet's task is constantly . . . that of finding ways and means of controlling feeling through metaphor' (PC, 223). For instance, in,

> Bright reason will mock thee
> Like the sun from a wintry sky

one notes how 'bright', introduced by the metaphor, brings in a certain tone. This tone can be best indicated by saying that 'bright' in the sense of 'clever' was used, at that time, 'chiefly of one's inferiors or children'; and it may fairly be called ironical. If 'bright reason' refers to the weak one's *own* cynical reaction, the implication of childishness has an obvious relevance. If it belongs to mocking observers of the situation, then they are 'inferior' because they *are* mocking, and not helping. The tone of irony modulates into a more strongly critical feeling as the metaphor leads up to the forceful word 'rot', and this feeling moves, in turn, into the sharp threat of the last line.

It may be that Leavis, in such analyses, is betraying the tendency which Richards saw in Hulme, and mistakenly demanding realisation of the vehicle, rather than realisation of the whole metaphor. This seems to be the case in some comments on Blake, at a point when Blake's 'concreteness' is being favourably contrasted with Shelley's lack of it. Leavis says of the opening of 'O Rose thou art sick': 'The vocative establishes the Rose "out there" before us, so that it belongs to the order of visible beings and we don't question that we see it.' (*Scrutiny*, xiii, 69). Leavis himself notes that 'see' can be misleading in a context like this, and insists that he is not guilty of the 'visualist fallacy', but even so one feels inclined to insist that Blake is not talking about a real rose; the poem is metaphoric and the rose is the vehicle. The point may be re-inforced by noting that his claim is a surprisingly large one for the mere use of a vocative. The same can be said of his remark that 'found out thy bed/Of crimson joy',

> is voluptuously tactual in suggestion, and, in ways we needn't try and analyse, more than tactual – we feel ourselves 'bedding down' in the Rose, and there is also a suggestion of a secret heart ('found out'), the focus of life, down there at the core of the closely clustered and enclosing petals. (*Scrutiny*, xiii, 69)

If one devotes oneself so strenuously to 'realizing' the actual rose, one has insufficient attention left for the tenor of the metaphor, and the evidence, of course, that the poem is more than a literal presentation of a rose is given by the poem itself. It would be a waste of time, for example, to try to 'realize' the 'invisible worm'.

The role played by Leavis' views on poetic language in his estimate of Shelley is, it seems, much the same as in the case of Milton. He has little sympathy with the poet's characteristic attitudes, and possesses convenient, but actually inapplicable critical principles which can be brought to bear to re-inforce the lack of sympathy.

We have already touched upon the other noticeable area in which Leavis too simply applies the criterion of concreteness: Shakespeare's dramatic poetry (*Scrutiny*, xiii, 69). The process here is like that exhibited in the foregoing analysis of Blake. As we saw, it is, with regard to Shakespeare, only occasionally evident, and Leavis commonly talks of Shakespeare's poetry in terms of tone, feeling and intention. This is to be expected, since he frequently speaks in those terms when discussing poetry in general. For example, one readily recalls his analyses of Donne (*Revaluation*, 13–14).

However, Leavis' occasional tendency to talk as though a speech in a Shakespeare play is 'concrete' in the way that, say, Keats' 'Ode to Autumn' is concrete, is important because it gave powerful impetus to that sort of Shakespeare criticism which is practiced by L. C. Knights, or by Wilson Knight. For instance, Leavis says:

> Shakespeare's marvellous faculty of intense local realisation is a faculty of realizing the whole locally.
>
> A Shakespeare play, says Professor Wilson Knight, may be considered as 'an extended metaphor', and the phrase suggests with great felicity this almost inconceivably close and delicate organic wholeness. (*Ibid.*, 60–1)

A representative remark by L. C. Knights may be set alongside this. He says of an image in *Macbeth*:

> Previous images of darkness and torpor have helped to determine the way in which we receive the quoted passage when it comes,

and goes on to speak of the 'larger pattern that lies behind the plot and the characters' (*Some Shakespeare Themes*, 18). Newton, in a plea for a return to an emphasis upon the study of character in Shakespeare's plays, makes a general condemnation of the study of Shakespeare's 'themes'

('*Scrutiny's* Failure with Shakespeare'). There is no objection to the study of themes; what is untenable is the view that the study of thematic imagery does greater justice to Shakespeare's *poetry*, than does the study of 'character'. As we have seen, the study of thematic imagery inevitably ignores a large part of the subtlety and power of Shakespeare's poetry. Any analysis of dramatic poetry, unless it is to place artificial restrictions upon itself, must quickly enter into questions of tone, feeling and intention in the language, and, in entering into them, it finds itself discussing 'character'. A real delicacy of response to Shakespeare's poetry is that which is exemplified in, for example, Dr Johnson's account of Polonius.

9. Summary

It has been argued that Leavis' views on poetic language contain a basic cluster of ideas which are similar to Richards', but that he shows biases in the particular application of them. These biases consist of too narrow a view of the 'exploratory-creative' use of language, a tendency to overemphasise disparity-action, and to apply too simply the principle of 'concreteness'. These biases are, as one would expect, largely related to certain emphases in the poetry and criticism of T. S. Eliot. They are most noticeable at strategic points where they conveniently re-inforce judgements which spring from Leavis' lack of sympathy with certain poets.

On the positive side, it is not being claimed of course that Leavis is a great critic because he has a core of sound critical principles similar to Richards'. Such principles are worthless unless they are accompanied by a capacity for full response to poetry, a capacity which Leavis possesses to a rare degree. The role of analysis in such response is, as we have seen, well described by Leavis himself:

> What we call analysis is, of course, a constructive or creative process. It is a more deliberate following through of that process of creation in response to the poet's words which reading is. (*Education and the University*, 70)

The word 'creation' here serves as a convenient reminder that Leavis' style of analysis, being concerned with complexity, is geared to the ideas of 'realisation' and 'self-realisation' which lie at the centre of his claims for the value of poetry; the analysis is in close touch with the wider interest. It is this effective and simple core of principles which, combining with a gift for vivid and delicate response to poetry, gives Leavis' criticism its characteristic energy and point.

The key word there is 'simple'. It seems unlikely that anyone would deny that these elementary principles are indeed at the heart of Johnson's criticism, as of Leavis'. What is not to be found is a proper recognition of the fact and its implications. In tracing those implications the foregoing account has, it will be seen, offered one kind of answer to the problem posed (to take a representative manifestation) by George Watson. Watson postulates a 'tidy school' of historians of criticism which he typifies by quoting Allen Tate's remark that the 'permanent critics ... are the rotating chairmen of a debate only the rhetoric of which changes from time to time' (*The Literary Criticism,* 11). Watson himself disagrees with this school:

> where they see a continuing debate down the centuries around the same questions, I see a pattern of refusal, on the part of the major critics, to accept the assumptions of the existing debate. (*Ibid.*)

My own account, dealing with its particular area of critical history, agrees with neither Tate nor Watson. I see both continuity and change; the continuity being more than a matter of the identity of questions for debate, and the change being more than a matter of rhetoric. Some such recognition of change and continuity – a recognition that has to be framed in such a way as to be capable of being turned into an analytical tool – seems essential to any balanced approach to the history of English literary criticism.

BIBLIOGRAPHY

Abrams, M. H. (1942) Unconscious Expectation in the Reading of Poetry, in *Journal of English Literature History*, ix.

Addison, Joseph.

(1914) *Joseph Addison, Miscellaneous Works*, ed. Guthkelch, A. C., London.

(1965) *The Spectator*, ed. Bond, D. F., Oxford.

Bateson, F. W. (1953) *Essays in Criticism*, iii.

Blair, Hugh (1965) *Lectures on Rhetoric and Belles Lettres*, ed. Harding, H. F., Southern Illinois.

Boswell, James (1971) *Life of Johnson*, ed. Hill, G. B., revised Powell, L. F., Oxford.

Brown, J. E. (1926) *The Critical Opinions of Samuel Johnson*, New York.

Buckley, V. (1959) *Poetry and Morality*, London.

Burke, Edmund (1958) *A Philosophical Enquiry into the Origin of our Ideas of the Sublime and Beautiful*, ed. Boulton, J. T., London.

Coleridge, S. T.

(1958) *Biographia Literaria*, ed. Shawcross, J., Oxford.

(1969) *The Friend*, ed. Rooke, B., London.

(1884) *Table Talk*, ed. Morley, H., London.

(1969) *Shakespearean Criticism*, ed. Raysor, M. Everyman edition, London.

Dennis, John (1943) *Critical Works of John Dennis*, ed. Hooker, E. N., Baltimore.

Downes, P. (1962) Johnson's Theory of Language, in *Review of English Literature*, iii.

Eliot, T. S.

(1933) *The Use of Poetry and The Use of Criticism*, London.

(1951) *Selected Essays*, 3rd ed., London.

(1957) *On Poetry and Poets*, London.

(1965) *To Criticise the Critic*, London.

Elledge, S.

(1947) *Theories of Generality and Particularity*, in *Publications of the Modern Language Association*, xlii.

(1961) ed. *Eighteenth Century Critical Essays*, New York.

Empson, William.

(1935) *Some Versions of Pastoral*, London.

(1953) *Seven Types of Ambiguity*, 3rd edn. rev., London.

(1951) *The Structure of Complex Words*, London.

(1965) *Milton's God*, rev. edn., London.

Fowler, R. (1970) The Structure of Criticism and the Language of Poetry, in *Contemporary Criticism*, Stratford-upon-Avon Studies, xii, ed. M. Bradbury and D. Palmer.

Gallie, W. B. (1966) *Pierce and Pragmatism*, New York.

Gardner, Helen (1949) *The Art of T. S. Eliot*, London.

Harding, D. W.

(1934–5) Aspects of the Poetry of Isaac Rosenberg, in *Scrutiny*, iii, 365.

(1963) *Experience into Words*, London

Heath, B. (1765) *Revisal of Shakespeare's Text*, London.

Hobbes, Thomas (1889) *Leviathan*, ed. Morley, H., London.

Hooker, E. N. *See* Dennis, John.

Hotopf, W. H. N. (1965) *Language, Thought and Comprehension. A case study of the writings of I. A. Richards*, London.

Johnson, Samuel.

(1765) *The Plays of William Shakespeare*, London.

(1968) *The Yale Edition of the Works of Samuel Johnson*, esp. Vols. vii and viii, ed. Sherbo, A., New Haven.

(1825) *The Works of Samuel Johnson*, London.

(1905) *Lives of the Poets*, ed. Hill, G. B., Oxford.

(1825) *Rasselas*, London.

Kames, Lord (Henry Home) (1762) *Elements of Criticism*, Edinburgh.

Krieger, M. (1956) *The New Apologists for Poetry*, Minneapolis.

Knights, L. C. (1969) *Some Shakespearean Themes*, London.

Leavis, F. R.

(1936) *Revaluation, Tradition, and Development in English Poetry*, London.

(1948) *Education and the University*, new edn, London.

(1952) *The Common Pursuit*, London.

(1955) *D. H. Lawrence, Novelist*, London.

(1959) *New Bearings in English Poetry*, London.

(1969) *English Literature in our Time and The University*, London.

Leavis, F. R. and Q. D. (1969) *Lectures in America*, London.

Locke, John (1884) *An Essay Concerning Human Understanding*, ed. Fraser, A. C., London.

Monk, Samuel Holt (1935) *The Sublime*. Modern Language Association of America.

Newton, J. M. (1965/6) 'Scrutiny's Failure with Shakespeare', in *Cambridge Quarterly*, i, 144–77.

Ogden, C. K. & Richards, I. A.

(1949) *The Meaning of Meaning*, 10th edn, London.

& Wood, J. (1922) *The Foundations of Aesthetics*, London.

Pope, Alexander (1967) *The Twickenham Edition*, Vol. vii, ed. Mack, M., London.

Richards, I. A.
  (1926) *Principles of Literary Criticism*, London.
  (1926) *Science and Poetry*, London.
  (1929) *Practical Criticism*, London.
  (1932) *Mencius on the Mind*, London.
  (1936) *The Philosophy of Rhetoric*, New York.
  (1938) *Interpretation in Teaching*, London.
  (1942) 'The Interactions of Words', in *The Language of Poetry*, ed. Tate, A.
  (1950) *Coleridge on Imagination*, 2nd edn, London.
  (1955) *Speculative Instruments*, London.
  (1968) *So Much Nearer*, New York.
  (1970) *Poetries and Sciences*, London.
Riffaterre, M. *Yale French Studies*, xxxvii / xxxviii.
Roberts, W. Rhys (1907) *Longinus on the Sublime*, London.
Russell, Bertrand (1961) *A History of Western Philosophy*, London.
Ryley, R. M. (1967) William Warburton as New Critic, in *Studies in Criticism and Aesthetics, 1660–1800*, ed. Anderson, H. & Shea, J. S., Minnesota.
Schiller, J. (1969) *I. A. Richards' Theory of Literature*, Yale, New Haven.
Sherbo, A. (1956) *Samuel Johnson, Editor of Shakespeare*, Urbana. *See also* Johnson, S.
Smith, J. (1930) *The Criterion*, x.
Sprat, Thomas (1667) *The History of the Royal Society*, London.
Tate, Allen.
  (1942) ed. *The Language of Poetry*, Princeton.
  (1949) Johnson on the Metaphysicals, in *Kenyon Review*, xi.
Tuve, R. (1950) On Herbert's 'Sacrifice', in *Kenyon Review*, xii.
Unger, L. ed. (1966) *T. S. Eliot: A Selected Critique*, New York.
Upton, John (1746) *Critical Observations on Shakespeare*, London.
Wimsatt, W. K.
  (1960) ed. *Johnson on Shakespeare*, London.
  (1970) Battering the Object: The Ontological Approach, in *Contemporary Criticism*, Stratford-upon-Avon Studies, xii, ed. M. Bradbury and D. Palmer.
  & Brooks, C. (1959) *Literary Criticism: A Short History*, New York.
Winters, Yvor (1947) *In Defense of Reason*, Denver.
Wellek, R. (1955). *A History of Modern Criticism: 1750–1950*, Vol. I (The Later Eighteenth Century), Yale, New Haven.

INDEX